A JOURNEY AROUND OUR AMERICA

THE WILLIAM & BETTYE NOWLIN SERIES
in Art, History, and Culture of the Western Hemisphere

LOUIS G. MENDOZA

A JOURNEY AROUND OUR AMERICA

A Memoir on Cycling, Immigration, and the Latinoization of the U.S.

University of Texas Press ⟠ *Austin*

Requests for permission to reproduce material from this work should be sent to:
Permissions
University of Texas Press
P.O. Box 7819
Austin, TX 78713–7819
www.utexas.edu/utpress/about/bpermission.html

⊗ The paper used in this book meets the minimum requirements of ANSI/NISO
Z39.48–1992 (R1997) (Permanence of Paper).

LIBRARY OF CONGRESS CATALOGING-IN-PUBLICATION DATA
Mendoza, Louis Gerard, 1960–
    A journey around our America : a memoir on cycling, immigration, and the
Latinoization of the U.S. / by Louis G. Mendoza.—1st ed.
        p.   cm.—(The William and Bettye Nowlin series in art, history, and
culture of the Western Hemisphere)
    ISBN 978-0-292-74208-6 (cloth : alk. paper)—ISBN 978-0-292-74387-8
(paper : alk. paper)
    1. Hispanic Americans—Social life and customs.   2. Immigrants—United
States—Social life and customs.   3. United States—Civilization—Hispanic
influences.   4. Social change—United States.   5. Mendoza, Louis Gerard,
1960- —Travel—United States.   6. Cycling—United States.   7. United
States—Description and travel.   8. United States—Social life and customs—
1971–   9. United States—Emigration and immigration—Social aspects.
10. Latin America—Emigration and immigration—Social aspects.   I. Title.
    E184.S75M454   2012
    973—dc23   2012020601

To "dreamers" across the nation who actively and courageously seek full inclusion as part of "our" America

To Marianne Bueno for her extra-diligent friendship and support while I was on this trip, most especially for being there when I needed help or to hear a friendly voice

PEOPLE TRAVEL TO FARAWAY PLACES TO WATCH, IN FASCINATION,
THE KIND OF PEOPLE THEY IGNORE AT HOME.

Dagobert D. Runes

TRAVEL IS FATAL TO PREJUDICE, BIGOTRY, AND NARROW-MINDEDNESS.

Mark Twain

CONTENTS

ACKNOWLEDGMENTS

This project would not have been possible without the support of the University of Minnesota's faculty sabbatical program. Additional assistance was received from the College of Liberal Arts, the Office for Equity and Diversity under the leadership of Vice President and Vice Provost Rusty Barceló, the Department of Chicano Studies, and a McKnight Foundation Summer Research Grant.

Edén Torres, Edna Day, Lisa Sass Zaragoza, Miguel Vargas, and Jennifer Nevitt of the Department of Chicano Studies provided much-needed logistical support along the way. My beloved parents (Joe and Mary Mendoza) and siblings (Rosemary, Mary Ann, Robert, Beatrice, Margie, Cynthia, and Gilda) as well as their spouses and my nieces and nephews provided support, encouragement, and faith in me. Many of my dear friends provided me with lodging and/or emotional nourishment along the way. Among these are Marianne Bueno, Ben Olguín, Sandy Soto, Miranda Joseph, Sherry Edwards, Jennifer Caron, Emiliano Compean, Omar Valerio and Cathy Komisaruk, Yolanda Chávez Leyva, Verónica Carbajal, Ralph Rodríguez, Luis Marentes and his wife, Negar, and their children, Kasra and Katayoun, Sheila Contereas and Salah Hassan and their daughters, Paz and Noor, Rita Alcalá and Raúl Villa and their son, Joseph, Tamara Belknap, Kisa Takesue, Brent Beltrán, Consuelo Manríquez, Antonio Díaz and Beth Ching and their son, Antonito, Cristal Casares, Kelly O'Brien, and George O'Brien.

Even after I returned from my travels and completed writing the manuscripts for this project, it has continued to live in numerous ways. A special thanks to the many people who have provided me with opportunities to speak about this project at academic conferences, universities, K–12 schools, and community settings.

At the University of Texas Press, editor-in-chief Theresa May and her staff deserve thanks for their skillful guidance in preparing the manuscript for publication. Research assistants Naomi Ko and Fartun Abdi assisted me with preparing photos and obtaining permissions.

Finally, it must be said that above all other types of support, this project absolutely depended upon the willingness of strangers to meet with me and trust me with their stories. Likewise, there were many, many people who reached out to provide friendship and words of support along the way via the Internet, at rest stops, in stores, and on the road. Among these were strangers whose acts of kindness reminded me of my connection to others through our common humanity.

To all those listed here by name and the many out there who believe in a vision of the United States that is enriched by our multicultural, multi-lingual, and multinational heritage, I thank them for working to make this vision a reality.

This is my story.

This is our story.

This is true whether or not you claim it as yours.

I hope you do.

Across Our America

i journey across our America
over the hills and through the plains of urban and rural realities
wheeling my way across streets and highways of endless disrepair
i join the multitudes who wonder what America is
becoming, has become, what happened to its roots.

Along highway 1 i pass workers in fields of corn and wheat,
patches of strawberries, groves of grapes and olives,
who move all day long up and down the rows hauling the food
        in
so you and i can take our time diligently picking their harvest
        under the fluorescent lights of air-conditioned
        supermarkets.

if Sally and Sam feel especially connected to madre tierra
they pay a fee to a local organic farmer
for the privilege of picking fruits and vegetables
playing like farmworkers along the seashore on Saturdays
while the campesinos who tend the farm are out of sight and
        mind.

These hijos and hijas del sol shield
themselves in long sleeves and hats
from the sun—who is their god and who is their enemy.

They toil for endless hours for wages unwanted by homegrown
        workers,
yet they are an unwanted and unwelcome harvest of a broken
        system.
Rumblings of "Go back to where you came from" shadow their every
        move
as they follow the sun and the picking season across the
        nation's horizon
so we can have affordable food at our tables.

Lorenzo, a farmworker in northern California, tells me,
as we ride a commuter bus over a treacherous hill,
of a wife in Michigan and a sister in Tejas
under the same sky but not in each other's sight or touch
because their arms are filled instead with sustenance for
        others.
Yet, even with the scorn steadily heaped on their backs, this is
        a better life
than the home where the food was ever absent.
We trade bike tales, his a bright yellow $20 garage-sale refuge,
my black dream machine 150x more expensive.
With an incredulous whistle he smiles and waves as we cycle
down different roads
of Our America.

A JOURNEY AROUND OUR AMERICA

INTRODUCTION

TRENCHES OF IDEAS ARE WORTH MORE THAN TRENCHES OF STONE.

José Martí

NO DOUBT THIS JOURNEY WILL BE A HUGE PHYSICAL AND MENTAL
CHALLENGE TO ME. THOUGH I HARBOR FAINT MEMORIES OF BEING
ATHLETIC, I CAN'T FOOL MYSELF ABOUT WHAT I NEED TO DO TO MAKE
THIS TRIP—ABOUT HOW FAR I AM FROM BEING READY AND HOW FAR
I NEED TO GO. AND YET, IN WHAT I HOPE IS NOT JUST AN EXERCISE
OF THE IMAGINATION, I LIKE TO THINK THAT MY OWN STRUGGLE
TO REALIZE THIS JOURNEY CAN BE SEEN AS A METAPHOR FOR THE
JOURNEY AND CHALLENGE THIS NATION MUST UNDERTAKE TO MAKE
ITSELF RIGHT AGAIN. AT BEST, THEN, IT WILL BE A JOURNEY OF
RECONCILIATION BETWEEN THE IDEAL AND THE REAL THAT IS PREMISED
ON THE NEED TO CONFRONT CERTAIN TRUTHS ABOUT AND LIMITS WITH
OUR PRESENT CONDITION. MY HOPE IS THAT THIS JOURNEY AROUND
OUR AMERICA WILL BE NOT ONLY MY STORY BUT THE STORY OF MANY
WHOM I ENCOUNTER WHO ARE PART OF THE PROBLEM AS WELL AS THE
SOLUTION. NO DOUBT MY VOICE WILL BE FOREGROUNDED HERE, BUT
I HOPE TO OFFER MUCH-NEEDED INSIGHT FROM VOICES THAT AREN'T
OFTEN HEARD IN FORMAL MEDIA VENUES.

IT'S MID-FEBRUARY AND I HAVE TO GET SERIOUS ABOUT PREPARING
MYSELF. PART OF THAT IS ABOUT WRITING REGULARLY, ABOUT PRE-
PARING TO EXPOSE MYSELF, MY FEARS, HOPES, DISAPPOINTMENTS,
THE PAIN AND LONELINESS I AM SURE TO EXPERIENCE FROM DEMONS
WITHIN AND WITH CHALLENGES I'M SURE TO ENCOUNTER ON THE
ROAD. EVEN BEFORE I START I FIND COMFORT IN KNOWING THAT
ALONG THE WAY MY SPIRIT, ENERGY, AND ENTHUSIASM WILL BE

RENEWED BY THE ENERGY, HOPES, AND IDEALS OF PEOPLE I WILL MEET.
THOUGH I'LL BE TRAVELING ALONE, I KNOW THE ROAD AHEAD IS FULL
OF FELLOW TRAVELERS.

Blog entry, February 13, 2007

A JOURNEY IS CONCEIVED

What can possibly shed new light on the immigration question
and the changing demography of the U.S., issues that are both uniting the
Latin@ community and making us individual and collective targets of big-
ots, nativists, and everyday folks who think of all of us as outsiders without
regard for facts about when, how, or why we came to be here?[1] What information and whose voices are missing from the increasingly hostile debates
about immigration and national identity that surround us? How can we in-
terrupt the incessant media hype and sensationalism that pit "us" against
"them"? In the season following a series of immigrant-rights marches
that rocked the country in the spring and summer of 2006, these questions gnaw at heart and brain. Never before having the luxury of funding to
write for an extended opportunity, my first instinct is to think about places
where I might retreat from "real-world" distractions to write in seclusion—
the typical removal of the self from society that many writers make to facil-
itate the articulation of experience, analysis, and reflection of internalized
feelings, thought, and imagination. As I ponder geographic relocation, perhaps to Mexico or Europe, to write from a distance, distance that would perhaps give me perspective, I admit to myself that this appeals to me because
it represents an opportunity for new experience. Heretofore my travels
have been limited to, at most, a two- or three-week trip, with two weeks in
Cuba in the spring of 1990 providing the starkest contrast to life in the U.S.
What I am searching for this time is an extraordinary, if not life-altering,
experience.

With that in mind I begin thinking of what to write about. Will this be
my chance to launch a traditional research project, or will it provide me the
opportunity to face my insecurities about writing within a more imagina-
tive framework, to discover once and for all whether I have the skills to ren-
der experience through an aesthetic and creative lens. Like many Chican@
scholars, I've always wanted my writing to matter, to be relevant. And so in
thinking about the form and substance of a new project, I began to realize
the absurdity of removing myself from the cultural and historical context of
my work.

Let me be clear—place matters to me. Place is intimately related to culture and history; a sense of place is how community manifests in time and space in the actions, words, and feelings of individuals relating to one another and creating a mutual sense of belonging. If I wanted my writing to be relevant, then complete removal of myself from a Chican@ cultural context suddenly seemed like an absurd proposition.

Having moved to Minnesota in the summer of 2004, I found myself obliged to think about migration and immigration in new ways. Though I politically came of age in 1986 as an undergraduate in my mid-20s during a wave of immigration-reform fervor, living in Minnesota, a state that is one of the nation's exemplars of the new geography of Latin@ immigration, was eye-opening. My position at the University of Minnesota as chair of the Department of Chicano Studies carried unique expectations and obligations to be a resource of information and facilitator of people's understanding of this emerging population and to be an ally and advocate for immigrant rights.

Wanting to get beyond the mostly superficial accounts of media coverage on conflict among newcomers and "citizens,"[2] I reached the conclusion that the best way to really explore this problem was to travel across the country and see firsthand the impact of new (im)migrations, to speak personally with folks within and outside the Latin@ community about what their presence here means, to learn lessons from their experiences as a way of broadening and deepening my perspective. And to let the experience of others become part of my own experience as a Chicano in the U.S. My first impulse was to drive across the country, to follow the lead of those before me who had hit the highways and back roads to rediscover America in all its complexity. But as I thought of previous cross-country trips I'd taken, I began to think of all I missed as I sped past places, towns, landscapes, and others in their cars or on foot.

Because I'd also hoped to use my sabbatical to get back into an exercise regimen, the idea of traveling by bike struck me as having multiple benefits. Undoubtedly, I'd get in shape, but going by bike would also force me to go slowly, to travel back roads and encounter the natural environment in a new and meaningful way—a way that would give me an appreciation for nature, the climate, the landscape that is an integral part of migrants' experience as they see a new land for the first time and imagine their place within it.

The decision to bike across the country added new dimensions to this newly formed research project. To be sure, the sedentary lifestyle of a professor and administrator doesn't lend itself to burning too many calories during the workday, even if I do feel like I'm constantly scrambling to meet deadlines and running all over campus to attend meetings. But as a teen and in my 20s I battled the bulge by becoming a runner. This became a passion for several years, and I participated in a few not-too-well-planned marathons, including the very first Houston-Tenneco Marathon held in the early 1980s.

I gave a lot of thought to the benefits of driving. How much easier the trip would be if I could follow my whims to stay or go—or follow leads near or far. How nice it would be to know that I'd always have a roof over my head—even if it was only the roof of my Jeep! And believe me, once the trip began I had many moments of regret about cycling. It was then that I had to remind myself that I was riding the bike for numerous reasons—some more symbolic and metaphorical than practical, though there was a practical element to it. Riding a bike required me to move slowly—to appreciate the journey's difficulty, not because I'm a masochist but because I thought I would see more by seeing less. What I mean by this is that my experience traveling by bike was fundamentally different than the experience I would have had by car. We are a car culture and I am a product of that. Its insular nature can bring us together by allowing us to cover great distances at a fast pace, but it can also keep us apart from each other as we travel in this metal cocoon with all our creature comforts protecting us from the elements and, in some ways, from each other.

Riding down the back roads and through towns and cities on a bicycle, I would experience nature and the road and people, as well as architecture and infrastructure, entirely differently. Cycling forced me to have a different kind of interaction with the world. It wasn't always better, but that may well be the point. The journey was difficult, but each day I gained better appreciation for the world around me—be it the power of the sun or the wind or the limits of my own body. Each day I encountered people in ways that I would not have if I had been in a car. When I needed to reach out for help, especially during these times, I experienced goodness and trust and had opportunities to interact with people that I wouldn't have had otherwise. Cycling inspired interaction with people I otherwise would not have had because it earned me instant respect from them. They wanted to know what I experienced, to share what knowledge they could of this or that town, of their own cycling experiences, or what was up the road, and to wish me luck on my journey. I found in these small acts of kindness a form of human solidarity—a gesture of giving me something they perceived I needed that would benefit us both—a gesture of mutuality. When these conversations had a chance to go further and I had an opportunity to tell them what

I do for a living and what I was researching and hoped to write, people were always intrigued.

At a personal level, I wanted the physical and mental challenge of doing this—to make me stronger, more fit, and capable of countering the many challenges this nation, this world face—not because I expect to single-handedly offer solutions but because I believe that the better we are each individually prepared, the better we are all prepared for the battles that lie ahead. I found my ability to be empathetic with immigrants enhanced by the trip. When I was dog tired and wanted to make this trip easier for myself, I thought of the many people who continue to travel across nations and borders by foot in search of food, job, a better life for themselves and their children, and I knew I had no room to complain because I had the luxury to take such a trip as this.

I also began to see getting myself in shape as a metaphor for the hard work this country needs to do to get itself right. We have become not only heavier but lazier as whole generations have moved away from the physically laborious work of our ancestors. I'm talking across cultures here—we have forgotten that there are lots of folks who still do the manual labor of the fields, the services we take for granted, our dirty work. Our dependence on basic sustenance and the comfort we experience from this invisible labor force is an integral part of our social body, but like so many vital organs of our physical bodies, we fail to appreciate the necessity of it until problems occur. What will it take to get people to truly appreciate the role everyone plays in making the success and well-being of this nation possible?

There is no easy answer. But what I learned from people, particularly people in small towns, is that they are acutely aware that the livelihoods of their towns depend on an influx of new people. Over and over again I heard from people that these small towns would die if not for the immigrants working in their factories, fields, mills, mines, and dairies. Ironically, it's the new immigrants who make it possible for some of the elderly of the towns to continue to hold onto their quaint lives—even as many elderly Euro-Americans have to adjust to the existence of Spanish-language newspapers and radio, Mexican restaurants and *tienditas*, and Spanish in the schools and on the soccer fields. No doubt some resistance, resentment, and suspicion exist, but I think many, if not most, see that the future is about change. The violence and pain accompanying the birth of a new era cannot be overlooked or taken lightly, but resistance to change does not forestall it.

Finally, another reason I felt it was important to do this despite concerns about my safety and vulnerability was that I wanted to exercise my right to do this. A great number of people, including strangers, expressed concern for my safety when they discovered I was traveling alone. I didn't see this as a test of masculinity or bravado, though I was always aware that being a man made me somewhat less vulnerable than a woman would be, even as I was simultaneously aware that I was also being perceived as a man of color. But I kept asking myself, "If other people take these trips, why not I?"

After giving considerable thought to the risks, I found it important to do this as an act of affirmation, to claim what we should all be able to claim—the right to go where we want, when we want, how we want. Having decided to do this didn't mean I could do so carefree. No, I knew a big part of doing this required that I act responsibly in what I said and how I carried myself. But I also knew that one cannot live life afraid of the worst possible people or accidents that can happen. To be free means to live in a world where we can all make choices that will allow us to grow and be a force in the world, even when that entails taking risks. In my own small way, in moving across the country at this time I was trying to both be changed and be an agent of change, to educate and be educated, to show others that we have much to learn from each other, to affirm firsthand what I already knew to be true—that people struggle through anger and injustice and constant pain to make this a better place and that this is a collective project in which we need to see ourselves mutually invested. These sentiments were confirmed for me by a number of people who expressed that they felt I was doing this for all of "us."

ANTEPASADOS

In thinking of literary antecedents for my journey, that is, travels across or around the United States to explore or rediscover what makes the U.S. unique, some obvious models come to mind, among them Alexander Tocqueville's *Democracy in America* (1835), John Steinbeck's *Travels with Charley* (1961), Peter Jenkins' *A Walk Across America* (1979), William Least Heat-Moon's *Blue Highways* (1982), and Jon Krakauer's *Into the Wild* (1996). There is, of course, a plethora of literature produced about the immigrant's journey to the U.S. and migration literature that chronicles the westward expansion of Euro-Americans across the continent. There is also a genre of travel literature from early colonizers that chronicles "discovery," conquest of the indigenous peoples, and the expansion of territorial acquisition for the crown or nation-state. We have chronicles by conquistadores and much more recent accounts by Latin@ immigrants, but very little literature by Latin@s exists about the deliberate movement across the land for the purpose of reflection and exploration not associated with conquest.

Some recent important contributions that document the Latin@ (im)-migrant experience are Ramón "Tianguis" Pérez' *Diary of an Undocumented Immigrant* (1991), Rubén Martínez' *Crossing Over* (2004), and Sonia Narzio's *Enrique's Journey* (2006). Each of these is clearly articulated from a Latin@ perspective and details the harsh realities confronted by the decision to leave home, the journey, and the reception by the respective new host community. These and the many invaluable collections of immigrant narratives documenting the crossing-over experiences of migrants in Arizona or the emergence of a sizable population of Latin@s in the northeastern or southern U.S. offer important insights into the experience of migrants. What I found different in my journey is not only my mode of travel but the geographic diversity of the destinations of new immigrants and the range of historical experience covered by including conversations with Latin@s from many different national backgrounds who have been in the U.S. for multiple generations.

In the volume *Conversations Across Our America: Talking About Immigration and the Latinoization of the United* States (University of Texas Press, 2012), I share with readers segments of interviews I conducted with numerous people on this trip. In contrast, this companion volume is intended as a travel memoir, a firsthand account of my experience in which I share the visceral, emotional, intellectual, and spiritual dimensions of traveling the country in search of a deeper, broader understanding of what it means to be Latin@ in the U.S. in the twenty-first century. To be sure, there is an emphasis on the issue of immigration as it shapes so much of the discourse on Latin@s these days, but that is not the exclusive focus. Even as I foreground my perspective, one of the challenges I face in writing this memoir is how to do justice to the voices of people I spoke with on my journey—those I encountered on the road, in stores and cafés, and those who so generously allowed me to record audio and/or video of lengthier interviews with them. As the reader will see, I include voices that complement and only minimally overlap those in *Conversations Across Our America.* As a memoir, the present book invites readers to appreciate the trip as a journey across the land by bicycle in a particular time and place—to see the interacting and mutually informing dynamics of the social, political, and natural climate that made up the summer and fall of 2007 as I traveled clockwise around the perimeter of the country. While I acknowledge meeting many of the people whose interviews are in *Conversations,* I include here segments of interviews with others that were not included in that book. More importantly, *Journey* allows me to discuss the multitude of people, places, and experiences that made this trip truly exceptional.

In addition to reading memoirs of other trips across the country during my trip, I read local and national newspapers on a daily basis to keep apprised of immigration issues as they arose during this time. I often found strong resonance between the two, but there were many instances in which local coverage of events was dissonant with what was occurring nationally or not in line with the conversations I had with community members.

In an effort to reconcile my interest in conveying the trip *qua* trip, one that was constantly informed by my experiences on the road and my consumption of local and national print media with the issues and themes that arose from my conversation with local informants, I have utilized a dual organizing principle to structure the book. First, the narrative of my trip that follows is organized chronologically, covering some of my pre-trip preparations in spring 2007 and then in more detail from July 1, when I departed Santa Cruz, California, to December 19, when I completed my more than 8,000-mile journey in Oakland, California. Like most travel memoirs, this book is organized linearly—the narrative by and large reflects the chronological and geographical structure of my trip. In part 1 I describe my preparations for the journey. Part 2 focuses on the segment of my travels from northern California back to Minneapolis, Minnesota, where I rested for ten days. Part 3 covers the ride from the Midwest to the East Coast and the South through Louisiana. Finally, Part 4 covers my journey in the Southwest through the borderland states and back to northern California. I have added a few segments of transcripts from my conversations with people in order to be inclusive of multiple voices. For similar reasons, select excerpts from local and national newspaper articles are inserted as sidebars to provide more context for the discourse on immigration during the trip.

Finally, a word about the book's title. While I hope that by now I have made my motivations and the literary antecedents for this trip clear, the title, *A Journey Around Our America*, was inspired by a provocative 1891 essay written by the famous Cuban poet, essayist, intellectual, and patriot José Martí for New York City's *La Revista Ilustrada*.[3] In this rhetorically charged essay Martí offers his readers a continental vision of the Americas that is set over and against the U.S.'s arrogant appropriation of the continental identifier. He thus speaks of two distinctively different Americas, that which is ours (Latin America) and that which is not (the United States). He argues against a stifling parochialism that pits communities against one

another and is politically counterproductive in the context of continental in-
equities and dangers posed by U.S. imperialism.

Warning against complacency and intimidation, Martí asserts: "Whatever is left of that sleepy hometown in America must awaken. These are
not times for going to bed in a sleeping cap, but rather . . . with our weapons for a pillow, weapons of the mind, which vanquish all others. Trenches
of ideas are worth more than trenches of stone." He advocates for a distinctively American culture, one that embraces rather than denies the dynamic
and organic relationship of place, language, and experience that shapes the
American continent:

> To govern well, one must attend closely to the reality of the place that
> is governed. In America, the good ruler does not need to know how the
> German or Frenchman is governed, but what elements his own coun-
> try is composed of and how he can marshal them so as to reach, by
> means and institutions born from the country itself, the desirable state
> in which every man knows himself and is active, and all men enjoy the
> abundance that Nature, for the good of all, has bestowed on the country
> they make fruitful by their labor and defend with their lives. The gov-
> ernment must be born from the country. The spirit of the government
> must be the spirit of the country. The form of the government must be
> in harmony with the country's natural constitution. The government is
> no more than equilibrium among the country's natural elements.
>
> To know the country and govern it in accordance with that knowl-
> edge is the only way of freeing it from tyranny. The European univer-
> sity must yield to the American university. The history of America from
> the Incas to the present must be taught in its smallest detail, even if the
> Greek Archons go untaught. Our own Greece is preferable to the Greece
> that is not ours; we need it more. Statesmen who arise from the nation
> must replace statesmen who are alien to it. Let the world be grafted onto
> our republics, but we must be the trunk.

Martí's vision is an internationalist one. And though he was critical of
yanqui imperialism, his stance was a defense of cultural and territorial integrity that would cultivate harmonious human relations from the ground
up. An important element to this cultural and political philosophy was a
commitment to respecting indigenous and mestizo peoples and values as
the foundation of any legitimate governance system in the Americas. Martí
poses a warning:

The disdain of the formidable neighbor who does not know her is our America's greatest danger, and it is urgent—for the day of the visit is near—that her neighbor come to know her, and quickly, so that he will not disdain her. . . . One must have faith in the best in man and distrust the worst. One must give the best every opportunity, so that the worst will be laid bare and overcome. If not, the worst will prevail. Nations should have one special pillory for those who incite them to futile hatreds, and another for those who do not tell them the truth until it is too late. There is no racial hatred, because there are no races. . . . The soul, equal and eternal, emanates from bodies that are diverse in form and color. Anyone who promotes and disseminates opposition or hatred among races is committing a sin against humanity.

While his rhetoric and gendered use of language is anachronistic, in many respects Martí was ahead of his time in his rejection of scientific racism and in his call for transnational harmony, not under the banner of a single nation-state but through a well-informed citizenry. His reminder that "our own Greece is preferable to the Greece that is not ours; we need it more" along with his admonition for "one special pillory for those who incite them to futile hatreds, and another for those who do not tell them the truth until it is too late" could well apply to contemporary discourse on immigration as it emanates from Arizona in its passage in 2010 of state SB1070 and HB2162 imposing anti-immigrant restrictions explicitly intended to rid the state of undocumented immigrants and eliminating ethnic studies, respectively.

As you embark on this literary journey with me, I hope you will explore and discover, as I did, a different face of America than is represented by those who would sow hatred and discord even as they conveniently forget that European immigrants seized and occupied native lands and evaluate human worth, indeed life itself, by legal categories.

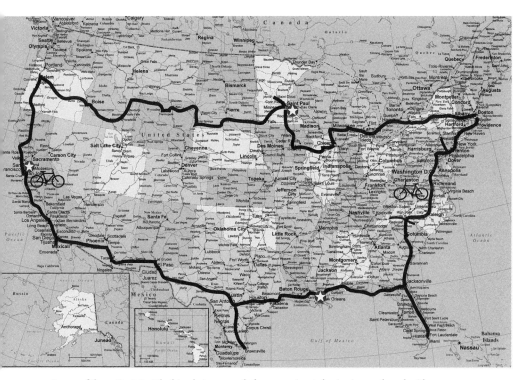

A map of the entire trip. The bicycle icons mark the approximate beginning, end, and midway points of the route. The stars indicate the segments of the trip covered in parts 2, 3, and 4 of the book. Louis Mendoza.

PREPARATION

TRAVELING IS A BRUTALITY. IT FORCES YOU TO TRUST STRANGERS
AND TO LOSE SIGHT OF ALL THAT FAMILIAR COMFORT OF HOME AND
FRIENDS. YOU ARE CONSTANTLY OFF BALANCE. NOTHING IS YOURS
EXCEPT THE ESSENTIAL THINGS—AIR, SLEEP, DREAMS, THE SEA, THE
SKY—ALL THINGS TENDING TOWARDS THE ETERNAL OR WHAT WE
IMAGINE OF IT.

Cesare Pavese

ONE'S DESTINATION IS NEVER A PLACE, BUT A NEW WAY OF SEEING
THINGS.

Henry Miller

¿Bicicleta Bato? I didn't even own a bike when I decided to take this trip!

I can't say that I've had a lifelong relationship with bikes. In a family of eight children, it's not like we each had our own. The bikes we had tended to be communal and generational as they made their way down the entire sibling chain. I remember we younger ones had a tricycle or two we shared, my two older sisters had big blue bikes, one of which my brother and I would later use for paper routes, and I remember the bright orange Stingray bike my brother earned when he was in high school selling flower seeds or some such item door to door. He was always good about setting a goal for some prize or another through his salesmanship. I recall the nice eight-track stereo he got a year or two after that. Of course, I was strictly prohibited from riding the prized Stingray with its chopper-style forks on the front wheel that simulated a motorcycle look. Naturally, this prohibition didn't stop me from taking it around the block when I knew I could do so before he came home. And naturally, doing so led to disaster one day when

I came barreling down the sidewalk, hopping the street curb at the end of one block, and bouncing onto the street at the corner of Lyons and Majestic—which was so cool because this bike had front shock absorbers, too—and ran full speed ahead into the side of a car that had pulled right into my path. I flew off the bike and landed on the hood of the car with a big thump that made a dent, and then I rolled off the other side. I didn't have the luxury of thinking about the cuts and bruises from the accident.

I saw trouble from two directions—the driver because of the dent on his car and the damage that was done to the Stingray, whose long front-wheel forks now seemed to have the elbows of a cricket. The driver was both mad and afraid as he hopped out and began yelling at me. For a moment I thought he might hit me, so I asked if he wanted me to go get the cop whose car was parked at the Dixie Maid Malt Shop across the street. When I said this I think we both assessed the situation and decided we'd better cut our losses. I was worried that my parents might have to end up paying for his car. He probably realized that he might be liable for not approaching the intersection with more care. So he said something to the effect that I should be more careful, and he took off.

With him gone I began to let the next level of fear sink in as I saw how badly damaged the forks, the wheel, and the handlebars were. In true Mendoza-kid fashion, I took that bike home and tried my best to twist it back into shape in the hopes that I would never have to tell my brother that his new bike had, uh, been really broken in that afternoon. It didn't work, of course, and it was one of those evenings when you're glad you have parents there to keep fraternal violence from getting out of hand. This incident may have had something to do with my partnering up for a while with a cousin of Raymond Nava, my next-door neighbor, who ran a sort of chop shop for bikes out of Raymond's garage. I didn't steal any bikes, but I did learn how to disassemble, reassemble, and paint them in various configurations. Like so many bikensteins, each went on to live another life in a new and improved form.

I can only recall owning two other bikes since that time, the first a ten-speed in my mid-20s that I would ride to my parents' house on Sunday afternoons—a good 20 miles each way. But going across town on Houston streets really requires an off-road bike, and I gave it up after a while because of numerous flats I'd pick up going over railroad tracks and pothole-riddled streets. I mail-ordered a pretty cool road bike in 2002 that I used to go on long rides on the paved mission trails in south San Antonio, alone or with a university colleague. When I moved away, I left it behind with him to give to his granddaughter.

Having decided I was going to make this journey on two wheels, in October 2006 I went to Erik's Bike Shop in Minneapolis to purchase the bike that would carry me across the country. Thus began my immersion into cycling culture as I learned about touring bikes, cycling apparel, and a myriad of bike accessories such as mirrors, a bike computer, lights, panniers, pedals with shoe clips, shoes with pedal clips, and so on. I left with a beautiful, black, very light, Cannondale touring bike and a new awareness of just how bourgeois a sport cycling can be. As I was to learn over and over again, most bike-store employees are avid cyclists, and short of embarking on their own excursions, nothing is more exciting to them than to hear about a cycling adventure. Their enthusiasm is contagious, and without exception, every time I needed help on my trip, the mechanics at bike shops dropped what they were doing to attend to my needs so I could get back on the road as soon as possible.

It wasn't long before the harsh Minnesota winter bore down, and being the still-novice cyclist that I was, I confined myself to cycling on a trainer rather than braving the winter winds and ice- and snow-covered streets. To say that winter in Minnesota is long is an understatement. To help give myself variety in my training I bought an elliptical trainer and set it up alongside the bike in the basement. Though I did use them, I have to admit it was only sporadically, as I found the basement workout boring and dreary. In mid-February I also began slowly preparing myself for the trip by launching a blog on which I hoped to document my motivation, preparation, goals, and eventually the trip itself. The heavy snows of winter gave me lots of time to ponder the issues, and I began to more closely scrutinize local and national media coverage of immigrants and the politics and punditry surrounding immigration discussions in this country.

LATIN@S AS PERPETUAL OUTSIDERS

Most Latin@s in this country know the experience of being perceived as an outsider. Much of this has to do with the perception of all of us as nonnatives, recent immigrants, and people from elsewhere who don't have a legitimate claim for social and political inclusion. Most often these assumptions are without regard for our actual personal or collective histories. And they are just plain wrong. Little distinction is made among the histories of various Latin@ groups, and little historical knowledge is transferred through the educational system, and thus the ignorance is institutionally perpetuated. For many Latin@s, our relationship to our immigrant heritage is unique and complex. And the lack of educational access, equity, and inclusion simply don't help, as Latin@s' self-awareness suffers first in how little many of us even know about our history or our own families' histories. Unfortunately, contradictions like this are integral to the very foundation of this country.

It's hard to call a place a true home if one cannot feel safe and respected. Of course, we can demand it and we must continue to do so, but doing so causes a restless psyche, a sense of both arriving and yet still having a long way to go. This is not something that only people of Mexican descent feel. It's shared by many immigrants. It's felt even more strongly by those who were here long before the so-called founders of this country. A few decades back, Chican@s saw in the label "Mexican-American" a sign of our second-class status in society. To be seen and respected as citizens we had to emphasize both our heritage and our legal status. Well, Chican@s may no longer be hyphenated Americans, but by almost any measure our community still doesn't enjoy social, economic, or political equality. For those who think about this and feel the continual dis-ease of not fully belonging, we feel a need to qualify our status with quotation marks to signify our awareness of this condition. We're "American," or as some would say, *americano*, to signify linguistically a broader sense of identity that is not fully aligned with official nationalism. We're stuck between the quotation marks; we're enmeshed in ambiguity, in suspended meaning. Sounds like we're in the same old place, no?

FEAR OF LATINOS

In recent months, the Latino community has found it necessary to show its strength and to demonstrate its ability to come together to deliver a very basic message: We are human beings with the same needs, values, desires, and dreams as our neighbors. It's a message that is both simply profound and profoundly simple. Our ability to come together across the country by the thousands and deliver this unifying message has been extraordinary. We have every reason to be proud of the way we carried ourselves and of the many supporters across ethnic groups who stood alongside us in solidarity with our cause.

Yet how sad it is that we continue to find ourselves under attack from so many directions as politicians in Washington debate our future. We are a community on trial. If the consequences were not so serious, it would almost be funny. Our need to defend ourselves from accusations as far-ranging as the subversion of American values to being threats to national security bring to mind the lyrics of Ritchie Valens' 1958 song "Framed."

> I was framed, framed, I was blamed, framed
> Well, I never know nothin', but I always get framed

It's fitting that these lyrics were written and sung by a young man whose desire to be successful in the mainstream music world was so strong that he changed his name from Richard Valenzuela to enhance his appeal to Anglo American music fans.

Some things never seem to change. As a community our sheer presence, our economic, social, and cultural contributions to the United States, has never been stronger, yet some continue to demand that we justify our existence, our loyalty, our rights by sacrificing our identity. How ironic that so many citizens of a country founded on the principles of religious and political diversity are so very afraid of those who seem outwardly different.

Only xenophobes would think that the language a message is delivered in is more significant than the message itself. How else do we understand the horror experienced by those who are offended by the Pledge of Allegiance being said in Spanish and "The Star-Spangled Banner" being sung in the same language? Heaven forbid! Why is it that translation provokes such fear rather than being seen as an opportunity for the building of greater understanding and community for all?

Rather than broadcasting an understanding of ideals of unity, liberty, justice, courage, and national identity represented in the Pledge and the national anthem, the any-language-other-than-English naysayers want to pass laws forbidding principals and musicians from delivering the message if it's not in English. How ridiculous! How sad that these so-called defenders of American patriotism are willing to kill the message to spite the messenger.

Perhaps we can teach those who are intolerant of linguistic and cultural difference a little bit of their history, and they will understand that we share a common past. Both the Pledge of Allegiance and "The Star-Spangled Banner" have had many multilingual translations. According to Wikipedia, recent research following the release of "Nuestro Himno" has turned up examples in German, Yiddish, Samoan, French, Latin, Polish, and Tohono O'odham. The U.S. State Department even has four Spanish-language versions on its website [subsequently removed]. The

Wikipedia author poses a good question: "Will this page be removed now that President Bush has declared that the anthem "ought to be sung in English"?

Of course, the language controversy aside, the real problem faced by English-only and anti-immigrant proponents is the legitimacy of our very presence here. Though many anti-immigrant proponents are careful to say they are not racist, their narrow-mindedness, their fear, their willful ignorance of the historical and economic causes of immigration as well as our many contributions to help build, improve, and sustain this society are evidence to the contrary.

The recent marches to assert our dignity, as well as our rightful place and our rights in society, made me proud to be part of this community as we continue to build a stronger and better society. Let us keep moving forward hand in hand with each other and with our allies across communities of difference.

Louis Mendoza, guest column, La Prensa de Minnesota, *May 29, 2006*

But we have to try to make change by being active agents of change and of resistance against cultural obliteration. I try to do my part in the struggle "out there," the so-called real world of action and decisions where people's life chances are made and unmade. I also try to be honest about my limitations—about what I can and cannot do. For the past few years, the Minnesota Immigrant Freedom Network has sponsored a day at the state capitol to advocate for passage of the Minnesota DREAM Act, a state version of the Federal Development, Relief, and Education for Alien Minors legislative proposal that immigrant-rights advocates support. Successful passage at the federal level would enable states to charge in-state tuition for undocumented youth to attend higher education if they meet certain qualifying residency provisions. The federal version contains provisions for obtaining permanent residency and the possibility of citizenship contingent on receiving a college education or serving in the military. Eleven states have passed a version of this bill, though they do not have the ability to establish a pathway to citizenship for beneficiaries.

The rally at the capitol is a day of affirmation in many respects. School youths express poignant *testimonios,* chant political slogans, and meet with legislators to try to convince them that recent immigrants have a dream of attending college one day. These youths embody not only democracy but what is best about this country. They are the latent potential and talent of our communities who are in the U.S. with their families often because U.S.

military, policy makers, and corporations were there—in the not too distant past in their homelands—systematically changing their economies, the political and social structures of their societies, even their cultures. Through no fault of their own, these youths have become a blank canvas upon which some of the worst elements of this country get projected. They want nothing more than to be like "us," and "we" hate them for it. There's some kind of self-loathing going on. Yes, "Americans" give mixed messages: "We want and need you to sustain our comfortable lifestyle by picking our food and working our factories and building our houses and serving our meals, but we don't want you to be our neighbors or utilize social services or have the right to be healthy or eat well or have insurance or, 'god forbid,' have the audacity to demand an education!"

From my contacts at the Idaho Community Action Network (ICAN) I received a copy of a booklet titled *In Our Own Words: Immigrants' Experiences in the Northwest*, put together by the Northwest Federation of Community Organizations in 2006. María Andrade, a lawyer with ICAN, speaks to one aspect of our "broken" immigration system: "With the current unavailability of visas, a legal resident alien can expect to wait anywhere from five to eight years to bring his spouse and minor children to the U.S. A U.S. citizen can expect to wait at least a year before they can get their spouse to the U.S. just because the internal processing is so delayed. Nobody I have ever talked to thinks this is reasonable—because it's not" (13).

My life has been a constant search for connection—between myself and others, between my inner and outer worlds, between my fears and hopes. I want to feel whole and loved. I want a place to call home that feels safe and secure, a place where I am wanted. Is that such an odd desire?

Blog entry, February 27, 2007

In March I realize that my training and preparation have not gone as well as I'd intended. Too many distractions with work and a lack of discipline on my part have made finding the time and *ganas* to bike ride and to write difficult. I am still very psyched about doing this. I want and need to

Left to right: Bobby, me, Rosemary (our oldest sister), Margie (kneeling on the ground), and Beabee, ca. 1964. Louis Mendoza family photo archive.

get away from the daily grind, so despite increasing concern about my lack of preparation, I remain intent on heading out July 1, the day my sabbatical begins. There are so many aspects of this trip to prepare for that I sometimes feel overwhelmed.

As I go through my personal things in preparation for this trip, I come across the earliest photo I have of me and a bike. I'm the little kid in a baseball cap squeezing in on my brother, Bob, who's on the bike. This is years before the infamous orange Stingray. It must be around 1964. I can't figure out where we are, but I assume it must be early spring since it can't possibly be summer in Houston if we're wearing coats and sweaters. We all look pretty happy here—though we're lined up, it's not the whole clan like photos taken during holidays.

In March I attend a conference in San Jose, California, and at the airport I pick up an interesting book by Terri Jentz titled *A Strange Piece of Paradise*. I am first attracted by the picture, but once I read the book jacket I am hooked and spend as much time as I can over the next three days reading it. It's the story of Jentz and another young woman who in the summer of 1977, following their sophomore year at Yale, decided to take a cross-country bike ride. Just a few days into their ride they experienced a horrifically violent attack as they camped near Bend, Oregon. It's an amazingly courageous book. While their story has to be understood in the national context of rampant and random violence against women during that time, the violence isn't exactly something this country has outgrown. Can you say Don Imus? Jentz and her friend were only six days into their cross-country bike journey when they were run over by a truck-driving misogynist as they lay sleeping in their tent, and the author's journey—her life path—was altered forever. The lessons one can take from her are many— courage, tenacity, perseverance, spiritual strength, how to channel anger and action into a creative force—and the book is also a cautionary tale about the fragility of life in both large and small ways. Reading the book makes clear to me that I'll have to think of issues of safety on the road, how I'm perceived by strangers as a curiosity, a threat, an opportunity, vulnerable. How do I account for unforeseen possibilities? These were already on my mind before picking up the book, but this has reminded me how much I need to both anticipate (control) and to let go (of the illusion of control) even before I get on the road.

Which brings me to another point. I have decided to change my route so that rather than travel only areas of new immigration, I will travel the entire perimeter of the country. This will give me the opportunity to go through Cline Falls, Oregon, where the events documented in *A Strange Piece of Paradise* occurred. I don't think I'm being morbid in doing this— it's curiosity, yes, but it's a tribute to the journey those two young women were never able to complete. This will add some miles to my proposed route, but the more I read of other people's journeys, I don't think I'll have a problem finishing this expanded route in my six-month time frame. I may start out slowly, but I think I'll be able to pick up speed and stamina as I go along. (I'd better!) My plan is to cross into Canada and Mexico at points along the way so I can add an international dimension to the trip. I'll begin the trip in Santa Cruz because my goal is to travel the northern route in the summer so I don't have to confront the Midwestern winter as I conclude the trip. What is left out is travel down through the middle of the country, though I still go through many states in the upper Midwest.

CINCO DE MAYO 2007

Two relevant news stories today. One is about a foiled plot by militiamen to attack Mexican migrant workers in Alabama with homemade bombs, assault rifles, and assorted other firearms. The other is an editorial commentary by a local Mexican American businessman in Minneapolis who poignantly expresses how painful and tragic it is to live as a target of conservative zealots who are trying to score political points by passing legislation that marginalizes all Latin@s in this country. The former provides support for the latter's claim that we are indeed random targets, that we are all perceived as illegal, that once someone is cast as illegal, the way is paved for random and deliberate acts of violence to occur. It's not so illogical as it might seem—after all, the fantasy that we are a people that lives by the rule of law and that laws somehow serve as the basis for a just, fair, and humane nation are so powerful a myth that many become blind to legal injustices that pervade our society. Criminalizing people and legitimating the language of criminalization—that a human being can *be* illegal rather than merely commit illegal acts—is the same language that justified the atrocities of Nazi Germany.

Anger and sadness, those are the daily psychological and emotional boundaries that define many people's lives. It can be hard not to lapse into despair or do like so many others do and simply exercise whatever privilege we may have to make sure people know we are not one of *los ilegales*. One would think that being a cynic protects one from being surprised by the everyday nature of random and deliberate violence, be it in Alabama or by police against people at the May 1 pro-immigrant rally in L.A., where clearly the Latin@ media became legitimate targets of the police. I was shocked, however, that the foiled attack in Alabama did not make national news as an act of terrorism. Why do you suppose this was so? Could it be because the target was a bunch of brown folks who were presumably "illegal"? Does that somehow lessen the severity of this intended crime? Imagine, if you will, that the foiled attack had been planned by brown men (of any ethnicity) against a community of whites? What do you suppose the news coverage would have been like in that case? I can only imagine the national headlines framing this as an act of terrorism occurring right here on American soil—warning us to be on the lookout for suspicious groups gathering to plot against national safety. Oh, before I forget, happy Cinco de Mayo!

TRAINING DAYS: MAY 2007

Toward the end of the spring semester my work schedule begins lightening up to the point that I can devote more time to prepare. Of course, I should be able to integrate exercise into my daily life, but finding balance is not a forte of mine. I did commit to a 100-mile ride in Chippewa

Falls, Wisconsin, on May 28, so that's a nice short-term goal. And if you're thinking I'm crazy to think I can do that, I might just surprise both of us. I went on a 65-mile ride this past Saturday and felt pretty good. If I can build up my time and stamina, I'll be just fine. It was a wonderful ride out past the town of Excelsior to the Chanhassen nature reserve. I have to say that though I didn't map out the ride in advance, Minnesota has such nice trails that I was able to get on Cedar Lake Trail and just keep on going west. A few weeks back when it was still cold I went the same route but not nearly as far. I was pleased to see that I got to the point where I turned around last time in a half-hour less. I attribute that to being a little stronger but also because the weather is so much nicer. Last time there was still snow and ice on the ground, and I experienced a full-speed fall when I hit an ice patch. Besides a few scrapes and a bruised ego, I was fine. It also helped this time that I have since outfitted my bike with a few more gadgets, like a computer that tells me my pace and distance. It's very useful in motivating me to keep a steady pace. I find that it doesn't take a lot more effort to pick up my speed when I need to.

Long, steady inclines up hills are hard, as one would expect. I hit a big bump coming down a decline and stopped to inspect the bike and could not get going up the hill, so I had to walk. That was humbling. Going down one hill I almost hit 40 miles per hour and had a flashback of a time in high school when my cousin Paul and I stayed out at his parents' beach home in a small town near Galveston and rode to the island. On the way there we rode over the drawbridge after the bridgeman chastised us for going that route, but he let the bridge down for us anyway. To avoid his attitude on the way back at the end of the day, we rode over the steep bridge connecting the island to the mainland via I-45. It was a pretty foolish thing to do, though we didn't realize how much so until we made it safely back to the other side. There was no bike lane or sidewalk, so we crept along the right-hand lane as cars going 55 mph passed us. Riding behind Paul, all I could think was that if he fell, that was it for both of us—we would spin out into the traffic and get crushed. When we got to the other side, we were pretty freaked out about what we had just done and swore we wouldn't tell our parents because we would be justifiably chastised by them. It was thrilling and frightening.

I expect a lot of that on this trip. Being in the nature reserve was quite beautiful as deer ambled across the bike path without fear of me. To be sure, the ride back home was long and hard, and I just wanted to be done. I also realized how much energy I burned and became aware that I would need to plan my nutrition intake very deliberately. One website I read from a cross-country biker said that you should feel free to consume lots of food when it's available because riding six or so hours a day for many days a week you will burn lots of calories. Of course this makes sense, and I look forward to carrying less weight as I put the miles behind me.

Six weeks to go, and I've a lot of challenges in front of me, including starting to ride with my panniers fully loaded and doing a couple of two- or three-day trips so I can get used to camping. One thing I'm not sure I'll be able to train for is the solitude of being on the road. The truth is, I'm something of a loner anyway, though my daily life is steeped in interactions with folks. Perhaps because of the intensity of my work schedule, I often want nothing more than to be home alone, though Shadow, my cat, is a constant companion. Spending time alone is how we introverts recharge.

Here's the rub—this trip will push me to minimalize in a serious way and simultaneously require me to be more outgoing than I usually am if I am to engage people in conversation every chance I get. My instincts will have to be sharpened and my shyness set aside. A number of people have expressed concern for my safety. Basic road safety is one thing, and any long ride reminds you that this is not like casually driving in a car. You really have to keep your eyes on the road and your peripheral vision active. My sense is that the concern they have for me is above and beyond this. People have cautioned me about riding through certain states (Idaho, Wyoming, Nebraska, Alabama, and Mississippi, to name a few), and I understand and appreciate the concern. Heck, I get the creeps driving a car through the South. It's not only memories of Jim Crow days when our family had to go to the back of the store to buy food in West Texas but much more recent trips where people can't stop staring, as if I'm an alien or something! But that's part of why I feel compelled to do this as well—to know that I can, not to prove to the world that I can but to gather the courage to find out if I can. And yet I know two things: first, I will carry a certain amount of privilege with me, and that will be signified in numerous ways, from my bike to my clothing. And to some extent this will shield me from being misread as foreign. And yet, secondly, as a man of color, I know that I cannot forget that my very body will mark me in ways that are inescapable and my safety can spin on a dime depending on whose path I cross any given moment. At the same time, as a man I carry male privilege. It may be considered risky for me to make such a trip, but it would be considered absolutely foolish for a woman to go alone. This is not to say women shouldn't have every right to do so or that many women don't take long solo trips.

RAISING THE STAKES: MAY 26, 2007

Early tomorrow morning I am heading out to Wisconsin with two friends to participate in the Chippewa Valley Century Ride. My friends Yectli Huerta and Gilberto Vásquez did one of these recently, but the 65 miles I rode a few weeks back was my longest ride yet. A 100-mile ride will be a new milestone for me. If successful I'll feel much better about the challenge ahead. I have trips planned for the next two weekends in a row to get a better sense of the feel of daylong rides and camping. Next weekend I'm heading out to Lake Itasca to the headwaters of the Mississippi. The week after that I'm going to Melrose, Minnesota, where Kelly O'Brien, a colleague of mine, has arranged for me to speak to townsfolk about the changing demographics of Melrose. I'm going to bike back. It's about 110 miles to Minneapolis, but as best I can tell I'll have to take an indirect route that will add a few miles.

As I head into the last month of preparation, I'm accumulating supplies and equipment, refining my route, and getting ready to let go of my life as I know it for a while. I'm both anxious and excited as I hope to learn a lot on this trip—about others as well as myself. I hope I'm not disappointed. The recent debates on immigration policy have proven to be as polarizing as one might have expected. Listening to talk radio on the road I am struck by the vitriolic rhetoric of talk-show hosts and callers about all these so-called unwanted illegals. It is painful and sad to hear. So much misinformation, so much willful ignorance, so much disdain for other humans beings. I have to wonder over and over again what it would take, if it's even possible, to change people's minds and hearts. I don't understand the lack of compassion. I don't understand the blindness that people have to how they are connected to immigrant labor by the food they eat, the industries where immigrants work that help sustain the quality of life in this country. How can people not see that their well-being is linked to the well-being of others?

CHIPPEWA VALLEY, WISCONSIN: MAY 28, 2007

Well, I could not keep up with my cycle mates, and somewhere around the 40-mile mark I inadvertently took a left when I should have taken a right and ended up on the 75-mile route instead of the 100. I realized my mistake a few miles down the road, but by then I had to admit that I would not be able to catch up and that I didn't think I had it in me to finish—at least not before the ride organizers called it a day. Counting an early misturn and a short postride, I logged 80 miles. The weather was very, very cool and the winds hard. It seemed like the winds were always in our faces whatever direction we were going. The organizers said it had been years since it was that cold and windy and that a larger than usual number of people were given rides back to the base site because the combination of wind and hills was just too much. I really felt my lack of stamina and strength training, but it was a good reality check. Still, all in all, it was useful for me to confront my limits, to get this many miles in, to enjoy the beautiful Wisconsin countryside, and to have some brats and beer at the end! The folks we met at the park and on the ride were all nice, though I have to say Yectli, Gilberto, and I were the only visible signs of a diverse population out there!

ITASCA AND CASS LAKE, MINNESOTA: JUNE 8, 2007

The trip to Itasca last weekend was a chance to try out my camping gear and get another long ride in. Lisa Sass Zaragoza, my friend and colleague from work, went with me. It was a great chance to see an area of Minnesota that I'd never seen before—Paul Bunyan country, you might say. As a kid I remember reading the legend, so seeing the statues of him and Babe the blue ox was entertaining. We made camp at Cass Lake and tried out the mini-stove, set up our tents, and played cards while we fought off mosquitoes, which also gave me a chance to test my insect repellent. It started raining in the middle of the night and continued the entire next day. After a breakfast of oatmeal and coffee we set out to ride to Lake Itasca, which we both thought was only 35 miles away. Riding through a steady stream of rain wasn't that bad, and I figured it was good practice for a scenario I'm likely to encounter. I don't intend to ride through storms, but so long as visibility and maneuverability isn't compromised I'll trudge along. The only time the rain became a major factor was when we took a shortcut through a country road of unpaved limestone. This slowed us up considerably, but we made it through.

About 25 miles into the ride we were looking forward to having lunch, and we saw a sign that said Itasca Park was another 20 miles away. It was more than we bargained for, and as game as she is and a much better athlete than I, Lisa hadn't planned or trained for that long of a ride. So we decided to stop in the little town of Kabokane and head back, still giving us a 60-mile ride. We took a nice break at a gas station where the owner let us rest on some chairs as we ate lunch indoors. He let us know that the rain wasn't going to let up, so after a good rest we headed back and were oh so happy to discover that the campground showers had hot water. Afterward we decided to drive to Bemidji and get a good hot meal. Later we went by Itasca and saw the headwaters of the mighty Mississippi and a beautiful rainbow. The mosquitoes were much less of a problem that night due to the rain. After breakfast the next morning we returned to Minneapolis, tired but content with a good experience.

The two most important things I learned from this experience are that I have to give my meals and calorie intake lots of consideration and that I have to better find my rhythm going up and down hills using my gears more strategically. I visited a nutritionist this week, and she informed me that I need an intake of probably 6,000 calories a day—a heckuva lot! Blogs from cyclists who have traveled long distances have said as much, but thinking through that from the practical standpoint of carrying food is an important thing to get my head around.

MELROSE, MINNESOTA: JUNE 12, 2007

This past weekend Kelly took me up to her hometown of Melrose to introduce me to folks whom her equally gracious father had arranged for me to meet. It was an eye-opening experience and gave me the chance to try out my conversations with a wide array of people as well as to cycle 130 miles back home. Melrose, like many small towns of middle America, has undergone a dramatic demographic change in the past decade. Repeatedly I heard from folks that prior to 1996 there were only about 16 Latin@s in town, all part of the Cruz or Carbajal families. During the '90s economic boom a great many Melrose citizens took better jobs in St. Cloud and subsequently moved. It was then that Jennie-O, the turkey-processing giant, began hiring large numbers of recent immigrants, and thus the chain-migration process began that resulted in a significant population from Michoacán migrating in to take entry-level jobs at the plant. These workers were an asset to the plant, helped the local economy grow with their entrepreneurship and spending, and boosted the housing market by buying and renting homes so Melrose did not experience a hard economic downturn despite losing lots of its Anglo residents. Now, Latin@ migrants from other parts of the country and more recent arrivals to the U.S., many of whom are *sin papeles*, comprise more than one-fourth of the local population.

A sign above the entrance to the Jennie-O Turkey Store in Melrose, Minnesota. Louis Mendoza.

My host for the day was Kelly's dad, George O'Brien, a retiree and former two-term mayor of Melrose from 1996 to 2002. It was during his tenure as mayor that the influx of Latin@ immigrants began in Melrose—and it was clear that George's leadership and open-mindedness toward Melrose's newest residents had a tremendously positive impact. In his own words, townspeople have tried to learn from the mistakes made in other Minnesota towns like Willmar and Worthington where the change in population has not been so smooth. To this end they are working with the Latin@ community and immigration advocates in the Twin Cities to develop a response plan should ICE (U.S. Immigration and Customs Enforcement) make Melrose the target of an immigration raid. More impressively, George was the catalyst for the formation of Communities Connecting Cultures (CCC), a nonprofit immigrant service organization whose single staff person, Ana Santana, works 25 percent of her weekly work hours running the organization and whose pay is supplemented by Jennie-O, her employer. The CCC has a board that offers Ana advice on issues that arise and direction for the organization's growth. George had heard about a similar organization in another town and approached Jennie-O about providing staff support and some office space to start the program locally.

Ana, her husband, and their three children live in a trailer park in Albany, a town about 10 miles from Melrose. Like her, many of her co-workers live in surrounding towns and make the short commute daily. Originally from California, Ana said her father moved them to Melrose in the late '90s for better working conditions. In California her father worked in the fields, and she shared memories with me of spending days in the vicinity of the fields while her family worked. Her father has since moved to find work in the southern U.S., but with a family and a stable job, she doesn't foresee leaving Melrose. She said when she saw the position advertised she was immediately interested and felt that her English-language proficiency and interest in helping her co-workers would be an asset. Over the past few years the range of support services offered by the CCC has grown expansively, from offering basic advice to newcomers about employment, social services, and cultural events to providing free tax counseling to people in the surrounding communities. Young kids take advantage of Ana's diligence, sincere desire to help, and resourcefulness—I heard one anecdote about a young man who wanted to learn to break dance, and she was able to find some online information for him so he could teach himself. Her work with the CCC is not limited to 10 hours a week, as folks approach her at home

Ana Santana and her children in their trailer home in Albany, Minnesota. Louis Mendoza.

or church with questions. The Santanas' house is decorated with Mexican Catholic religious and cultural icons. The kids gathered around as we spoke, and they were happy to pose for a picture with their mom. I asked her what her hopes and dreams were for her children, and she replied that she wanted them to have a good education so they could have even better opportunities than she has had.

Kelly, George, and I then met his wife, Barbara O'Brien, for lunch at El Portal, the best restaurant in town, I was repeatedly told. We met the proprietor, José, and his daughter. George's familiarity with people became evident as adults and children alike greeted him when they entered. We spoke about the longtime townspeople's attitudes toward changes over the past decade, and the O'Briens acknowledged that not all folks are as open as they are. Change has been rapid. According to the O'Briens, the 1990 Census showed that there were 16 Hispanics in Melrose. In 2000 there were 338. When we spoke, approximately 20 percent of the population of Melrose was Hispanic, officially about 650 but counting the undocumented closer to 750. The 2010 Census identified the Hispanic population in Melrose at 27.5 percent. Many work in meat-packing plants in Melrose or Long Prairie, while others work year-round in local dairies. Here is an excerpt from our lunch conversation over a plate of the best *migas* I've had in Minnesota:

GEORGE: It's hard to discriminate against people who work so hard. One of the things we did when Jennie-O's said we could hire Ana Santana was put her out there. She's probably better known than the governor of Minnesota to most people around here. She's helped 390 people this year, filling out taxes, et cetera. The church has a Spanish-language mass.

BARBARA: This is a highly Catholic area, and the priest has been very active . . . They put in a statue of Our Lady of Guadalupe.

ME: Do folks accept this?

BARBARA: Yes, but not everybody.

ME: Where does it come from with people like you and others, this willingness to be part of positive change?

BARBARA: I think it's just good Christian people practicing faith. I belong to a group of ladies. There may be disagreements with the national issue of illegal immigration, but locally it's different. We are neighbors; we meet and have meals with them.

ME: So actual interaction helps?

BARBARA: Yes, it helps.

 ME: *I don't see any local tension.*

GEORGE: Well, our chief of police has made a difference. He's changed, too. He's different from just two years ago. Many of us have been involved in what to do in case there was a raid by ICE. The chief of police, the mayor, and city administrators have been involved in discussion at various levels. We're trying to work with Pillsbury United. I talked to Francisco Segovia there, and they are coming up with a booklet [of what to do] before, during, and after a raid. We've met with Gloria Edin at Centro Legal. She's been really helpful. We just keep going along and deal with things as they come up. Sister Adela is the diversity coordinator for the diocese. She's met with a number of people locally and nationally to plan on how to be helpful. She's our lead person in planning for a raid.

 ME: *Have there been issues in schools?*

GEORGE: Yes, we need more Spanish-speaking teachers for sure. Scott told me at a basketball game some of the students started verbally harassing the Hispanic kids from Melrose, and all of a sudden a bunch of Anglo kids from Melrose stepped up and said, "Hey, these are our friends. You mess with them you mess with us!" Scott said he was so proud of them. Cold Springs has a large Hispanic population. We were down there on a Saturday, and we saw only one Hispanic lady downtown. You come here on Saturday, and you'll see lots of Hispanics.

 ME: *Obviously, they seem more comfortable here. With all the discussion on immigration, this is a good example of how people live in the shadows. They stay invisible if they don't feel safe. What would happen in Melrose if Hispanics weren't here?*

BARBARA: I think they came here because Anglos wouldn't do the jobs. It's very hard, dirty, and monotonous work. They came because these companies needed the employees.

 ME: *So what would happen if they didn't come?*

BARBARA: They wouldn't produce as much. They have two shifts right now.

GEORGE: A lot of the dairy farms have switched to machines, but manual labor is still needed. Jennie-O used to close down in December and stay closed until March. Now they're open year-round. At Jennie-O they probably have about 50 Somali workers now. They didn't have a liaison person for Hispanics until we forced the issue. We sold this to Jennie-O.

> ME: *Where did you get the idea for Communities Connecting Cultures?*

GEORGE: We studied what was happening in other places like Worthington. We tried to take the best of everything we knew from other places. So we talked to Jennie-O and the city. We started with a job description. We had to file 501(c)(3) status—Kelly helped with that. We only had about 15 people in the first few months. But now we're running several hundred a month. It's about developing trust. During last tax season we had people come from Fergus Falls, which is 80 miles away. We even had someone come up from Iowa. It's the trust factor that has made a difference.

Kelly later expressed her chagrin at her mom's response to why the local community is accepting of newcomers; she thought it was a bit too convenient an explanation that didn't get to a more complex social and political explanation, but I believe Mrs. O'Brien was sincere. I could hear my own mom offering the same rationale because the Catholic disposition to be charitable to others and to follow the golden rule is a simple and profound guide for living; having compassion and doing good deeds offers one a way to find personal salvation—and therein lies a framework for understanding one's self-interest but also a lens through which to see how people's well-being is tied together.

After lunch I met with Tim King, the publisher of *La Voz Libre*, a Spanish-language newspaper published in Long Prairie, and Herman Lensing, assistant editor at the *Melrose Beacon*, to discuss my trip. We had a lively conversation about other literary sojourns taken across the country and in other nations by foot, car, and train. Tim indicated that he would cover my trip from time to time so the local communities could stay apprised of my progress. This was followed by an opportunity to meet with Angel Vargas, a young entrepreneur who owns two stores in Melrose and one in Long Prairie. Two of these are clothing stores that specialize in *ropa mexicana*, and the other one is a small automotive accessory store in downtown Melrose that specializes in electronics. While the clothing stores target the Latin@ community, Angel spoke of wanting to draw a more diverse crowd to the accessory store. Angel is from Fresno, California, and came to Melrose with his family about five years ago. Besides being a young entrepreneur, he is active in the community as the director of one of the youth soccer leagues. He and Tim King spoke about the prospect of buying one of the local radio stations and wondered aloud if advertisers would support a Spanish-language station. After chatting with them I met with John Jensen, the chief of police, at a coffee shop across the street and had a very insightful conversation on his perspective on Anglo-Mexican relationships in the town.

Kelly gave me a brief tour of downtown Melrose that included a visit to St. Mary's Church—where a Spanish-language mass is held on Sundays and a side altar has been set up to honor the Virgen de Guadalupe—and a quick trip to Earl's Bar. Kelly then took me to the soccer game at the park to meet Peggy and John Stokman, retirees who relocated to Melrose from Nebraska with the intention of finding a community where they could be advocates for new immigrants. As with the O'Briens, it was evident that the Stokmans were known and liked in the community as children and adults went out of their way to greet them. Having spent some time in Central America on a mission, the Stokmans returned to Nebraska and became involved in the immigrant-rights movement, mostly through their church. Though their involvement is something that is frowned upon by their children, who take a more legalistic approach to people's rights, they have not allowed that to abate their passion for their work.

Aware of how their presence as outsiders might be perceived, the Stokmans' entree into the Latin@ community of Melrose began through their regular attendance of the Spanish-language mass. After a few weeks some parishioners began approaching them, letting them know they appreciated the couple's presence, and inviting them to social outings. As trust was built and genuine relationships formed, the Stokmans said residents told them what they needed most was English language instruction. Having experience with this in Nebraska, they put together a free ESL (English as a Second Language) program and solicited volunteers from among Melrose residents who served as instructors after receiving some training. This program involved more than 60 tutors, most of whom knew no Spanish! Notwithstanding the impressive involvement of residents in the ESL program, when I asked them about Anglo-Mexican relations, they admitted that for many folks, particularly the elderly, there was reluctance to accept change. Scattered throughout the mostly Latin@ crowd at the park were some young white youths who were clearly friends of the players. To help me get an answer to how youths were adapting to this change, the Stokmans took me to a high school graduation party to which they had been invited so I could find out for myself.

There I met the guest of honor, Elena Cruz, who aspired to go to St. Benedict College in St. Joseph. In her view, socializing among youths

My shadow on the road as I make my way back to Minneapolis from Melrose. Louis Mendoza.

of different backgrounds in the high school was somewhat limited. However, her younger brother, who just passed to the sixth grade, said the kids were all friends despite their backgrounds. I also had the pleasure of meeting Mr. and Mrs. Carbajal, some of the longtime *mexicano* residents of Melrose who are considered community elders and often looked to for advice. Mr. Carbajal is now retired from Jennie-O, while his wife continues to work in human resources at the plant. Mr. Carbajal was fairly adamant that things have changed for the better for the Latin@ community as it has grown. He said it is incumbent on new immigrants to earn the trust of locals through their actions and behavior.

I left Melrose about 5 p.m. feeling very satisfied with the range of people I met and the conversations we had. My goal was to reach Watkins, about 45 miles away, by nightfall. When I got there, I could not find a place to camp or a hotel, so I rode into the dark to the next town, about 16 miles up the road. Highway 55 has a nice, broad shoulder, and though there was no moon out and I had to ride a lot more slowly, I made it to Annandale a little before 11 p.m. Unfortunately, I ended up having to go two towns farther, to Buffalo, before I could find lodging. By the time I arrived it was close to 1 a.m., and I had gone 85 miles. Very, very tired, I slept late and rode the final 45 miles home the next morning.

The next weekend, Yectli and I rode the Willard Munger Trail from

Hinckley to outside of Duluth and back. I rode 120 miles in a single day for the first time and declared myself ready to go—physically, at least.

NOS VEMOS: HEADING DOWN THE ROAD, JUNE 28, 2007

News from Capitol Hill. The immigration reform bill is dead, and the Supreme Court shows its colors by dismantling desegregation efforts in the K–12 system. 'Tis a sad day when our legislators show once again that they are unable to take action on one of the most pressing issues facing the nation. Is it 2007 or 1967? At least in 1965 and again in 1986 the nation's leaders were able to pass legislation that accounted for the world we lived in. Our leaders today are moving us backward by failing to figure out how to move us forward. And I'm starting my trip.

I spend Monday and Tuesday leading a seminar on immigration called American Crossings at the Minnesota Humanities Center for a group of 50 impassioned educators who know that education is the key to our future, as is the need to find a just and fair solution to our immigration policies. The goodwill and sentiments from many who have expressed concern for my safety inspire me and lighten my load as I pack to leave for Santa Cruz, where my longtime friend Marianne Bueno, a PhD student in history at the University of California–Santa Cruz, will host me as I make final preparations for hitting the road.

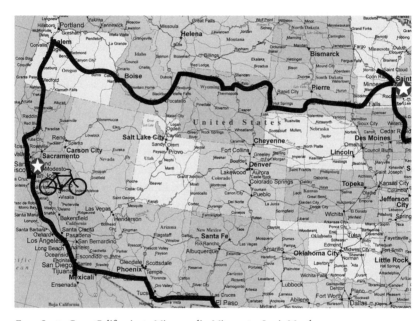

From Santa Cruz, California, to Minneapolis, Minnesota. Louis Mendoza.

PART TWO

THE START OF A JOURNEY
Ready, Set, Go!

A JOURNEY IS LIKE MARRIAGE. THE CERTAIN WAY TO BE WRONG IS TO
THINK YOU CONTROL IT.

John Steinbeck

WHEN YOU'RE TRAVELING, YOU ARE WHAT YOU ARE RIGHT THERE
AND THEN. PEOPLE DON'T HAVE YOUR PAST TO HOLD AGAINST YOU.
NO YESTERDAYS ON THE ROAD.

William Least Heat-Moon

On the first day of July 2007, with some trepidation in my heart for what
lies ahead, I say goodbye to Marianne on the outskirts of Santa Cruz, California, and begin pedaling my bike and 50 pounds of gear northward on
Highway 1. Day one is all about learning firsthand why you should ride
from north to south along the coast with the wind at your back and not in
your face. I make it to Half Moon Bay, about 50 miles from my starting
point in Santa Cruz, and realize that going into San Francisco will be almost impossible due to headwinds, hills, and construction. I kid you not
when I say coming down steep hills where one would normally expect to
coast at speeds of 25–30 mph, I am barely going 12. More than once I have
to walk the bike up a hill as the winds bluster the oceanside flowers flat.
It is otherwise a beautiful day, and cyclists are out in full force—but they
are all heading south. I am excited and nervous, and I remind myself not
to think of the entire length of the trip, as doing so is daunting. A huge
shadow of self-doubt lurks; rather, I tell myself, I should focus on one day
at a time and have faith in my ability to adapt and cope with what the road
brings me.

Between Santa Cruz and Half Moon Bay are numerous beach farms and places that advertise pick-your-own strawberries and cherries. As I look at the beautiful landscape of these farms with ramshackle boarding for farmworkers I wonder about the workers' quality of life and can't help but think how migrant farmworkers remain the bellwether for how Latin@s, mostly Mexicans, are treated in this country. To be sure, when migrants are able to settle out, they often do well and their families tend to obtain a better education and become upwardly mobile. Both sets of my grandparents worked the cotton and agricultural fields of Central Texas when they first arrived in the U.S. in the early twentieth century—so my family history is testimony to this. But why is it acceptable and necessary for us to allow such horrific double standards of workplace laws regulating safety and wages? Do most Americans even know that migrant farmworkers have a lifespan that's more than twenty years less than the U.S. average? Do they know that farmworkers earn an average annual salary of around $10,000, that laws allow children in the fields to enter the workforce at a younger age, that until 2008 minimum-wage laws didn't apply to most farmworkers, that children often attend six or more schools in a given year as their families follow the crops?[1] Do most Americans even care? Or is it simply better to be willfully ignorant?

TALK ABOUT INCONVENIENT TRUTHS

I, like many others, understand the appeal of enjoying the fruits of one's labor symbolized in the pick-your-own fruits and vegetables cottage industry on some of these small farms where people can feel eco- and labor-friendly by spending a couple of hours picking their own food straight from the fields. There is something quaint and romantic about this when we experience food and labor as less separate. It's one of those rare moments in today's world when we can feel like we are directly producing something that nurtures and sustains us. But, in truth, this too is only a minuscule portion of the real sweat and muscle behind farmwork. As I pass signs with images of low-flying planes warning of crop dusters, I hope they are off duty this Sunday even as I realize these are the working conditions of people in the fields every day.

At the end of the day I take advantage of still being near my point of departure and call Marianne for a ride to San Francisco. The next morning we drive down the road and go through Devil's Pass. I feel less disheartened by my decision to ask for assistance so soon into the trip when I see that it was a good decision, as the construction, traffic, and steepness of the mountain pass all combine to make this virtually impassable for bikes because the shoulders of the road are shut down. As I soon learn, this will not be the only time I need to forsake riding a road to be safe. Not wanting to face the winds all the way up to Oregon, I alter my route to go up Highway 101 and eventually parallel I-5 through northern California.

In Sausalito, I realize Highway 101 isn't bike-friendly, so I head back to the coast and ride up to Reyes Point Station and then cut back over to Santa Rosa. Along the way I encounter many friendly bikers who are openly envious of my trip and profoundly generous in expressing their best wishes to me. My gear is a sure sign that this is no casual ride I am undertaking. I am especially inspired by one man who tells me he crossed the country the previous year and was loaded down with more gear than I. Already I've unloaded some items and am constantly thinking about what else I can dispense with to keep the load light.

Every day is a new adventure, and I find I need to increase my tolerance for the unknown. After a ten-hour ride on day two, I check into a Motel 6 in Santa Rosa when I find the high visibility of the regulations against camping in a local state park backed up by patrol cars. The next day I go over more hills as I head toward Calistoga. It takes me three hours to ride 15 miles over the mountain, and by this time my thighs hurt every time I see the road swing upward. I stop at the Petrified Forest to watch a geyser and check in at a gas station for drinks and directions before getting on the road over the next mountain toward Clear Lake. The *mexicana* attendant says *Dios mío* and shakes her head when I tell her I'm riding on a bike. Half an hour later I will be saying the same thing as I head up the pass and realize there is no shoulder and a sign indicates 10 miles of an uphill climb to go. I've found the reward of coming downhill exhilarating, but going up and down with no shoulder and heavy truck traffic kicks my survival instinct in, and I remind myself that the goal is to survive to tell this tale. I turn around and go back to Calistoga, where I eventually find the bus depot and learn that for three dollars I can get a ride to the next town on the other side of the mountain.

On the bus I converse in broken Spanish with Lorenzo Martínez, a farmworker who has also placed his bike on the rack in front of the bus. He evades my questions about where he's from and instead tells me where he might be going. He likes working in this area because it's beautiful and the pay is okay, but he says the price of $300,000 for a casita is out of reach for him and his wife. She has taken off to Michigan for the picking season, and when she returns they may move to Texas to join his sister who moved there last month. He doesn't know where in Texas she is because he

hasn't heard from her yet, but he understands that it might be more affordable. I assure him it is, but I can't say what the pay is like. When we get off
the bus I regret not taking his picture, but its feels so touristy and I worry
about being perceived as endangering his security, so I refrain from doing
so. I have to figure out how to do this without feeling like I'm objectifying
the subject of the camera's gaze.

At night I sleep on a ridge overlooking a vineyard outside of Clear Lake.
It's a restless sleep with the traffic nearby and the temperature not cooling
down significantly until late in the evening when the moon rises. Feeling
lonely and a need to record my thoughts, I speak into my recorder.

> It's the evening of July third. I'm about two miles south of Highway 20
> on Highway 53, just a few miles north of Clear Lake, California. I'm
> watching the sun set over some grape vineyards. It's a warm night.
> It's been a crazy day. I haven't really had a chance to start interviewing
> folks. I'm just trying to get my distance in each day, and each day has
> been a different challenge.
>
> . . . I made it into Santa Rosa about eight o'clock or so and was look-
> ing for a place to camp and couldn't find one. I asked some young kids
> in a Subway sandwich shop for directions to a Motel 6, and they pointed
> me in the wrong direction. So, I spent about an hour trying to find it.
> I thought of camping in some of the nearby woodlands, but the many
> signs indicating that camping was not allowed dissuaded me, as the
> thought of being confronted by police so early in the trip didn't sit well
> with me.
>
> I got off the bus near Clear Lake. I was told I could transfer and
> get a little closer to Highway 20, but I decided to ride the eight miles to
> Clear Lake and then head up five more miles toward Highway 20. I kept
> my eyes open for places to camp because so far every night I've stayed in
> hotels. I really can't afford to do that all the time. I found a place that is
> something like a plateau along the opposite side of the road, and it's hid-
> den from view enough, so I decide to lay low and camp here. To mini-
> mize my visibility, I decided not to set up the tent, so I'm just lying on
> my sleeping bag. I'm wearing my jacket, and as the sun sets and a wind
> picks up I expect the night to be chilly. I'm between the highway and a
> fence, and I'm hoping I'm not going to ruffle anyone's feathers if they
> see me here. I don't think I'm visible from the road or from the other
> side, where there appears to be a vineyard. Maybe with the holiday, busi-
> ness won't be as usual if there is any activity on the farmland. Maybe
> the workers have the day off.

I would say that so far I haven't got into a rhythm. I've struggled so much with the ongoing mountain terrain that it takes all I have to just keep pedaling. Despite my training, I know there is nothing like the real deal to help you understand your limits. Each day has been a real challenge of one sort or another, which is okay and it's good to know I can adapt. I'm reading *Blue Highways* by William Least Heat-Moon, and it's a pretty good book, along with John Steinbeck's *Travels with Charley*, which are helping me think about how to frame my trip. Obviously a road is a road is a road. One thing is for sure, you don't really know what's around the corner. I think cycling makes a road trip very different because you feel it in such a deep way as opposed to riding around sleeping in your car or motels. I've certainly had the luxury of hotels, but you feel quite a bit more vulnerable in an unofficial campsite like this. If anyone comes along and says I shouldn't be here I'm not going to argue with them—I'll respect that and take off. I'm certainly not looking to get into confrontations.

Lots of things to think about with respect to things I've seen. I haven't had conversations with people about Latin@s as workers or as immigrants who are historically here. This is California, so we're everywhere. I asked one young white kid in a pickup truck if he knew where the bus depot was in Calistoga, and he was like, "I don't know if we even have one," but he pointed me in the direction of a gas station, which didn't exist, but it did take me to the county fair lines where at the entrance were two young Chicanos who knew exactly where it was and gave me directions on how to get there. Partly I think that whether or not they have cars themselves, they're probably just more familiar with how the bus lines work.

Taking the bus over the hill today was a good idea. There's no way I could have survived that road. I just don't see how anybody could bike that road. The cars were hugging each other, and there was a serious car wreck at one end of the road, and at one point the traffic came to a complete standstill, and there just was absolutely no shoulder, and the steepness of it was just unbelievable. Riding along the road you certainly notice other things as well, besides just road kill. You see where cars have wrecked, and it makes you feel vulnerable when you see broken glass and crumpled windshield wipers where cars have flipped over.

You always have to be careful. You can't control everything, and life spins on a dime in that way, and you don't want to take any more risks than you have to. This trip is not about being ultra-courageous, nor do I need to be purist in my cycling. My goal is much larger. As I think about all the stuff I've seen, you have to be really careful. You have to also think about the difference between riding a car and cycling. One of the reasons I like to ride long distances in cars is because it's relaxing. Your instincts take over, and you can ride, and I don't think it's uncommon at all for people to say they drove from one state to another without even realizing it because they were deep in thought. Your eyes and hands and feet know what to do in terms of being safe and just following the rules of the road. Of course I may not be paying 100 percent attention to the road, but it's not all that uncommon. Bicycling, however, you don't really have that luxury—not that I haven't been thinking about things, which you are more able to do on a flat road with a good, nice, clean, wide shoulder. But so much of what I've been doing so far has involved really intense concentration.

It's all the more taxing for that reason because you have to be so deliberate about keeping your eyes on the road and making sure that there aren't—in a place like California—falling rocks, drivers swerving outside their lane onto the shoulder, or branches. Or the overgrowth is so bad that you whip into it with panniers. You have to be careful about hugging the shoulder but not so much so you don't hit a mailbox, which sounds ridiculous, but if a pannier hits or gets snagged on something it can make you lose control. Today my right pannier was ripped on a news rack, and I felt a strong jerk.

People have been pretty gracious overall with respecting cyclists. Only once did I have people honking at me. As I started going up the steep hill a couple of people yelled at me something to the effect that I was crazy to think that I could go up there. They were probably right, and their yells made me think twice about what I was doing. Otherwise, this Asian American guy pulled over today in a van and told me he thought he saw something drop from of my pocket and thought it might be money. I knew it couldn't be much money, but he insisted on walking with me to find it, and sure enough, it was a one-dollar bill crumpled up. His kindness touched me. He asked me about my cycling trip and wished me luck and told me to be safe. Other than him, the people I've talked to on the road so far have mostly been cyclists. Coming out of Sausalito toward Santa Rosa, a number of them made a point of asking me, as they cycled by, where I was going because of course the panniers signaled a long trip, and they were in awe of the fact that I was going not just across the country but around it.

I've been wondering if I'm overpacked. I don't really know how much more I could unload with the exception of a book or two. I find these very important, especially the kinds of books I've selected, which are travel books and immigration books. Anyhow, one cyclist I spoke with today told me that he actually stayed in a pretty good mood the whole time he traveled across the country, though he was aware that many people talked about how you have to psych yourself up for a melt-down or two. I'm not close to a meltdown yet by any means, but my legs are so tired of mountainous roads that each time I see a curve going up my body gets tired faster and faster and I long for a flat stretch.

People have stopped while I'm resting on the side of the road to see if I'm okay, which I've certainly had to do in unexpected places. But when you need to rest you need to rest, I've found. More than one person has turned around and asked me if I'm okay or needed a ride. It's been mostly women who've stopped, and I thought that was very nice of them, though I have to say I'm a bit surprised that they offer to pick up a stranger. Clearly I'm marked by my clothes and the quality of my bike and gear as not being some casual cyclist.

Tomorrow holds another day of hard riding. I've learned that scenic routes marked on the map are oftentimes mountainous routes, although that's not always true. Today it was true for part of it and not for other parts. Right now it is relatively flat and straight and seems to have plateaued. I don't see any foreboding mountains in the distance, but you only have so much perspective on that. Even as you go up mountains, you think you're at the top, but it just keeps going up and up, and even when you think you're going down, there will just be another ridge going up. My goal now is to make it down Highway 20 across Highway 5 to Williams, northward up toward Red Bluff and to Redding. I'm looking forward to finding a daily rhythm that includes writing because the days are so taxing that I've not been able to find energy to write in the evenings.

Right now I'm still feeing pretty good. I'm riding with a cell phone, of course, which makes it a lot different in terms of being able to be in touch with folks. I'm not using it much, but it's nice to know I have it. It is also good to know it's only a few days away from last Friday, when I was up till two in the morning trying to take care of last-minute business at work. I have to keep in mind that much of the first portion of this trip is simply about finding my groove on the road. There are not going to be many places once I get into Wyoming where I will encounter people who have had much interaction with Latinos because it's a lot of open land that, as far as I know, hasn't experienced a lot of demographic change. Nonetheless, I will still try to have conversations. I also feel like a big portion of this first part is to prepare myself physically to do the rest of it. I'm hoping that as I go west to east the roads are going to be a lot flatter.

EVERY TURN BRINGS A NEW VIEW: JULY 7, 2007

It's the seventh day of travel, and I'm feeling lucky to be taking a break in Redding, California. As I noted earlier, the first leg of the trip is all about finding my riding rhythm. It hasn't been easy. As I head toward Williams on July 4 I rejoice that for once the day begins with a downhill ride before reaching a set of rolling hills. What I've learned, however, is that up in the hills or mountains you can never really tell where you are or what's around the corner, so about 18 miles from Williams when I spill all the water out of my CamelBak while transferring water from my jugs, I worry about having enough to last me, particularly since I tend to drink more when going uphill. I decide not to risk it and make a sign for a ride to Williams.

About 15 cars and 15 minutes later, a blue van blaring rock music pulls over, and I'm greeted by John and Mindy and their dog, Maggie, who are on their way to a camping trip in Mendocino National Forest. They are hippies in every sense of the word; the bumper stickers plastered inside the van's sides and roof bespeak their worldview—quotes from John Lennon ("Give Peace a Chance"), "We are all the HUMAN Race," "Animals feel pain, too!"—as do the Zig Zag rolling papers on the floorboard. Over the next 25 minutes we discuss politics and they, mostly John, are clear in their sentiments that the country is in sad shape because the government has sold out to corporations, and both national and international business interests dominate U.S. policies. John says people are feeling more and more powerless but that he's aware that resistance occurs in small ways and he thinks people have to band together and refuse to capitulate. He's pretty disgusted with the electoral process and sees little difference between the parties, but at the same time John and Mindy both seem to have a strong belief in the essence of Americans, a spirit that will not allow injustice and imbalance to dominate forever. They drop me off at the first gas station in Williams, accept with pleasant surprise my donation for the ride, and wish me luck on my journey after they pose happily for a photo.

I make it to Colusa by early afternoon and decide to rest. I ride around town and learn, as I will over and over, that as inviting as the little parks are in the center of town, police are watchful that you don't get too comfort-

John and Mindy pose for me when they drop me off in Williams, California. Louis Mendoza.

able and are quick to let you know that camping there is out of the question. The local casino is having a discount on hotel rooms, so I take refuge there and engage in friendly banter with the casino staff about my bike ride. The next day I go to Corning, and the weather is dramatically hotter. I am enjoying the flatness of the ride through this valley, but I find myself having to stop every hour or two for shade. At the edge of Hamilton City under a tent I meet an elder from Nayarit, Mexico, selling an ice-cold sweet-and-sour lemon-lime-sugar concoction called *tejuino de Colima*. It's fantastic. As I roll into Corning, I cut through a neighborhood to look for downtown, and I hear an ice cream vendor. A minute later I'm enjoying a strawberry *paleta* as I pedal down the street with one hand on my handlebars. At night I stay at a rest stop along Highway 5 and have to fix two flat tires I picked up when I went off the road and a bunch of burs from a plant punctured both tires. As I will learn, these goathead thorns are a curse of bikers. They require pliers to pull them out of your tire. The next day I make it to Redding, but the temperature has reached new heights, and when I find out in Anderson, just 10 miles outside of Redding, that the reason I'm feeling so hot is that it is 116 degrees, I decide to take a long, long break. I go into a movie theater until the sun sets before completing my ride for the day.

REDDING, CALIFORNIA: JULY 8, 2007

YOU CAN CHECK OUT ANYTIME YOU LIKE, BUT YOU CAN NEVER LEAVE.
"Hotel California," The Eagles, 1977

I arrive here Friday night with the intention of resting on Saturday. I have a fairly mellow Saturday running some errands, catching up on e-mail, renewing supplies, and visiting bike shops looking for lightweight, long-sleeve jerseys to protect me from the fierce sun that is slowly but steadily baking any exposed skin into a leathery, deep red-brown color. The owner of one bike shop gives me a wonderful book about riding through Shasta-Trinity National Forest. He suggests strongly that going over the almost 15,000-foot Mount Shasta will be a pretty difficult ordeal. After reviewing the book with its color-coded charts of the grades and the mileage, I agree. I reluctantly decide to take a bus to Yreka, near the Oregon border.

Sunday morning I get up early to put together the makeshift box I need to pack the bike. I call the Greyhound bus station all morning to buy a ticket in advance, but no one answers. When I don't get a busy signal a machine answers, telling me, "The machine is off." After a few moments I hear, "The machine is now hanging up." With two and a half hours before my bus is to depart I call a cab to make sure I get there early. Fifteen minutes, I'm told. A half-hour later I call back and am told they're busy but I should see a cab in about 15 minutes. This goes on for almost two hours. I want to scream at the operator, but this is the only cab company in town with a van to carry my big box, so I'm afraid to get listed as a problem customer. Between the no-show cab and the unanswered phones at the bus station, I feel like I'm in a Motel 6 Twilight Zone. At 15 minutes to departure time I cancel the cab and check into the motel again. There isn't another bus leaving today, so I unpack the bike and explore Redding.

While in Redding I have the chance to patronize a couple of Mexican food establishments. Here's a cultural quiz for you. Consider the names

Signs for Tortilla Flats and The Whole Enchilada in Redding, California. Louis Mendoza.

and guess which one is a "family-owned restaurant," which, from what I can tell in the Northwest, is code for "authentic" Mexican food. In the Southwest you don't need to state this, but the farther into the Northwest I get, the more one can read this as a signifier of the ambience, the quality of the food, and the prices one can expect. One is called The Whole Enchilada, the other Tortilla Flats. One is very small with eight small tables; the other is gaudy, pricier, and kept dark during the day, and it has a cheap, plastic, neon-lighted cactus on each table.

If you guessed that The Whole Enchilada is the family-owned one, you were right. With a name that evokes the John Steinbeck novel about Mexicans in northern California, Tortilla Flats has a certain irony, given that the owners probably intended to give it a name with a ring of authenticity. However, like Steinbeck's novel *Tortilla Flat*, it's pretty far removed from the real thing, but the entirely non-Latin@ staff and clientele seem pretty content with their own little cultural fiction.

I will say that when I first read Steinbeck's *Tortilla Flat* I was profoundly disappointed in him. I expected more from the author of *The Grapes of Wrath*. I read it in the early '80s before I was exposed to much Chican@ literature and was still searching for our literary presence. I found his depiction insulting and crass—that of an outsider who was trying to evoke sympathy or pity rather than empathy or critical awareness of the relationships of culture, class, and protest. In preparation for this trip I read his 1962 book, *Travels with Charley: In Search of America*, and my respect for him was renewed. William Least Heat-Moon says in *Blue Highways: A Journey into America*, a book I finish while on the road, that *Travels with Charley* isn't one of Steinbeck's best. But I found the memoir very insightful and revealing of Steinbeck's own worldview, particularly when he confronts the raw and muted emotions that the emerging civil rights movement is causing in people of the South.

FROM MEDFORD TO COTTAGE GROVE, JULY 9–10, 2007

I arrive in Medford, Oregon, and bike 45 miles to a campground in Treehorn. I'm feeling good with two days' rest. On Tuesday (day 10), I get an early start and have a long and very productive day shadowing I-5 off and on as I try to stay on Highway 99 as much as possible. I've been told by an Oregonian that I-5 was built on top of old 99, so it is a bit unreliable at times—the road is fine, it ends, then it reappears, and so on. Unfortunately for me, what this means is that several times I am left with no choice but to hop onto I-5 for a few miles.

Traveling the interstate on a bicycle is not what I'm in this for. I learn that without even trying, you tend to go faster because your adrenaline rises as the traffic zooms by you. One time in Roseburg when I-5 dead-ended across a bridge that was being reconstructed, I had to go back five miles to get on the freeway despite urging from a local who told me to hop the train tracks and a fence and climb up the hill to the highway. It was tempting because it was right there, but going up a hill and crossing a fence illegally didn't appeal to me, especially while carrying the bike and 50 pounds of gear. When I came back on the highway across the river the bridge narrowed significantly and the shoulder disappeared. My best guess is that this reduces the cost of the bridge, but if you need to cross this on anything not motorized, you put your life in the hands of others. About three-fourths of the way across this bridge as I am coming down the other side, I see a man walking on the right side. By his stiff walk, his straight back, and his arms hanging by his side I can tell he is an elderly man. Rather than yell "Passing left" at him, I decide it is best just to keep my eye on my rear-view mirror and squeeze by him and the traffic, hoping that my panniers will hit neither. They don't, but unforeseen moments like this are what make riding the interstate enormously risky.

Because I am riding through a lot of level ground and my speed is up several miles per hour, I think I might actually make it into Eugene. But twice more this day I take roads I thought were Highway 99 that turned into dead ends. Both times I do take shortcuts to the interstate. One time I come down a long and steep road into a dead end that goes into property that is fenced off and has multiple "No trespassing" signs. The thought of going back up a steep hill to the interstate entrance so discourages me that I decide to cut through this property to get on the interstate, which means one less barbed-wire fence to get over. In fear that I will be caught, I push my bike through chest-high grass at top speed, cross a small stream of water, get to the fence between this property and the interstate, quickly unhook all my bags from my bike and toss them over the five-foot fence, lean my bike on a pole, climb it, hop over the fence, reach over it, and yank the bike over the top. I then move everything beneath a tree near the highway where I am forced to take a break before putting everything back in order.

I barely make it to the small town of Cottage Grove that evening, 20 miles outside of Eugene. The extra physical and emotional exertion of these cuts to the interstate have worn me out, and though I have possible contacts in Cottage Grove, it is all I can do to get to the first small motel in town and crawl into bed. The amount of sweating I have been doing thus far has also taken its toll on me. My clothes are drenched by mid-morning each day, and this causes serious chafing on my thighs, buttocks, and crotch. For the next two weeks, I make sure to use generous amounts of anti-chafing cream or Vaseline to heal it and prevent a recurrence. Though my tailbone hurts from the hard, solid seat of my bike, already I can tell that what I was told when I first bought the bike—my butt would adjust and develop muscles to adapt—is coming true.

News and controversy about the building of a fence along the U.S.-Mexican border continue unabated. An Associated Press article by Elliot Spagat (printed in the Bend, Oregon, local paper, *The Bulletin*, on July 14, 2007), quotes Don McDermott, a Border Patrol supervisor who worked the U.S.-Mexico border near San Diego in the 1980s, as saying, "'It was a never-ending battle, and we were losing very badly.'" According to Spagat, "The Border Patrol made 800 arrests a day in the five-mile stretch from the Pacific Ocean in the early 1990s. . . . Now arrests in that area and six adjoining miles are about 50 to 75 a day."

Riding through the small towns of Oregon, I see evidence of the demographic and cultural changes that are occurring. Some of the social and economic dynamics are similar to what is happening in Melrose, Minnesota, and elsewhere, but they have their own variations as well. Cottage Grove, for instance, was a logging town that has seen a sea change in that industry since the housing market dropped in the 1990s. Now, it has be-

My bike and mural art at Dave's convenience store in Cottage Grove, Oregon. Louis Mendoza.

come a bedroom community to Eugene because its housing is so much more affordable. New immigrants work in the firefighting and service industries, and they are entrepreneurs, as evidenced by the abundance of small restaurants. The appearance of these restaurants has caused longtime establishments like a cafe on the main street in Cottage Grove to adapt its menu. I learn this firsthand by eating there, and I can't help but notice a new insert in the menu with Mexican food offerings.

As I head out of town, I discover that something even more complex is going on. I photograph a Virgen de Guadalupe mural outside Dave's convenience store in Cottage Grove and go in to speak with the owner about its reception by the local community. It turns out my assumption that it is a Mexican-descent owner is wrong. The Anglo cashiers tell me that the owner is a great believer in the Virgin Mary and that he'd had this painting commissioned in her honor because she has helped him straighten out his life and end his drinking problem. One of the cashiers says that though he's not Mexican he's come to believe in her in all her forms and that his new Mexican clientele from the neighborhood had told him how this mural was a good way to pay tribute to her. It's a reminder that cultural exchange and adaptation are a two-way process—immigrants adapt, but the communities adapt to their presence as well.

FROM EUGENE TO BEND, OREGON: JULY 11, 2007

Made it into Eugene. Very sore today, though the good news is that clouds were out and the weather was a lot cooler. For the last week it seems that every weather report I've seen has made note of record high temperatures. I've arranged to meet with Guadalupe Quinn, the regional director and one of the co-founders of CAUSA Oregon, an immigrant-rights organization started in response to the anti-immigrant climate precipitated by California's Proposition 187 in 1994. I speak briefly about my trip on KOPT, an Air America radio station, and then meet with Guadalupe at an IHOP for a great two-hour conversation. She is generous in spirit, and her admonition "Take care of yourself, m'ijo" when we depart makes me feel blessed with a friend.

Guadalupe's story is both complex and common. As young newlyweds she and her "American" husband moved to Eugene from Oxnard, California, to start a new life. She was a teacher's aide with a high school diploma. In the early '80s a friend took her to a Quaker meeting on solidarity with Central America—in opposition to U.S. intervention. She went because they needed a translator, and she offered her service. Her act of translating proved to be ideologically transformative. She had never seen or heard such criticisms of government policy and abuse of power, nor had she experienced the power of people coming together to make social and political change. From that moment on, her life changed as she became part of this movement and then part of the immigrant-rights movement. She acknowledged that she had to renegotiate her marriage with her husband because no longer would she be the traditional domestic wife and mother he thought he had married, but their marriage survived this transition.

As the sole contact for CAUSA in Eugene, she works out of her house. Her work involves implementing education campaigns, building alliances with progressive organizations, working with the campus MEChA (Movimiento Estudiantil Chicano de Aztlán) to sponsor events, advocating for Congress to pass the DREAM Act (originally titled simply the American Dream Act), and much more. She tells me the groups had about 600 people at last year's immigration rally, a turnout they consider highly successful. She speaks with pride about successes the community has achieved, like the naming of a new local elementary school after César Chávez and the growth of the community evidenced by *tienditas*, restaurants, and *panaderías*.

Thursday evening I stay with Tamara Belknap, a friend of a friend who owns a beautiful home in the mountains near Corvallis. Her partner, Robin, cooks a great BBQ, and we sit down with Tamara's dad, Jim, for good food and conversation. From Jim, a resident of Cottage Grove, I learn about the decline of the logging industry and the transformation of some of the smaller towns. The next day, Tamara drives me to Lebanon to get back on the road. She tells me of the racial tension she witnessed as a high school student in what was then (mid-'90s) a majority-white town. Now, she says, the demographics have shifted dramatically, and change is not always easy but an ongoing process.

HEADING ACROSS THE CASCADES: JULY 13, 2007

From Lebanon I begin my ride eastward across the Cascade Mountains heading toward Bend. I'm happy to be making my first major directional shift. It takes me two days to cover a 105–mile stretch, much of it tortuous uphill climbing. The terrain is beautiful. I had assumed there would be running water in the national forest campsites, but I was wrong. After nine hours on the road, I begin an earnest search for a campground where I can eat, sleep, and replenish my water supply. I have to walk uphill a number of times, and late in the day as sunset appears to be only an hour or two away, I worry that no open campground or supply store has appeared. Pushing the bike uphill has produced sharp pains in my back because of the weight and the angle at which I need to hold the bike as I push. As I rest along the road before beginning one last, long push, I reassure myself that I can sleep anywhere off the road and have several days' worth of food on me, but I worry about my very low supply of water. And not for the first time I begin to have doubts about the wisdom of conducting my research

On the Oregon Trail across the Cascade Mountains. Louis Mendoza.

this way. A car suddenly seems much more appealing! I let myself briefly consider what it would mean to get to a safe place and take a bus home and get my car before heading onward. I force myself to snap out of this train of thought and try to refocus on the present moment.

As I lie against my bike, I think I hear running water. I can't see it, but I feel cool moisture in the air, so I put my bike in the brush and take my CamelBak and water jugs and begin walking around. Within ten minutes I find a stream flowing down the steep mountain and replenish my water. Not wanting to take any chance of getting sick, I use a filter and a water-cleansing ultraviolet light I have to kill any bacteria. Feeling rested and emotionally reinvigorated, I get back on the road, and after a few more miles uphill I find a picnic site. No one is here, but I welcome being off the road near a portable toilet, and I set up camp. The food is great, though the night is cold, dark, and eerily silent. My phone doesn't get a signal, so I've no way to connect to anyone, but I feel some small triumph for not letting fear or despair get the best of me.

The next day I continue this beautiful if a bit treacherous ride over the Cascades. I see three snowcapped mountains in the distance. I learn later that these are the three sisters, North, South, and Middle Sister, sitting between the towns of Sister and Bend. Coming down the mountains I pass a large area that has experienced a wildfire—eerie and sad. I am unable to get pictures because I am on a steep downhill grade and can't easily stop. As I approach the town of Sister, I barely avoid a rock with my front wheel, only to run over it with the back. The impact bends the rim so it rubs hard against the bike frame with each wobbly turn. I try in vain to straighten it and only make it worse. Even pushing it is difficult. I make it to Sister after a couple of hours. It's very crowded with traffic, and I learn that the annual quilting convention is in full swing with 30,000 attendees. There are no cabs in Sister, but there are in Bend, so I call one to come get me. I have a long wait, the cab arrives, and I chat with the driver.

BEND, OREGON: JULY 14, 2007

The cabbie lets me know where I can get my bike repaired, and I ask him to take me to any inexpensive motel in town. He's curious about my ride, so I tell him about my project. He tells me Bend used to be a logging town but it has begun to develop as a tourist destination. I tell him I've been talking to people around issues of immigration. I turn my recorder on, and this is what I record:

CABBIE: Well, Bend has a hard-working class. The Hispanics that come to Bend are families and work.

ME: *Is the Hispanic presence new?*

CABBIE: Yes, the way Bend is growing it's getting bigger and become a magnet for Hispanic families to get away from crime and gangs. They work real hard.

ME: *What kind of work do they do?*

CABBIE: Construction, landscaping, painting, all that kind of work.

ME: *It sounds like Cottage Grove, where people told me it'd been a logging town and died out. But they said it was a bedroom community.*

CABBIE: Yeah, Bend's real estate was ranked as one of the highest. Went up way too fast and now it's plummeting. You can't sell anything here now, but that's a good thing. It just went out of control. Yeah, we are a little like Cottage Grove. Logging, millworks, pretty much gone out of this town now.

The harvester is a powerful and controversial symbol as Oregon and the nation struggle with the economic realities of immigration. As public pressure drives a border crackdown and increased enforcement, farmers nationwide face labor shortages as high as 30 percent to 50 percent during harvest. Further complicating matters, larger numbers of migrant laborers have switched to construction jobs for the higher pay and year-round stability.

Angie Chuang. *Excerpted from "Picker puts steel in immigration debate."*
The Oregonian. *July 16, 2007: A1. 2007 © The Oregonian.*
All Rights reserved. Reprinted with permission.

From the local paper I see that I have just missed a huge, five-day bike competition. One of the local youths with the last name Chávez was shown on the front page giving a victory salute. The winner of the previous day's stage was a Cuban American named Domínguez, dubbed the Cuban Missile Crisis by the locals for upsetting the local favorite. I'm not sure whether to be amused or insulted and wonder what Domínguez thinks of this.

The next morning, a Sunday, I attend Spanish-language mass at St. Francis of Assisi community center in northeast Bend. I'm not a practicing Catholic, but unable to find a geographic concentration of Latin@s, I figure this is a sure way to locate the community, the laundromat being another one, as I discovered on Saturday evening. The church's central parish in downtown Bend offers a Saturday-evening mass in Spanish and then a Sunday-noon one at the community center several miles from the city's center. Initially I think maybe this is a secondary location in the boondocks, but as I ride out there I realize it is an expanding part of the town. The location is home to a K–8 school, and a new church is being planned. Though plain, made mostly of cinder blocks and wood with a vinyl tile floor, the center is quite nice. It is furnished with about 500 plastic chairs. There are about 300 attendees present, almost all Latin@. It is evident to me, an insider-outsider, that this is a close-knit community of folks who know one another as friends and family in the way they acknowledge one another with hugs, nods, and handshakes. This same intimacy comes through in the priest's homily when he addresses parishioners by name as he actively engages them in questions and calls the men by their first names—Manuel, Felipe, Víctor, Jesús.

The sermon is quite interesting; the priest entreats the members of the

The after-mass gathering at St. Francis of Assisi Church in Bend, Oregon. Louis Mendoza.

congregation not to be seduced by American values of materialism. They should measure the quality of their lives by their love of God and their loving actions toward one another, not by what they own or what they can buy. "Don't think you can buy your way to happiness or salvation like Americans. *Esta religión no vale* [This form of religion has no value]," he says. Live your beliefs; don't be hypocrites. Don't be fooled by outward displays of happiness such as big smiles because these are jokes if you go home to an empty house and an empty heart. (This is a paraphrased translation of his Spanish.) It isn't anti-American or even pro-Mexican. I take it as a cautionary tale for new immigrants not to assimilate uncritically. What I also find interesting is that many single men are in attendance at church. After mass parishioners sell ice cream cones and cups of fresh fruit with slices of lime sprinkled with pepper. I have a *paleta* and make polite small talk. I try to find the priest but am unable to.

In the evening, as I smoke a cigarette outside my motel room, a red-eyed, red-faced, unshaven man with tousled hair approaches me with a "How you doing, amigo?" I say, "Fine, how about you?" He introduces himself as John Cassady and tells me that he is just floating around the country. His brother in Florida had told him Bend was a nice place to land. He says he just got back from Ireland a few days ago. When I ask where in Ireland, he says Dublin and Galway. He tells me his grandparents came from Ireland, and he was visiting cousins there. He tells me his wife died nine months earlier, and before I can say anything he says, "Don't, whatever you do, tell me you're sorry. I hate that shit." So I tell him that I, too, am traveling around the country. I tell him that I've always wanted to visit Ireland, and he tells me that it is a crazy place, as he proceeds to recount drunken brawls in the pubs of Galway. He says that as a Yankee he was everyone's friend as they proceeded to show off their hospitality.

I tell him that other than firsthand accounts of Ireland from friends and teachers, most of my knowledge came from writers like Joyce and Yeats. He adds names of a few others he thinks I should know. I tell him

John Cassady outside the motel where I stayed in Bend, Oregon. Louis Mendoza.

that he has a great name to be traveling the country, since the only other Cassady I know of was Neal Cassady, one of the Beat poets. He immediately says, "He was my uncle, no, not really, my second cousin." I say, "You're messing with me," and he says, "Hell, no, I'm serious," at which point he pulls out his Florida license to show me, though I don't know how this proves his point. In any case, we talk for a while. He says he knows a little Spanish, having grown up in New York. His first wife was Dominican. He says he's been up all night drinking. Every time he hears a crow caw he points out that it is death chasing him. He says he isn't afraid but that he isn't sure about making plans for the future.

TO BROTHERS, TO BURNS, AND INTO BOISE: JULY 21, 2007

I leave Bend on Monday a bit late and arrive around 6:30 in the small town of Brothers about 50 miles up the road. I stop at the only place in town to eat and learn that the next town is 95 miles up the road with nothing in between. I decide to stay the night at a rest stop and leave early the next morning. I make it to Burns reasonably early the next day, about 4:30, and learn that this is one of the communities that has been surrounded by wildfires in the nearby arid basin. At times authorities have found it necessary to close the road I am traveling due to fires all the way up to the road or smoke that reduces visibility.

The next morning the hotel clerk tells me I can expect delays on the road due to the fires, and this causes concern for me since I am more susceptible to the smoke inhalation for a longer time on bike. I go to the local pizza parlor, where a shuttle bus going east stops, and I am told I can't be guaranteed passage on the afternoon bus since it is small and if it arrives with lots of people it may not have room for me or the bike. I decide to wait, but there isn't enough space, and the driver is pretty skeptical about my chances the next day. I spend the afternoon trying to find someone I can pay to take me past the first mountain pass, where the fires are. I even go back to the local Laundromat, where I had seen a business card for Antonio Rodríguez, a drywall specialist, and call him to see if a more personal plea might help. No answer. My message with an offer to pay him goes unreturned.

I speak with employees at the local "authentic" Mexican restaurant, but they don't know anyone who can help me out either. Once again, I am obliged to stay another night because the day has gotten away from me. I go to the local casino that evening but retire early resolved to get up at five o'clock the next morning so I can get an early start and see what happens when I go up the road. I ride about 30 miles and stop at a gas station and "Indian" museum and gift shop (not run by Native peoples) and learn that I am very near the main area of the fires, though no smoke is yet apparent. I've arranged a meeting with the co-founder of the Idaho Migrant Council, Humberto Fuentes, for Thursday evening, and the delays I've faced are putting that meeting in jeopardy because he is leaving town on Friday. I decide to post a sign offering to pay for a ride when a man approaches me. His spouse and two children are inside the store, and we chat about my trip. After some initial uncertainty about whether he can fit my stuff in his van, we decide the bike can go on his luggage rack.

Danny and his family are wonderfully kind people returning home from vacation somewhere near Portland. In addition to speaking to me about his numerous jobs he's had over the years, his other seven kids, and his cowboy and hunting exploits, he also shares with me his experiences as a Mormon missionary in Latin America and working with Mexicans in Idaho over the years. Danny is a devout Mormon who begins asking me about my own spiritual beliefs. We speak about his faith, and he foregrounds his comments with the belief that Native peoples were chosen people. He asks me if I am Native, and I say, well, I'm of Mexican descent. He replies, well, then you're Native, right? I smile, and say that as mestizo, yes, I am, but this is not often recognized in the U.S. context.

Danny explains that he spent two years as a young man in Ecuador and Bolivia and was required to study Spanish before going and learned some Quechua while there. He offers to take me to the Idaho border, and I accept. We talk nonstop, and we pass the fires and then enter the steep mountain terrain with strong wind tunnels that rock the van. I begin to think the ride is a blessing. As we descend from the mountain, some of the most lush landscape I've ever seen hugs the beautiful river running alongside Highway 20. After our discussion about religion, I explain the purpose of my ride to him, and he happily exclaims: "Hey, I know a whole bunch of wetbacks!"

My body tightens, and I unwittingly hold my breath, trying to decide whether to tell him how offensive I find his words, even as I remind myself of my decision to be a listener and not be reactive to oppositional perspectives. So, I say, "Oh yeah, how so?" What he says next belies his offensive language and earns my respect:

Well, I used to work at a potato farm, and we had a lot of Mexican workers there. They were good men who worked harder than most other
men I knew. We would ask them to send word home for others to come
up if they could promise to work as hard as they did. And lots of them
came. Sometimes these men would get dropped off by coyotes in Colorado and would have no way of getting up here. So me and my friends
would go pick them up. I knew it was illegal and that I could get in a lot
of trouble, even get my car impounded, if we got stopped, but I tell you,
these were just good men trying to work, feed their families. I became
really good friends with some of them and even served as best man in
a couple of weddings. One of my best friends married a white girl. It
didn't work out and he moved to California. We stay in touch. I'm teaching my kids to learn Spanish because I think it's important for them to
be able to communicate to this community. The world is changing and
they need to be ready.

As I relax, we speak about the immigration debates and hostilities dis-
played by many people. He says he knows it is controversial and that something has to happen but that so long as there is work, he doesn't see the

Danny, Brenda, Keisha, and Cody when they drop me off in Ontario, Oregon. Louis Mendoza.

Outside Machuca's Restaurant in Ontario, Oregon. Héctor González.

problem. They drop me off in Ontario, Oregon, and Danny and I hug. He lets me know that if I go through Rexburg, I have a place to stay.

In Ontario I regroup and have lunch at Machuca's Mexican restaurant. As I am leaving, Héctor González, a nine-year-old boy whose mother works there, asks a lot of questions about my bike and gear. He takes a photo of me but declines to have me take his. I am amazed at the pervasive presence of Latin@, primarily Mexican, culture everywhere I go; even the smallest towns between point A and point B seem to have a restaurant, a *tiendita*, a garage, a Spanish mass—all profound evidence of the strong culture and entrepreneurial spirit that is making our presence felt. As I enter Idaho, I can't help but smile as I ride past the Tejano Bar on the outskirts of town. How strange and comforting to have Tejano culture evoked in this place so far from Texas!

In Nampa I have a great conversation with Humberto Fuentes, of the Idaho Migrant Council and an active participant in numerous organizations and community-action groups in Idaho over the past 40 years. As a student at Treasure Valley Community College in the '60s, Humberto was linked nationally to Chican@ movement activities and leaders in Colorado, Texas, California, and elsewhere. The next day I call the Idaho Community

Action Network (ICAN), as Humberto recommended. The executive director is out of the office, and when I ask to speak with someone who can tell
me about their programming, I am directed to Fernando. We agree to meet
at a mall the next morning. When I arrive there I lock up my bike, and over
breakfast Fernando shares his life as a migrant who came when he was 16
fleeing Mexico because as the son of a single mother he kept finding himself in conflict with family, friends, and local police. He is able to attend
Boise State because his father received amnesty in 1986. He tells me about
his work with ICAN and as a student activist.

MOUNTAIN HOME, IDAHO: JULY 23, 2007

I've been taking pictures of the various sizes of the road shoulders
because riding on the margins makes one hyper-aware of their quality and
width. The roads in Idaho remind me of the streets of the Houston barrio where I grew up—rock mixed with asphalt, potholes, and cracks with
weeds pushing their way through. The preferred method of repair seems to
be asphalt patching over the cracks, which makes for a rough and bumpy
ride. Nor are the shoulders kept very clean. Between the trash on the shoulders and goathead thorns on the road, I have numerous flats. Idahoans
have proven friendly so far for the most part, but the roads are less kind.
I arrive in Mountain Home on Saturday night.

What a long day cycling in the hot sun to end up in a very cold place!
I think I am in luck because there is a KOA campground here in Mountain
Home—but I encounter my second Jim Crow experience on this trip. The
first was in Rosebud, California, when I went to a small motel where the
sign said "vacant" and the parking lot was empty. The woman who helped
me was sweet but said immediately that the motel was full. I told her it
might be a good idea to change her sign—which she did. I went down the
road to find another place, and when I came back by the motel an hour later
looking for dinner, the "vacant" sign was on again. At the Mountain Home
KOA I enter the office behind one man, and a few minutes later two other
travelers come in. They are acknowledged and helped by the elderly white
guy overseeing the place. One of the travelers apologizes to me and indicates that I was there before him. I tell him thanks for noticing but that
it is the clerk's job to notice that. Because things have come to an abrupt
stop, the clerk gives me a look of annoyance and asks, "What do you need?"
I say, "A campsite," and he says, "Well, I guess I can give you #7 across
the street," as if he is doing me a favor. I ask about the price ($22) and af-

ter looking at it—a bare site with no shade and adjacent to the road—I tell him I'm better off going to the motel down the street. Experiences like these are downers, but quite frankly, I am prepared for worse. The goodness I've seen from people has outweighed these shameful acts. I'm feeling very, very tired and looking forward to exiting Idaho in a few short days and spending some time in Yellowstone. I'll cross the Rockies there, but it will be beautiful and cooler due to the forest.

In the morning I make a quick stop at Wal-Mart to get some universal tire tubes as backup. When I'm packing them in my gear, a guy comes by and asks about my trip. As I tell him about it, I can see the envy in his eyes. He looks at me and says, "I would so love to take that kind of trip." After a pause, he adds, "You must not be married, huh?" I say, "No, why?" "Well, if you were, I'm pretty sure your wife wouldn't let you be doing this and leaving her at home by herself or with kids." I laugh and say, "That might be true." He is only one of a number of men and women who make that observation. But I also meet many people who tell me of cross-country bike trips with partners and/or future spouses. They all say it really allowed them to bond and get to know one another. I leave early, hoping to get a head start on the sun into the mountains to the east. About 20 miles out I have a flat. When I find out the local bike shop is closed, I learn the hard way that universal bike parts are not so universal, as the valve stem does not fit through my rim. So I walk most of the way back before a guy in a U-Haul with a big German shepherd in the cab is kind enough to give me a ride.

As expected, this part of the trip has been physically grueling. I'm pleased not to have hurt myself (no pulled muscles or crashes). Somewhere along the way I've developed heat and poison-ivy rashes on my arms and legs. They are itchy and uncomfortable, but they seem to be healing. My endurance is building, my breathing has been good, I think I'm slowly losing weight from my midsection, and my legs are definitely much stronger. I've been very frustrated at times but not yet near a breakdown. Loneliness is constant, but I'm thankful for a cell phone and the many, many people along the way who've helped me, engaged me in conversation about my trip, and otherwise acknowledged my presence.

A QUICK STOP IN TWIN FALLS: THE THINGS I CARRY

When I finally get back on the road I make speedy progress, and a long day gets me into Twin Falls. I keep finding myself on the Oregon Trail and have to begrudgingly admire the fortitude of pioneers who would travel

The sparse ruins of the Minidonka detention center. Louis Mendoza.

with no sense of what lay ahead. Some of the historical markers are pretty good about identifying relationships of cooperation, conflict, and contestation over the land with native peoples once the settlers became so numerous and greedy. Others gloss this over. In Twin Falls, while the derailleur on my bike is being fixed, I rent a car so I can see some sites. The Perrine Memorial Bridge crosses the Shoshone River and overlooks a beautiful valley to the west. The bridge is about 480 feet high, and skydivers jump off it regularly. I try but cannot find El Milagro, the housing project now owned by the Idaho Migrant Council that Humberto Fuentes told me about.

I visit the falls, and while looking at a map of the region I see that about 20 miles away is the Minidonka Relocation Center, a former World War II detention center for Japanese Americans. I drive out there and have a difficult time finding it because there is no historical marker at the turn-off or sign designating the actual site. All that is left are a few ruins of the entrance and visitor waiting room. The surrounding area is farmland. When one recalls that many of these detention camps were mostly tent cities, it makes sense that there would be very little infrastructure, but the absence of something more substantial to commemorate this sad and hor-rific history makes me feel empty. I try to imagine what life was like for the detainees here. It is hard not to think of how harsh the winters must have been. I note that the historical marker identifies this as Idaho's largest ghost town. What a bizarre and disrespectful designation for a detention center! However, the plaques on the ruins do offer a more critical perspec-tive about how this history should remind us of what happens when peo-ple's civil liberties are violated, something we sorely need to be reminded of more often.

I think about how even now so many tent cities dot the landscape in hidden places around the country, serving as detention centers for immi-grants. The beautiful and often barren and harsh landscape and the pro-fane injustices of the past, a few of them eventually leading to greater social justice, sometimes mill around in my head and make me dizzy. Though my mind would like it all to be simple, I realize this is history in the mak-ing—what we make of it, not as passive witnesses but how we create fairer conditions and change the world for the better. Better for whom and how? Well, those are the questions that really matter, aren't they?

REFLECTIONS

I anticipate arriving in Yellowstone in a few days. Along the way, I've been blogging when I can—though my mini-PDA with Internet ac-cess isn't doing me much good. From time to time I stop and use libraries in small towns to post blog entries and answer friends' questions about my trip, like these from Sandy:

Sandy: *I keep wondering what it's like to live day by day with only 50 pounds of "gear," the same gear day after day. Can you give us a listing of what you're carrying?*

Me: I have a tent, a mini-stove and small bottle of fuel, a sack of food (oatmeal, tuna and chicken packets, easy-to-cook dinners, PowerBars, energy gels, three bottles of water plus a CamelBak, three changes of clothes, a fourth shirt that's not a biking shirt to wear "out," a pair of zipper pants, a windbreaker, a thermal undershirt, a skull cap to wear under my helmet, a pair of hiking shoes, a hygiene bag that has my chamois towel and washcloth, toothbrush, toothpaste, comb, nail clip-pers, deodorant (I was going to rough it and forgo this, but after a few days, I realized it was a necessity if I expect people to talk to me!). A really good first-aid kit that has all kinds of neat stuff I hope I never have to use. Suntan lotion, moisturizer, insect repellent, an ultraviolet water purifier, a water filter and iodine pills, a mini-AM-FM radio, three pairs of riding gloves (one long-fingered that I've needed for the cold nights on the road), vitamins, prescriptions, multiple kinds of over-the-counter pain pills (Aleve, Motrin, etc.), a journal to write in, a folder full of news articles, a couple of student papers I need to read, a book (*New Destinations*), a GPS/PDA with wireless keyboard, a bag of AA and AAA batteries and wires for all other gadgets, cell phone, digital voice recorder, two mini-USBs, a digital camera and minicam recorder, solar-powered battery charger, sleeping pad and sleeping bag, toilet paper, numerous forms of flashlights, headlights, a tool bag with spare parts, tools, tubes, a folding tire, a hunting knife, bear mace, two compasses, sunglasses, reading glasses, maps, pens, highlighters, a bandana, camp soap that works for everything (dishes, body, hair, etc.), a trowel, business cards, postcards about my trip and ones I've picked up along the way, and lots of other small stuff.

Sandy: *And what do you find that you've used the most often thus far—that you can't live without?*

Me: Tools, air pump, spare tubes.

Sandy: *What have you had to pick up along the way that you hadn't anticipated needing or simply wanting? What have you gotten rid of?*

Me: I dumped a folding chair that my sleeping pad fit into and replaced a small shovel with an even smaller trowel. I mail things home as soon as I can so I carry as little as possible. My bags feel a bit lighter than when I started, but maybe I'm just stronger.

Sandy: *What have you lost?*

Me: A pair of sunglasses and a pair of reading glasses.

Sandy: *And what has broken or torn or become unusable?*

Me: Tubes. I'm very unhappy about the PDA/GPS and wireless keyboard. They are not entirely useless, but almost so. I'm going to have to rethink things when I get back to Minnesota. I think I need to bring a PC with wireless capability, but I will have to give up other things to make room.

Edén Torres asks a different set of questions:

Edén: *Since you are not taking the usual tourist path across the West, are you seeing things you might like to return to someday? Are you paying attention to the daily news, or does the primitive feel and slow pace of the journey make news seem to live in another dimension?*

Me: I do think a lot about how different this trip would be if it were by car. The choices one makes are so delimited by the mode of transportation. I read the news fairly often, but it feels a bit surreal. I am paying particular attention to coverage on Latin@s and Latin@ issues both locally and nationally. I clip and save articles I read because these provide the context for my journey for me. That may seem a bit self-centered, but these external touchstones produce internal maps for me to recall where I was when I heard this or that. Being in so many rural settings has made me really think about the margin and the center of daily life in interesting ways.

A JOURNAL ENTRY FROM
YELLOWSTONE NATIONAL PARK

It's the evening of Friday, July 27. It's my second and last night in Yellowstone before heading to Cody to return the car. I was strongly advised not to cycle alone through Yellowstone by the park rangers because 1) the buffalo might attack me, 2) the roads were not made with bikes in mind and many of the most dangerous places have no shoulders, and 3) people are distracted when driving because they are looking for animals. Good advice—as I was to learn when I rode the big outer loop for about five hours yesterday. I saw a number of wondrous things, including bison, elk, deer, two bald eagles, and other, small critters. The bison and elk were very regal. The male bulls would snort walking with their mates, very aggressive. The park is mystical in numerous ways with the thermal regions constantly spewing steam.

Today was a good day. I went to the Grand Tetons and saw the beautiful lake up there and more bison. I saw one bull chasing a car. It was pretty exciting. It seemed like it was going to attack it. It rained a lot today, but it cleared up rather early. I also went over to Jackson Hole today to see what was there. It's like a big mall with lots of motels, stores, restaurants, mountain gear, a bit overwhelming. I haven't had too much

occasion to interact with people here except when we're sharing the animal sightings. I'm feeling very mellow. It came to mind today that being here is under-overwhelming. It feels very disconcerting to not have
anyone to share it with, to affirm the wonder and beauty that is so rare
to many of us from urban environments. It's humbling—as it should
be—for nature to make you feel your own smallness in time and space.
I have a constant sense of aloneness. Not that it's not beautiful in the
absence of others. I did see some other cyclists today going through
the Grand Tetons. Most of them were cycling for the day. I did see one
woman coming toward Yellowstone with saddle bags. She was moving
right along, very strongly. I got back from over there a little before five
and set up camp and picked up a pint of whiskey and am having a little drink and enjoying a little buzz as I cook dinner. Got a nice fire going this evening. Cooked one of my dinners requiring water. Not bad.
Somehow managed to burn my Jiffy Pop popcorn. Spent some time
writing notes in my journal to record both minor and major experiences
I don't want to forget.

Last night I listened to talk shows on the radio because I couldn't
pick up anything else. Glenn Beck was making a big deal about having acquired a "Come and Take It Day" flag. If you're not a Texas history buff, you might not know that this is a flag used by Texans in Go-
liad during their war for independence against Mexico in 1836. The flag
has a picture of a cannon that the Mexican government had outlawed.
The local patriots flaunted their resistance to this law and dared the government to come and take their cannon. Beck was making a big deal
out of it as an antiterrorism statement and encouraging others to buy it
and display it. He got a call from someone in Texas who said he had one
and could tell others where to get them, and they were going to post it
on the website about where to buy it. He said one of his Mexican American neighbors had told him he was being a Mexican hater by flying that
flag. Then they had a discussion about its relevance to Texas independence. Beck did know some of the history behind it but emphasized that
he thought the main purpose of the war for Texas independence was
about opposing a dictator who had given license for his soldiers to rape
and pillage. Beck's effort at moral justification seemed to rely on a dis-
tortion and simplification of history.

I've been sleeping very well here. It's nice to be in a tent where I
can hear the pitter-patter of the rain falling. I've experienced very little
rainfall on my trip, but doing so here is pleasant. I've mapped out the
rest of my week. I should be able to get through Wyoming by the week-

end. From here I go to Cody, then to Greybull, then I go over the Big-horn Mountains. From there I'll go to Buffalo, from Buffalo to Gillette on I-90. Hopefully it's okay to ride on the highway because otherwise it's a huge circle around on small roads to get to the same destination. I may be able to take a shortcut into South Dakota. I'm thinking that by Thursday or Friday I may be into the Black Hills and make it through South Dakota in a week or so. I want to go to Mount Rushmore and the Crazy Horse monument. I'm looking forward to being back in Minnesota. The comfort of my own home will be nice. Even though I don't hang out with lots of people, sleeping in my own bed, seeing Shadow, all these things will make me feel less lonely. I'm sure it will be hard to leave again.

Hopefully I'll leave there with a renewed sense of purpose and a new plan. I have to figure out easier Internet access and how to camp more regularly. I look forward to riding with other folks, perhaps Omar in Iowa and maybe Lisa at some other point during the trip. I know people in Chicago, Michigan, New York, Boston, Washington, D.C. Having a sense of something to look forward to will be good. Those are really long distances. Though it's a long ways away, I'm worried about the eastern corridor. So much traffic. I don't know what the back roads will be like. I'm going to enjoy my campfire here and go to bed early so I can get an early start tomorrow.

I enjoy my time in the park immensely. My interactions with folks are fairly limited—though when you happen to see something wonderful in the presence of someone else, there is a knowing exchange of glances that you've witnessed something special together. My exit from Yellowstone on the east side is delayed as cars carefully wind around a recent landslide. One other observation: I've seen very few people of color while at Yellowstone. Interestingly, the only Latin@s I encounter are working in service positions, one at a restaurant in Yellowstone—she's from Colombia (the staff all wear name tags that identify their home communities)—and another young woman in Jackson Hole who took my order at a small diner. I ask her if there are many Latin@s in the area and she says yes. I ask "Where?" to which she replies, "They're hiding, but they work in businesses and on the ranches on both sides of the mountains." She is a high school student whose family moved from California. She says she likes living in the area.

NOTES FROM WORLAND, WYOMING: JULY 29, 2007

You leave town feeling pretty good. Things are going well two days out of Yellowstone. Your heart is leaning toward home because your body and spirit are feeling tired. But after a couple of days' rest and a good ride yesterday you think, "I'm good, I can do this. I can get to the mountains today and over by tomorrow and across the state and be in South Dakota by the end of the week." But not even five miles out of town you have a flat. That's a bummer. You change it. And you think, "Well this is not going to continue. It's not a bad pattern; it's just a flat." So you fix it and go on. And then your bike computer quits working, and you're bummed about that because you use that to help gauge your speed to monitor your progress. On this highway there are no mile markers, and you have no idea where you are or what your rate of progress is. Without that you feel a bit lost; you wonder if you're going too slow or too fast.

You face some hills, and they slow you down a bit but nothing too bad. You're hoping for a break about 15 miles out, which is usually a decent first stopping point for the day. You can stretch your legs, get some rest, and get moving again. But in Wyoming you're facing the desert, and there's not a bit of shade to be found anywhere. No trees. The only trees you see are on the other side of the fences, and the shade is not coming into the road so those trees do you no good. You see trees by the houses that people smartly planted. Those look great. You envy the coolness of how the residents must feel embraced by all that shade.

You start to get a little disgruntled and a bit disillusioned, but you keep moving on. And pretty soon you start to see illusions of water on the road caused by heat. Every once in a while someone will pass by and honk and wave, and that lifts your spirits some. After a while you're just wondering if you can make your goal for the day, about 80 miles, partway up the mountains. You start having these negative thoughts and try to beat them back and not let them enter into your psyche at all because they will just escalate out of control, and that might make you vulnerable to one of those emotional breakdowns you've heard about. And the last thing you want is to have a breakdown with no one around and you in the burning heat. You think of stopping for a rest, and you realize with no shade you won't be able to sit down. The sun will just soak up your energy. So what's the point? You might as well keep on moving.

At some point you realize you're going to have to go 40 miles to Worland before you get a break. But you can't tell how fast or far you've gone, what kind of progress you're making. You think you'd be doing good if you can get there in three hours or so. That's really not too bad. It's a pretty average rate for what you've been doing. And so to keep yourself strong you start thinking all these things about being tough, about being a man. And you think of how recently someone told you to "man up" and how that really hurt your feelings because you were expressing your vulnerability. And you know that the expression is something she herself didn't like when it was told to her son by her husband because she wants her son to be emotionally expressive. And he should be. She had expressed her disgust with that expression. And so a chasm arose between you and her.

And you're tired of always having to be strong, of not being able to express your vulnerability, so you think about life and death on the road and try to focus on the next hill, on the next marker in the road, on the long and short goals. You take it one pedal revolution at a time. You realize this is the way you learned over time to be a man. To not feel those thoughts, to not let yourself be vulnerable. And you think if you can just keep the emotions at bay and focus, to repress those hard feelings, to focus on the task at hand for the next few hours, then you're going to be all right and this wave of vulnerability will pass and you won't really have to deal with it because this is not something that's complex, after all, even though today being on the road makes you feel your aloneness in the world. It's not that you can't reach out, but will anybody understand? And maybe this is part of being a man, too, wondering and being afraid that no one will understand.

After a while you start seeing signs for Worland, and you realize that hey, in a half-hour or so you'll be there. When you get closer you finally see a tree. But you think, Oh, there are going to be more comfortable places in town to rest. When you see the time you think, Wow, hey, you did better than you thought you were doing. Wow, what a man. So now, get some rest. Man up. Move on.

I push on. In the afternoon I experience some of the strangest weather of my life. Clouds come in fast, pushed by hard winds that are alternately very hot and very cold. This is followed by rain and then hail. I look for cover, but I am surrounded by hills covered with boulders that offer none. I pull out a tarp and drape one end over the bike and duck underneath it, holding out the other end of the tarp with my outstretched hand. The rain and hail end within minutes. They are followed by intense humidity and

newly awakened droves of flies and crickets. Completely bizarre and uncomfortable. I ride as fast as I can to make it difficult for the insects to land
on me. A short way up the road there is an RV trailer on its side, blown
over by the winds. No one is hurt, and others have already stopped to help,
so I press on. I'm glad I wasn't there to see this happen because I can only
imagine how freaked out I would have been.

FROM TEN SLEEP TO BUFFALO, WYOMING: JULY 25, 2007

I arrive in the very small town of Ten Sleep in the evening. I stay
in a campground cabin at the foot of the Bighorn Mountains. Tomorrow
will be an intense ride, and I'm worried about my bike because the gears
have begun slipping. Two people in town tell me the first 27 miles will be
the hardest, as this involves a constant incline—particularly the middle
12 miles. I prepare myself mentally and start off early and slowly. About five
miles out of town the highway begins winding through the mountains. I
decide to take a parallel road that follows Highway 16 and a river because a
sign indicates that it will intersect with the highway eight miles down the
road. This road turns into gravel, but it isn't too bad. However, the gears
start slipping really badly, and this makes riding uphill impossible. About
four miles up the road I decide I should hide the bike in the brush and get
to a town where I can rent a car and retrieve the bike to get it fixed. The
parallel road and the highway are separated by a gully and the Ten Sleep
Creek, a fairly rapidly moving body of water. I decide to go up and down to
save time, but it isn't easy. When I reach the highway, I am unable to get a
ride. After a couple of hours in the heat, I decide that though I've brought
my CamelBak full of water, there is no way I can risk trying to walk
12 miles back to a town so small it has no transportation services at all—
or forward close to 50 miles. I call a co-worker in my office back home at
the university and ask her to help identify a cab in Buffalo, the next town,
despite a fare that was sure to be exorbitant. Thankfully, she is persistent,
and when she finds out Buffalo does not have a cab company and the local
police will not help, she contacts the Wyoming State Highway Patrol—and
a trooper eventually comes to get me.

When the trooper arrives he is pretty annoyed to be on this rescue mission and says he is going to give me a ride back to Ten Sleep or to Worland,
where I can figure out my next steps. I know there is nothing in Ten Sleep,
and Worland is 45 miles or so back in the direction I've just come from.

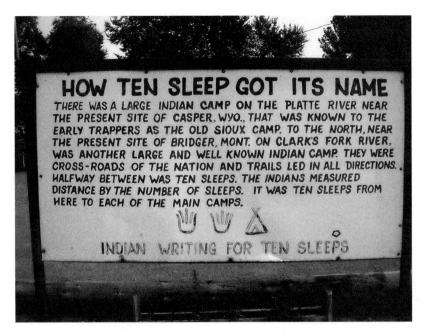

An explanation of the origin of the town Ten Sleep's name. Louis Mendoza.

I'm not sure what I expect him to do, but I am very unhappy with the prospect of going backward. I decide to talk to him and see if any new possibilities pop up. I ask him about his work and eventually tell him about my research. Wyoming Highway Patrol trooper Lieutenant David Gluyas tells me there is little controversy on immigration issues in Wyoming because the work new arrivals perform (agricultural, ranching, and sheepherding) are not areas of high job competition, and they are much needed to get the work done. He says it is clearly the case that they are performing jobs few others want to do. I learn that most sheepherders in Wyoming are from Peru and have expertise in the field; because it is such a lonely and difficult lifestyle means few locals want to do it. He points out that in Worland, where he lives, the most common and popular restaurants in town are the five Latin restaurants, most of which are family-owned. He says it is a running joke among his friends that if you go out to eat, it is going to be Hispanic food. Particularly since these are family-owned, he says, you get to know the owners and the restaurants are a great place for the different communities to interface.

Our conversation seems to warm him up to me. He then asks where my bike is and if it is still rideable. I say yes, but with the derailleur shot I can't make it up and down the mountains' twisty road. He says if he takes

Trooper Gluyas at the peak of the road going across the Bighorn Mountains. Louis Mendoza.

me to the top of the mountain, about 12 miles up the road, I can coast 40 miles into Buffalo. It makes sense to me to go forward rather than backward, so I gladly accept his offer. We retrieve my bike from the back road, and off we go into the clouds. As exhilarating as it is, the other side of the mountain isn't all downhill, so it still takes me several hours to arrive, but I am happy to see Buffalo, thankful for Lieutenant Gluyas, and glad to have friends at the university I can count on. When I arrive in Buffalo, the manager of the motel I go to is so impressed with my trip he gives me the manager's discount. I celebrate with a large pizza and lots of cold water. In the morning I learn that there is no bike shop in Buffalo, so I ride to Gillette on the flat interstate. My first task is to find a place to sleep and a bike shop where I can get the derailleur replaced.

I am near South Dakota and should be there soon. Motorcycles are all over the place heading toward Sturgis. At a rest stop on the highway I hear some cyclists checking in with friends on the pay phone. They brag about having ridden four to five hours nonstop on the road and say how hot it is. I'm amused and envious as I figure that four or five hours on a motorized vehicle is the equivalent distance I cover in four to five days by bicycle. Meanwhile, I hear about the tragedy back in Minneapolis—a bridge on

I-35 right by the university collapsed last night. I understand several people were killed and many hurt.

BUFFALO, WYOMING

Much of Wyoming is sparsely populated. Sometimes this makes planning tricky because I can't assume that I can find places to rest or eat in any given town. As I pass a sign identifying the population of Emblem at 10, I wonder if it was larger in the past; presently it only has about four houses and nothing else to designate it as a town. What's the smallest population of a town in the U.S.? Is there a sign out there somewhere that says, "Population 1"?

I first see mention of Crazy Woman at a cafe in Ten Sleep, Wyoming. I think it is just a humorous name for a woman-owned business, but later I see many references to it in other business names and markets. I pass the creek bearing this name somewhere between Buffalo and Gillette. While waiting for my pizza in Buffalo, I ask a woman about it, and she tells me a version of the story having to do with a woman who was left behind by settlers. This makes me think of Woman Hollering Creek near Seguin, Texas, and the legend of La Llorona and how they both had to do with women dealing with death and abandonment. These tales strike me as stark examples of historical and cultural convergence centered on female disempowerment.

After the Bighorn Mountains adventure I am feeling extraordinarily

Signs in Wyoming referring to the legend of Crazy Woman. Louis Mendoza.

Names like Devil's Tower in Wyoming reflect the legacy of efforts to demonize sacred lands of native peoples. Louis Mendoza.

tired, so I decide to rest in Gillette for a couple of days. I rent a car so I can be more mobile. One of the places I visit that I would have bypassed if only on a bike is Devil's Tower National Monument. As soon as I see it advertised I recognize it from the film *Close Encounters of the Third Kind* and know I have to go to satisfy my curiosity about all things having to do with life beyond earth. I learn that it is a sacred site for indigenous peoples, and the awesome magnitude of the tower is beautiful. I walk completely around it and take pictures from many angles. I see some cliff climbers going up one side. That is intense. While I have the car I go to Deadwood and Sturgis because I intend to bike into South Dakota through a more southern route. Deadwood is a very modernized old western town with a plethora of casinos and bars. I visit one or two.

Bikers from every direction are heading toward Sturgis for the big motorcycle rally and accompanying festivities coming up in a few days. I appreciate that many bikers see me as a fellow traveler and take the time to honk and wave. This always gives me a little boost, especially on a back road where there is little else going on. Unfortunately, the festivities are an occasion for every motel in Wyoming, South Dakota, and even western Minnesota to jack up their rates. I pay $95 for a Motel 6 in Gillette, Wyoming!

By the time I enter South Dakota, I can't help but feel like I am hot on the trail of every vacationing family as I traverse the West during the middle of summer. In addition to motorcycles, RVs are out in force. I ride into the Black Hills through Hamilton, Wyoming, and go east to the towns of Custer and Keystone, where the Crazy Horse monument and Mount Rushmore are. By this time the heat has dissipated so it is only in the low 90s, and though there are some steep hills, they are neither as steep nor as numerous as those I have encountered before. It makes sense to me to go to Crazy Horse first since this was sacred land to native peoples. I cannot tell you the impressiveness of the project based on its sheer size. It was begun in 1948 by sculptor Korczak Ziolkowski, who had worked on Mount Rushmore under Gutzon Borglum. The Crazy Horse Memorial Foundation's history of the project tells us that in 1939 Mr. Ziolkowski received a letter of invitation to make the mountain carving from Chief Henry Standing Bear that states in part, "My fellow chiefs and I would like the white man to know that the red man has great heroes, too." But the project remains a subject of controversy among the Native community today due to the nonnative origins of the project overseers and the foundation caretakers, as well as the objections of those who see it as being against the spirit of Crazy Horse.

This is not a simple question to be swept aside. However, when one considers the history, artist, and purpose of Mount Rushmore, one can appreciate how the Crazy Horse monument dwarfs the national monument. Only from looking on the web do I learn the sordid past of the sculptor of Mount Rushmore. Gutzon Borglum not only carved this unfinished government-funded monument in tribute to the "founding fathers" responsible for fulfilling Manifest Destiny and U.S. territorial expansion, and thus

Crazy Horse monument and Mount Rushmore, two very different views of America. Louis Mendoza.

native decimation—he also was an active Ku Klux Klan member. I am in awe when I learn that the entire Mount Rushmore sculpture can fit inside the head of the Crazy Horse monument.

After visiting the monuments I camp out. As I lie in my tent at night I hear on the radio a broadcast from the Pine Ridge Pow Wow—it's the grand entry of the dancers. I listen and realize that I will be there before the pow wow is over. The next day I take a highway paralleling the mountains with plans to stop in a small town just west of Pine Ridge. When I arrive it is still fairly early, and I see a sign for a casino hotel on the reservation just 12 miles away. As I head east I learn firsthand how strong the prairie winds can be, so it takes me almost two hours to get to the hotel. At the casino I see a woman wearing a T-shirt with the quote "We didn't cross the border, the borders crossed us: Native Pride," and I feel an affinity with the slogan and her.

The next day I head toward Pine Ridge. I stop to rest at a convenience store in Oglala and press onward. Because of winds I make pretty slow time and begin to worry about whether it makes sense to stop at the pow wow since I also want to see the Wounded Knee memorial. In Pine Ridge I ask about lodging and learn that there is none. At a Pizza Hut I ask about campgrounds, and the young Native man behind the counter tells me, "Just go through the intersection over to where the pow wow is being held and you can camp there for free—there's no charge. This is not Amerika-ka-ka." I say, "I know that's right. I'm glad to be here," and decide to camp there for the night.

I ride around the camping area a bit and decide on a place to pitch my tent. In just a few minutes a guy comes up to me and asks where I've ridden from. When I tell him I left from California he says, "Wow, I want to hear more about that." He tells me he lives in Oglala and he and his family had seen me on the road and he wondered, "Who is that guy? Where's he coming from?" He says his questions must have led me to stop right in front of him. He then insists that we move my tent near his family's and he will introduce me to everyone. I accept the invitation, and he places my small tent right in the middle of their camp. His name is José Cervantes, his dad was from Guadalajara, his mom was full-blooded Apache from New Mexico, and he grew up on the Mescalero reservation with his sisters. He is living in Oglala because he married a Lakota Sioux woman, Olivia Yellow Cloud, and he's been there about 25 years. José is in his early 50s. They've pitched a large canopy over a wood-post frame they made, and they have picnic tables, chairs, and plenty of food and drink, to which they tell me to help myself. I feast on buffalo stew, which tastes just like *caldo de res* to

José Cervantes and two of his children at the Pine Ridge Pow Wow. Louis Mendoza.

me, and some fry bread. I am welcomed by the family members—an entire clan of extended family of all ages, though José seems to be the oldest and the one who is held in highest regard. Olivia and José have two kids, Mercy and Anton. I am happy to be adopted for the day. I sense no awkwardness as they joke and laugh and quibble the way any family does, and I have a great time. I meet spouses, sisters, cousins, nephews, sons, daughters, and in-laws, all of whom are relaxed and joking around. Some of the family members are up from New Mexico, and they speak a lot about how their pow wows are a bit different—no entrance fees, okay to drink alcohol, and so on. For a while I'm thinking we might not even go see activities at the pow wow because there is so much to enjoy underneath their tent. Several of them drink beer in cups. They offer me one with a warning that getting caught means sleeping in jail overnight. I feel like I'm with family. Eventually José decides we will go with the kids to the carnival and he will ride one ride, which he and I do together.

José was in the Marines for six years and traveled to Okinawa, Africa, and Europe. He and his youngest sister, Maria, tell me a bit about their lives growing up, which sounded very harsh; their father died when they were young, and their mother was alcoholic. He says he basically raised the family from the time he was 11. One of his primary motivations for staying in school was to save half his lunch and bring Maria food to eat when she was still an infant. Maria is a retired (disabled) security office from the schools in Mescalero, but she runs security for the pow wows there each year. Her youngest son, nicknamed Flaco, has driven up with her. He will begin college this fall. They know some Spanish and joke around by calling me *ese* (dude) and using slang when they can. I have a good time, and close to midnight we go see the dances.

Some of the cousins are singing and drumming, and we see the performance of the rabbit dance, another form of couple dancing, and fancy dancing, which includes a standing-horse dance and a dance-off of two finalists in a chicken dance to determine the winner. Beautiful dancing, beautiful garments, and beautiful people. At some point I ask José how life on Pine Ridge is and explain that I know it is one of the poorest reservations in the country. He says things have been improving, most people can get work, and the casino has helped a lot by creating some good jobs. I stay up until about 1:30, at which time I excuse myself, crawl into my little tent, take some notes on a recorder, and go to sleep to the sound of drums. The next morning I awake, and many are up before I am, sitting around the table. José and his immediate family had gone back to their house in Oglala to sleep after we'd said our goodbyes. I get some advice from Oliver, José's brother-in-law, about possible routes to take after visiting the memorial at Wounded Knee.

After stopping to get some breakfast at the gas station I head out toward Wounded Knee and make it there in an hour and a half or so. The memorial itself is modest, but knowing the history I feel humbled and saddened to be confronted with yet another example of government decimation of people without any regard for the sanctity of life. It's this history that makes me have little respect for those who would like to proclaim that we're a nation of laws that promotes freedom and social justice. I am honored to see the graves and surprised to see so many who served in the U.S. military, some dating back to World War I. I am also humbled by an elder, a woman in her 80s, who tells me she moved away from Pine Ridge at 18 and is now living in Wichita, Kansas. She walks the path around the monument praying and crying in honor of her ancestors.

From there I go to the town of Martin, South Dakota, and realize I am too far to make it to anywhere that might have lodging or campgrounds, so I check into the only motel in town. I have a good conversation with the manager, Rudy Requejo, a Mexican American originally from Nebraska. His grandparents immigrated to the U.S. in the 1930s. I ask Rudy about immigrants in the state, and he tells me there are some doing fieldwork, but their public presence is minimal. He says there are no controversial issues with immigration in the state because the numbers are small and the real concern is with the well-being of the Native populations. But, he says, in his opinion one of the reasons this doesn't get addressed is the denial of the persistence of racism. I ask him where the grocery store is because I want to buy a fresh, cold watermelon after a hot day in the desert sun. We agree that I should come back and talk with him some more later. However, by the time I eat and rest, it is late, and I want to get an early start the next morning. I pick up his card with plans to write him. I tell him I will send him a book on Chican@s, as he is reading *Aztec* by Gary Jennings.

For two days I face strong prairie winds that leave me tired and frustrated because I hoped to move faster once I hit flat terrain. I decide to cut up north toward I-90 to see if the winds will lessen. Immediately I begin to move faster with the wind at my back, but the road I am on ends, and I have to go a 23-mile stretch on gravel. I make it to a rest stop near Belvedere after being chased by some dogs. At one point when I see that I won't be able to outpace one ferocious-sounding dog barreling down on me, I hop off the bike and scream "STOP!" at the top of my lungs. To my surprise, he skids to a stop. I walk for a while before getting back on the bike. Shortly afterward, I settle down for the night. For the first time on the trip I feel a sense of danger. I select a picnic table near the back of the rest stop to draw as little attention as possible and to immerse myself in the darkness so I might sleep better. Camping is forbidden at most rest stops, so I've learned to sleep on the table either lying down or in a sitting position. Since at many rest stops the grass is watered at night, I learned the hard way to stay on the concrete. This particular rest stop has a road running behind it. A truck drives slowly by. I don't think much of it, but then it comes by again and again. I cannot make out who is in the cab, but I imagine that I am the only one who can be seen from the back. I get nervous and decide to forgo the darkness for a better-lit site near the parking lot. My sleep is restless even though, or perhaps because, there is almost no one else at the stop.

The next day I take off almost as soon as the sun rises and go to a rest stop called 1800s Town, purely a tourist trap. I eat breakfast and chat with some African American bikers from Florida who are part of a Buffalo Soldiers Brigade heading toward Sturgis on motorcycles. The next two days I fly across South Dakota because a strong and steady wind is now directly behind me. I go about 90 miles each of those days, and then on the third I go a miraculous 170! I stay at rest stops along the highway. My intention is to stop in Sioux Falls on the third night, but once I arrive there it is early and I am only 10 miles from the Minnesota border, so I rest and continue on. An interview has been arranged for me in Worthington, about 45 miles

into Minnesota, and I decide to try and make it all the way since I need a
shower badly as well as to wash my clothes. I end up riding into the dark
and arrive in Worthington close to 10 p.m. A triumphant day.

BACK IN MINNESOTA: AUGUST 17, 2007

The people of Worthington, Minnesota, like those in many small
rural towns, have worked hard to make adjustments to a rapid change in
demographics over the past two decades. Residents there will tell you it
hasn't always been easy but that most folks recognize this change is permanent, not a passing phase. As with so many other places I've visited across
the Northwest and into the Midwest, the growing pains have lasted a long
time, but most local leaders recognize that the present and future well-being of the community depends on the quality of government and institutional leadership provided during this time of change. In the meantime,
the local economy has flourished with the influx of workers and numerous
entrepreneurs. One has only to go down 10th Street (formerly Main Street)
to see evidence of this change; the many restaurants, *tiendas*, video stores,
and other businesses serve as a visible manifestation of Latin@ economic
contributions. Latin@ labor benefits U.S. industry giants, and here at the
local Swift meat-packing plant it has helped the company become a global
leader in food processing. On December 12, 2006, Día de la Virgen de Guadalupe, ICE conducted a raid at Swift meat-packing plants around the country including the one in Worthington. The terrorizing and polarizing ef-
fects on the local communities and families have been harsh.

The morning after arriving I call some friends with the Minnesota Immigrant Freedom Network, Alondra Espejel and Mariano Espinoza, to ask
them to help me identify contacts, and I discover they are in Worthington for a series of meetings. I leave 10th Street and take a leisurely ride on
the sidewalks toward the union offices where they are. A few blocks up the
road a police car pulls into the street, and the officer steps out and hails me
down. He proceeds to tell me that Minnesota law requires that I ride on
the road and if I am going to be on the sidewalk I need to go with the flow
of traffic. He asks if I am a cross-country bike rider, and I say yes but that
I am currently living in Minnesota and have just arrived into town on my
way back for a rest in the Twin Cities.

This piques his interest, so I ask him about the relationship between
law enforcement and the local immigrant communities. Sergeant William Bolt speaks very proudly of the efforts the police have made to develop

a strong and trusting relationship with the local Latin@ community. He makes a point of crediting the police chief with developing policies and incentives for this. When he sees a colleague pass by, he contacts him by radio and asks him to come back and talk to me. I meet Bob Fritz, the officer responsible for developing relationships with youths in the schools. Here is part of our conversation:

OFFICER FRITZ: We're getting to be a 24-hour operation. And of course, with that everyone is struggling to deal with the language and culture issues that we're not used to dealing with, some of the wanna-be gang stuff, graffiti. I'd say it's been four to five years now that it's taking us to get a handle on things. We have the largest elementary school in the Midwest to begin with anyway, and in K through fifth grades it's a good 50 to 60 percent minority. As it goes up [in grade level] it's a little less [minority].

It's a real melting pot. Spanish, Asian, African, American Indian, white people, it's an amazing mix. The young kids really get along. Everyone was very apprehensive at first on both sides. We didn't know how to deal, and the minorities didn't know what to do with us, because of the whole cultural difference thing. This year we had our 12th international festival [that] celebrates every single culture in town. I don't know if we could be any more inclusive now—any kind of food and ethnic group you can imagine. Our police and medical personnel have become very diverse. You should see the groups of people that come together. The city really embraces it.

ME: *What's your job?*

OFFICER FRITZ: This year my title is juvenile officer and school resource officer. My job is to work with kids through the school year to do preventive stuff—drugs, alcohol, tobacco, gangs, violence stuff. In summer I do general patrol, hang with kids to keep [the] relationship going at parks and pool, to keep [a] positive relationship going.

ME: *Did you grow up here?*

OFFICER FRITZ: I remember growing up here as a kid, and there was one black family and one Hispanic family, and I knew the kids from each family, and that was it as far as diversity. People would come in from the farm and think they're a novelty. And now they're practically the majority. If you see the businesses on Main Street, you see almost more ethnic businesses than anything else. [That's] the thing that really encourages me, and I think it takes a generation or two to get racism out of a community or coun-

Officer William Bolt of the Worthington Police Department. Louis Mendoza.

Officer Bob Fritz of the Worthington Police Department. Louis Mendoza.

try. I go to the elementary and see the young kids in K through fifth grade, and they play, hold hands, and color or race is the furthest thing in their mind. But as you see the middle and high school kids, it intrigues me, but they have all this stuff. Where are they getting this junk? They're getting it from home or somewhere, TV or movies. It's almost like a switch comes on and they say, "Hey, they're different than me."

> ME: *To be honest, I have my own stereotypes of small towns, and this trip has been really changing my view of small towns.*

OFFICER FRITZ: Yeah. Worthington is an amazing place. We make local, regional, and national news all the time.

The officers make it clear to me that though there is not a written policy to this effect, it is their practice not to formally cooperate with ICE because they feel it is important for local police to have a trusting relationship with immigrants so silence and fear do not prohibit communication regarding local law enforcement issues. Sergeant Bolt gives me a few names of other people I can speak with, and the officers send me on my way.

After meeting with Alondra and Mariano and some of the union organizers, I get a sense of the local situation with workers. Since the ICE raids, Swift has had trouble holding onto workers. This is a labor issue and has a chilling effect on workers who do not want to be vulnerable to deportation or harassment. I meet with a local reporter who publishes a nice story on my trip a few days later in the *Worthington Globe*. The reporter, Amanda Walljasper, is a part-time reporter and full-time teacher with the Integration Collaborative, a multicultural initiative of the school district funded by Minnesota's Department of Education. I had heard of this program through several people by this time and take her up on the offer to call the office to see if I can speak with people there. They invite me over, and I have a powerful conversation with four employees: Nancy Landeros, a young *mexicana* who moved from Iowa via Texas; Antonio Colindres, an agricultural worker originally from El Salvador; college student Antonio López y Sebastián, a refugee whose family escaped Guatemala's civil war of the 1980s; and Carrie Adams, a longtime resident of Worthington, of German-Scandinavian descent.

They share with me the vision and extensive work of the collaborative and its cultural initiatives, including the annual international festival. They explain how their work varies according to circumstances and say that in the immediate aftermath of the raids, their offices served as an informal clearinghouse for many support efforts. Each of them acknowledges that many people are involved in trying to foster positive social relations among different ethnic groups but also that this is a long process. They make it clear that change has to be deliberate and that the overall climate of the country and the recent debacle around immigration reform have only served to arouse suspicion and fear against Latin@s without regard for their immigration status. They bemoan the deep roots of tensions

Integration Collaborative staff members (left to right) Carrie Adams, Nancy Landeros, and Antonio López y Sebastián. Louis Mendoza.

between Latin@s and mainstream America. For instance, they say, active recruitment of workers to the region continues unabated, and thus strong mixed signals result in a fragmented sense of belonging. Carrie acknowledges that despite the slow pace of change, she sees a generational shift toward more acceptance occurring.

Worthington is no utopia, but that place doesn't exist. With hearts and minds working to build stronger cross-cultural relationships based on justice and a common sense of humanity, change can occur.

HOME IS WHERE YOU DON'T HAVE TO PACK UP AND LEAVE EVERY DAY!

It takes me two days to ride from Worthington to Minneapolis. I catch a lot of rain in Mankato but push on. I arrive home early Sunday afternoon. It's good to be in my own space after six weeks on the road. I'll spend the next ten days resting, regrouping, and planning my next moves. I catch up on my blog entries, respond to questions from people who have been following my blog, and write some larger reflections on what I've experienced thus far. While it would be hard to say that all has gone according to plan, given the unanticipated challenges I've encountered, in many respects it has because I knew from the start that I could not count on having control over every aspect of this trip. I've learned lessons and will move forward to the next phase all the wiser.

RURAL HISPANICS AT A GLANCE

Between 1980 and 2000, the Hispanic/Latino population in rural and small town America nearly doubled from 1.4 to 2.7 million and is now the most rapidly growing segment of the population in nonmetropolitan (nonmetro) counties. In 1980, Hispanics constituted just over 3 percent of the nonmetro population, a figure that rose to 5.5 percent in 2000. Since 1980, growth in the Hispanic population has contributed over 25 percent of the total nonmetro population increase and over 50 percent of the nonmetro minority population increase.

Hispanic population growth has helped to stem decades of small town population decline in some States, demographically and economically revitalizing many rural communities. Hispanic population growth in new destinations outside traditional Hispanic settlement areas in the nonmetro Southwest can drive change in local economies and can raise questions about social service provision, socioeconomic adaptation and integration, and other important public policy issues for nonmetropolitan counties (1).

While Hispanics make up less that 6 percent of the entire nonmetro population of 46 million, their growth rate since 1980 outpaces that of all other major racial and ethnic groups. Of the four major minority groups, only nonmetro Blacks outnumber nonmetro Hispanics (4.1 million to 2.7 million). At current growth rates, however, Hispanics are projected to become the largest minority group in rural America by about 2025, as they did for the entire Nation in 2003 (2).

Hispanic population growth has checked long-term population decline in many rural counties, especially in Midwestern and Great Plains States where natural decrease and outmigration by young native-born adults have been reducing population in some areas in the 1950s or earlier.

In rural areas, as elsewhere, Hispanics comprise many nationalities and range widely across virtually every socioeconomic indicator. These dimensions include education, occupation, median age, citizenship, race, and history in the United States—even within groups. For example, the largest ethnic group, Mexicans, includes many citizens who trace their ancestors' U.S. settlement back for hundreds of years, as well as new residents. Hispanic residents in newer rural destinations, while ethnically diverse, include larger proportion of recent U.S. migrants than are found in more established settlement areas (3).

U.S. Department of Agriculture Economic Research Service,
excerpts from Economic Information Bulletin no. 8, December 2005

REFLEXIONES, BIG AND SMALL

While resting at home I answer questions I've received on my blog and add some musings before departing on the next phase of my trip:

My brother, Bobby: *How is your mind? You must be playing some mental gymnastics at times just to stay sane.*

Me: Yes indeed, I do have to play all sorts of mind games to stay focused. This is mostly during the day while I'm biking as opposed to the evening when I'm resting or interacting with folks. Some of this I'll address in response to Otto's questions. But you make an important point—one plays these games to keep from getting emotionally down; that is, it's easy to get overwhelmed with the enormousness and emptiness of the open road. Being physically tired makes one emotionally vulnerable, and it works in the other direction as well.

My sister Rosemary: *Has this trip been harder than you anticipated? Is this trip something you had to do alone? Are there creature comforts you miss? Have you felt unsafe so far anywhere on this journey?*

Me: Yes and no. I knew it would be very hard, but knowing that doesn't make experiencing it any less severe. I can say that in many respects it's gotten easier as I've gotten stronger and learned new strategies for biking hills, eating, keeping my energy up, and avoiding pitfalls like running out of water. It's also gotten easier as the rewards accumulate— and by that I mean that by realizing my goals of talking with people, of seeing and experiencing so many good things, I feel like it makes sense, it's affirming. I don't think the trip would have been compromised by being with someone else, and in fact it may have been enriched. But I suppose at an individual level it's testing my ingenuity and persistence in ways that may benefit me down the road.

As for creature comforts, for sure I miss my own bed and a bath or shower on a regular basis as well as the ability to just recuperate in my own surroundings, but I haven't exactly been that deprived of basics since I've spent more time in motels than I expected to. I really need to get better at scouring around and finding alternate sites to rest. Truly, the only time I've felt unsafe was once or twice on the road when I was crossing a bridge with narrow shoulders and lots of fast-moving cars. There was one other time near Belvidere, South Dakota, at a rest stop when someone in a pickup seemed to be scouting me out. Not knowing what was up, I moved to a bench closer to the building and better lit.

Kamala Platt: *My thought today in terms of blog prompts that you asked for is that bike trips such as yours may be even harder in a few years as weather becomes less and less predictable . . . I heard a doctor/ environmentalist yesterday talking about global warming as disease (off kilter) of the earth. He talked about our bodies' abilities to heal themselves . . . (inherent here is also the adjustment to extreme change such as might be relevant more for you at the moment). Anyway, the earth also has bal-*

ancing acts to keep it "healthy," but these have been thrown off by global warming.

Me: I'm not quite sure how to respond to this other than to say that from a weather perspective this trip hasn't been predictable. I traveled across the northern region first so I could avoid it in the winter, but I didn't realize it would be so hot. For the first few weeks I was in the midst of a strong heat wave, and most people said it was hotter than it had been in years. Climate change is slow, so I don't know when or if it will ever get so hot as to make a trip like this impossible.

Ben: *I just got back from Cuba a week ago and thought of you after coming across a small photo of Che at the Museum of the Revolution: he was on a bike—non-motorized! Apparently, before his more famous motorcycle ride, he took a several-thousand-mile trip throughout his native country of Argentina asking similar questions about national identity that you are asking and investigating about the U.S. This trip, which preceded his Pan American and then world travels and activities, raised several questions that may serve as a good prompt. That is, what is the nature of the national identity you are seeing transformed, and how is this relating to the resurgent and militantly anti-imperialist Panamericanism?*

Me: A great question but one that defies any simple or easy explanation. I think that once we get beyond the dogmatic positions associated with U.S. official nationalism (patriotism) and reactionary nationalism (nativism), what is left is something that is an enormously complex dynamic of accommodation, resistance, and assimilation. I wouldn't say a new nationalism is emerging, but I do think that new immigrants bring a very different sense of national identity—one that is much more transnationalist. So, for instance, they may have dual loyalties. While many may have criticisms of the U.S., they also have many things they like about it—this is their new home even as they retain ties to their homes of origin. I don't think they see these as being in contradiction to one another as many traditional nationalists would have you believe— a love it first and last or leave it mentality that wants to see national identity as stable and fixed and absolute.

I don't know that the "internationalism" of today is the same as the internationalism of yesteryear, such as existed at the height of the anti-colonialist movement of the twentieth century. Even the more successful nationalist movements currently thriving in Latin America today are cognizant of making distinctions between governments and the people—whom they hold more faith in. In truth, this has a parallel with what I feel like I'm seeing and hearing from folks thus far. Notwithstanding those folks affiliated with anti-Latin@ or anti-immigrant groups, most people on the ground level simply want to understand what the human implications of new groups will be for them. And if intermarriage rates and relationships at work and in the churches and schools are any indication, the fact of the matter is that most people are getting along. In fact, some of them recognize the ways in which our destinies are mutually intertwined. In that regard, I think that despite the many problems with the discourse of globalization, the flow of human traffic in these times is leading to the disintegration of the idea of a stable sense of national identity and culture because actual interactions and relations with others do not allow folks to sustain perceptions of difference.

Gabriel Fernández: *We've read through the arduous physical aspects of your journey and the search for the answers to the various questions you have about the state of Latin@ization. Where are you as far as your own personal spiritual journey? I know that you feel that we are all connected, but with the solitariness of your journey do you feel yourself coming into closer contact with all around you, and even do you feel yourself becoming one with Nature? If you had these deep spiritual feelings before, are they growing, becoming more? Is this journey changing your mind about God or a Source of the Oneness or a source of the connections?*

Me: Again, a great question but one that I'm not sure I can articulate very clearly. I think I have a much more profound appreciation for nature, but I can't say I feel one with it—despite a sometimes contentious relationship with it, I do not feel in opposition to it at all. I find it sad to think of the privatization of land and the ways in which we, that is, most of us, are deprived of having a more authentic relationship to it because we cannot afford to buy it or because despite the large areas of parks, we cannot afford to travel to it. I do understand why making one's living off the land builds a spiritual relationship with it and all of nature because you both shape it and are at its mercy. Thus far, I must say that my sense of connectedness with people has been affirmed and strengthened. I don't have a lot to say about a higher being because I am mostly concerned with people realizing the goodness in themselves and acting upon it. For me, people taking action and resisting the anti-humanist and dehumanization of others would be an enormous stride forward for all humanity.

Sandy Soto: *Great photos. I especially like the one of you and your bike—which makes me wonder if you've given her a name yet.*

Me: I haven't named the bike yet—though it's certainly been on my mind. Given my intimate relationship with it, I should name her. In *Travels with Charley*, John Steinbeck named his truck Rocinante, a tribute to Don Quixote and a sign of his own quixotic quest to discover America. William Least Heat-Moon christened his van Ghost Dancing in tribute to Sitting Bull and Native American resistance. I'm open to suggestions.

My sister Margie Cortinas: *What do you think about when you are riding your bike, or do you listen to music?*

Me: I don't listen to music when I ride because I need to be able to hear cars coming from behind me. I think about the news I've read, about my life, where it's been, where I'm going, about the next mile, the hill right in front of me, my breathing, the next mile marker, the speed I'm going, the aches in my legs, butt, and hands. I think of the land around me and wonder why we don't have enough food to end world hunger or enough space to house anyone who wants a home. I think about the role of the privatization of the land and fences that keep me from getting to a shade tree. I wonder what those huge RVs look like inside and about ice-cold drinks. I observe all the road kill—snakes, rabbits, gophers, raccoons, deer, dogs, cats, and other, unidentifiable, furry things that are now flat and/or decayed.

Q: *Are you trying to meet people you know in certain places?*

Me: I've only met two people I know along the way—a friend of a friend in Oregon whose house I stayed at and two friends in Worthington, Minnesota, who I didn't know would be there doing work when I arrived. I do hope to see others I know in the Midwest, East Coast, South, and Southwest.

Otto, a University of Minnesota alumnus: *After graduating in '91, I made a bike journey with other U of M colleagues down the west coast of the U.S. We learned more of ourselves than of the places, actually. Don't drink and bike . . . no matter how cold the beer is on the forehead and/or how many are offered! After crossing Venezuela (and then S.A.) by bike, I could hardly remember the ride, for the Venezuelans were so happy to have a cyclist drink their offered beers.*

Me: I wish I had this problem!

Q: *I love your blogging contributions. How do you feel you're doing on balancing riding and meeting your goals?*

Me: I think it's been a good balance. There are many days, most days, in fact, when it's just about the riding. I worry that I'm not tending to my "research," but then I remind myself that I'm going through 33 states, and all I really need to have enough materials is a few good interactions with folks in each state, and I'll have plenty of material to work with. When I think about it like this, I realize that I'm doing pretty good.

Q: *Have you begun to calculate how many times your wheel has rotated since your departure yet? It'll happen on a very hot and dry day . . . especially now that I've suggested the task.*

Me: I've come close. I've calculated how many pumps it takes to get from one reflector pole to another (about 40) or if I'm on a concrete highway, how many pumps it takes to get from one crack to another (10). I really hope to push your suggestion you made out of my head—that would drive me crazy.

Rachel Jennings: *Have you needed the 6,000 calories a day that you were informed were required? Do you really live off the PowerBars and so forth that are in your baggage?*

Me: I have no idea. I don't think I eat near that much. Though I need to eat regularly—three good meals—I'm not pigging out each time I do. Even though I often eat lunch at a convenience store, I find myself eating healthier because the thought of eating anything fried for lunch or dinner grosses me out. I'm too hot!

What I don't mention in my response to Rachel is that I drown my thirst at the end of the day by drinking large quantities of soda and ice. And I stave off anxiety and loneliness by chain-smoking in the evenings. For those who know me, none of this may come as a surprise, though I think many are under the wrong impression that I've become a health nut.

My 10-day respite at home is quickly coming to a close, and I'm heading out Thursday morning. It won't be easy to leave, but I'm also eager to get back to my trip. While here I have given one radio interview and two for newspapers, had a chance to share some of my photos and observations on my trip thus far with friends and colleagues, and made plans for moving forward. Marianne has moved to Minneapolis from Santa Cruz to teach, and she will sublet my house until I return, so I'm happy that Shadow will be able to come home. Not counting the side trips I've taken when I rent a car, I calculate that I've traveled approximately 2,750 miles, with a breakdown of travel by bike, car, and bus:

> 2,750 miles total from Santa Cruz to Minneapolis
> 30 miles from Calistoga (bus)
> 150 miles from Redding to Medford (bus)
> 47 miles from Eugene to Corvallis (car)
> 22 miles from Sisters to Bend (cab)
> 106 miles from Buchanan to Ontario, Oregon (car)
> 85 miles from Mountain Home to Twin Falls (bus)
> 132 miles from East Yellowstone to Cody (car)
> 20 miles in Bighorn Mountains (car)

This totals 592 miles by motor vehicle and approximately 2,158 miles by bike.

My plan from here is to go south to Iowa City and visit friends who have alerted me to tensions arising in nearby communities related to immigration. From there I will go toward Milwaukee, down to Chicago, and then across to Detroit and into Ontario, Canada, where I will cross back into the U.S. at Niagara Falls. From there I will head east through New York and Massachusetts and begin a southward trek along the eastern seaboard. I hope the ride and my Internet access challenges will be easier, and I go forward a bit thinner, stronger, and smarter. I've lost about 16 pounds during stage 1. To make room for a small laptop, I decide to not take my stove and fuel and to lessen the amount of food I carry, since finding food has not been a problem and the denser population of the East will minimize that risk even more.

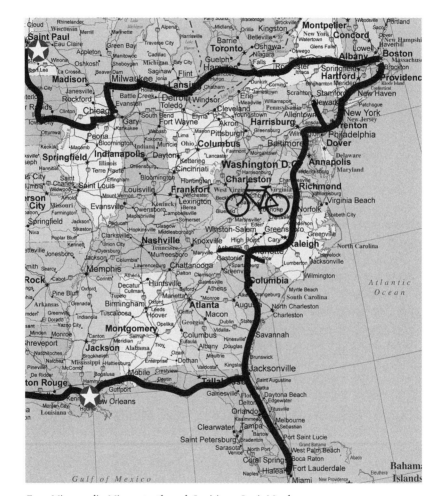

From Minneapolis, Minnesota, through Louisiana. Louis Mendoza.

PART THREE

REDEPARTURE
From the Heartland to the New South

A WISE TRAVELER NEVER DESPISES HIS OWN COUNTRY.

Carlo Goldoni

ADVENTURE IS A PATH. REAL ADVENTURE—SELF-DETERMINED, SELF-MOTIVATED, OFTEN RISKY—FORCES YOU TO HAVE FIRSTHAND ENCOUNTERS WITH THE WORLD. THE WORLD THE WAY IT IS, NOT THE WAY YOU IMAGINE IT. YOUR BODY WILL COLLIDE WITH THE EARTH AND YOU WILL BEAR WITNESS. IN THIS WAY YOU WILL BE COMPELLED TO GRAPPLE WITH THE LIMITLESS KINDNESS AND BOTTOMLESS CRUELTY OF HUMANKIND—AND PERHAPS REALIZE THAT YOU YOURSELF ARE CAPABLE OF BOTH. THIS WILL CHANGE YOU.

Mark Jenkins

ST. PAUL TO ROCHESTER: AUGUST 23, 2007

Severe thunderstorms are forecast for Thursday, so I delay my start until Friday morning. Marianne has recently moved to the Twin Cities to teach, so she takes me to St. Paul's West Side so I can head down Highway 52 going south to Rochester. With the first part of the trip still fresh on my mind, I am somewhat reluctant to leave. Nevertheless, I push off about 9:30 and have a nice day in the sun with minimal traffic. I arrive in Rochester about five o'clock. It takes me about an hour to get to the south side of town, which is where I want to be so I can take off in the morning. I have an interview with a local reporter, and she advises me that there are some Mexican stores and restaurants near downtown. After checking into a cheap motel, I get some advice from the motel clerk and ride around. Rochester is a pristine city of about 100,000 where the Zumbro River flows into Silver Lake. It's easy to discern that the renowned Mayo Clinic is the driving economic force of the city, as it dominates the downtown area, and it is evident that the economic base and well-manicured infrastructure of the city thrives on the money generated by this medical giant. To be sure, a strong service sector is needed to support the well-heeled employees of Mayo and its affiliated industries. The downtown area is peppered with ethnic and international stores to suit the cosmopolitan interests of doctors and scientists.

My great-grandmother was smuggled into the United States from Russia in a gunny sack by my great-grandfather years ago. I understand that it was a much simpler time, but did all of our ancestors get here legally? I believe we forget America is the land of opportunity and always has been, forged by people looking for a better way and new beginning. Which is better: to have this country rid of another illegal immigrant, or have an 8-year-old boy lost without his mother?

Steven M. Grehl, letter to the editor, Minneapolis Star Tribune, *August 23, 2007*

Walking down Fourth Street I encounter evidence of a thriving Latin@ population, such as St. Francis Catholic Church's announcement of a Sunday noon mass in Spanish and El Texano, a modest tiendita that serves the local Latin@ community. The store has lots of different specialty items, mostly food. I grab some *pan dulce* so I can patronize the store and justify my presence. I speak briefly with the proprietor and learn that he moved here from Eagle Pass, Texas, about seven years earlier. He tells me that most Latin@s work in construction, in restaurants, as janitors in offices, or on farms in surrounding areas. He says his business is so-so, enough for him to keep busy and do okay. I tell him I am from Houston but now living in Minneapolis and that being in stores like his makes me homesick. We talk briefly about the Latin@ populations in each city and wish one another well.

From there I go to eat dinner at Dos Amigos, a restaurant that seems to cater to mostly non-Latin@s, though it has an almost all-Latin@ staff. I sit at the bar and watch customers enjoy the ambience. A waiter changes the TV station to a soccer match for me. On the way back to the motel I come across a 24-hour *taquería.* I am impressed that it can sustain business, and

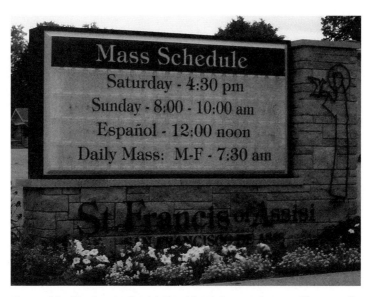

Sign outside of St. Francis of Assisi Church in Rochester, Minnesota, like many all over the country indicating that new immigrants are a growing constituency of faith communities. Louis Mendoza.

I snap a photo. One of the employees comes out and asks why I've taken a picture. She seems satisfied when I explain that I am traveling around the country and taking note of Latin@ businesses. I assume there is an underlying concern by some Latin@s that makes them worry about my intentions, such as whether I'm affiliated with ICE or some other government agency. Such wariness is something I encountered in Rexburg, Idaho, by a Spanish-speaking restaurant owner who had a lot of questions for me when I asked for an interview. He seemed satisfied with my answers but asked if we could wait a few days for the interview. His reticence and request for a delay was enough to ensure that I couldn't conduct the interview because I needed to keep moving on. I don't know exactly what motivated his concern, but I can only imagine the extraordinary caution one must feel when a stranger starts asking questions. That was the first of many times I would be reminded of how my lack of Spanish fluency limits my ability to more quickly earn people's trust.

In his youth, Leo picked beans and cotton in the South, where Mexicans and African Americans shared the rough side of segregation. He found his lighter skin tone could get him into a "white-only" society, but he rejected the system that belittled his friends. The injustice only fueled his determination to be a boss someday, so that he could treat his workers according to their merits, not their color. "I was going to prove to myself that what you are really doesn't mean much," he says. "It's what you do."

J. Carl Ganter, With These Hands: Lives that Shape the Land *(Grand Traverse Regional Land Conservancy, 2000), 19. Reprinted with permission.*

The next morning I go to Rico's for breakfast and then stop by a beautiful veterans memorial on my way out of town. On the roster of soldiers commemorated there of those who lived within 50 miles of Rochester, from the Civil War to the present, I find three Latino surnames. In the afternoon as I approach the Iowa state line, Marianne picks me up in Harmony to keep me company on my birthday. The horse-drawn carriages of the Amish and my bike seem to move along at the same pace. We drive to Postville and are surprised that almost all the people walking the streets in the center of town are Latin@s. There are numerous restaurants, some stores, and a local church that holds a Spanish-language mass every other week. We visit one well-stocked Latin@ store playing *norteño* music and buy a few items. Postville has been the subject of several studies because of its new immigrant populations; the Hassidic Jewish–owned kosher meatpacking companies and the Latin@ workers arrived hand-in-hand and were met with suspicion by the locals. More recently, Postville joined the ranks of small towns that have passed local anti-immigrant ordinances.

A year after we pass through here, Postville will make national news following an ICE workplace raid of the kosher meatpacking plant that will yield dozens of arrests and uncover horrific stories of workplace abuse. Proceedings after the raid also will become notorious for the use of mass hearings to expedite the detainment and deportation of workers.

The next day Omar Valerio and Cathy Komisaruk meet us in Waterloo for breakfast. Omar, a seasoned cyclist, brings his bike, and we ride from there to Iowa City. Well, almost. We run out of daylight, and the shoulders are made of soft gravel, so when it gets dark, we decide rather than risk the narrow roads to call Cathy for a ride. In any case, we have a beautiful 85-mile ride to Solon, much of it on a great bike trail. I spend Monday in Iowa City meeting people and visiting surrounding communities. On Monday morning we watch the news coverage on Alberto Gonzales' resignation as U.S. attorney general as a result of accusations of perjury before

Congress. Gonzales had been the highest-ranking Hispanic public official in the country. He was involved in several controversies in the aftermath of September 11, 2001, including his approval in 2002 of a memorandum that called the limitations on the questioning of prisoners under the Geneva Conventions "obsolete" when dealing with terrorism, his August 2007 testimony to Congress regarding unauthorized government surveillance programs, and his confusing accounts of having approved the dismissals of nine U.S. attorneys in 2006 while denying detailed knowledge of the circumstances or reasons. Hearings on the firings led to the controversy that ended in his resignation, though he was later exonerated.

We listen to Gonzales' statement in horror as he speaks of how much he loves this country and says that even his worst days in office are better than his father's best days in Mexico. I hope his father and others explain to him how insulting that statement is. His scheduled departure date of September 16 will give new meaning to Mexican independence— or should I say, our freedom from this tyrannical Mexican American? To be sure, many saw in Gonzales a shining example of American meritocracy in which an ethnic minority member of modest background could rise to the highest ranks of power. However, for many progressive-minded Latin@s, Gonzales has represented the limits of access to power unless one is willing to mimic the tactics and values of the ruling elite.

IOWA CITY AND WEST LIBERTY

Omar takes the next day off to show me around Iowa City and surrounding communities. I have a great meeting with Ángel González, a program coordinator with the University of Iowa's Labor Center. We visit La Reyna, a small store and restaurant in the area, and speak briefly with one of the co-owners and hear a little about how she started her business. She and her husband moved from Chicago so her children would not have to attend public schools there. I am fascinated with how new immigrants are able to open businesses, and they trade stories of how this is achieved through the pooling of money. Omar makes a point that will become more and more clear to me throughout my trip, that new immigrants of any background often take business risks here because their chances for mobility and entrepreneurial success are greater than in their home countries. Omar arranges a meeting for me next day with José Elizondo, the first Latin@ city council member elected in the town of West Liberty, about

20 miles east of Iowa City. Over dinner that night, Cathy and Omar inform me about some of the local dynamics and the lure of coming to settle in the small-town Midwest. Cathy makes the point that many recent immigrants are coming with an education and professional background that make them better equipped and more business-savvy.

The next morning as I'm preparing to leave toward Illinois, I read my horoscope in a local paper: "Not everybody wants to change the world, you know. So when you declare your own personal revolution, don't be offended if all you get is foggy looks. They'll understand later." It's muggy and in the mid-90s. I'm adjusting, somewhat painfully, to being back on the road. From Iowa City I go to West Liberty, a town of about 3,600 people. I speak with José Elizondo over breakfast at the restaurant he co-owns with his mother there. He says about half of West Liberty's residents are Latin@. With the exception of El Torito, all of the Latin@-owned restaurants are located within a two-block downtown area. The concentration of Latin@ businesses contributing to the local economy is reminiscent of those in Postville. Unlike Postville, though, West Liberty has experienced growing pains over the years yet has not resorted to passing local anti-immigrant ordinances, and there is lots of evidence indicating that the townsfolk and town leaders are embracing change. West Liberty has struggled to make change and has managed to do so with the tenacity of families like the Elizondos.

José's father was from Tamaulipas, Mexico, and his mother is from Weslaco, Texas. They came to the Midwest as part of the migrant stream, eventually settling out in Chicago. They then decided to begin selling Mexican food items to the Latin@s in the farm communities in Muscatine and the surrounding areas. This business venture turned out to be quite successful, and they opened a restaurant in West Liberty and became community leaders due to the elder Mr. Elizondo's business savvy and practice of bringing Tejano musicians to play on the weekend. Mrs. Elizondo served as a midwife, and together they became a resource for the entire community. José shares stories of working with his father and serving as his translator in business transactions with the large, mainstream, commercial stores. He has some fascinating stories to tell about his short tenure on the city council. The Elizondos represent a great example of the persistence and entrepreneurial spirit of Latin@s who start with little and fill important cultural niches in small communities all over the U.S. I hear similar stories of many folks in the Chicago area who started businesses out of their cars and eventually opened stores, restaurants, and/or delivery services.

LATINO INFLUX SHAKES UP IOWA'S POLITICAL PICTURE

MARSHALLTOWN, Iowa—Colorful piñatas hang from the ceiling, and Spanish-labeled goods fill the shelves of Angel Regalado's grocery in Marshalltown, a rural place with a bulging immigrant community.

Many of his customers lived in Mexico a decade ago. But the influx of Latinos to Marshalltown, with its large meatpacking plant, and else-where across Iowa has changed the political dynamics in what was one of the most homogeneous states in America.

Now more than 115,000 Hispanics live in Iowa, almost 4 per-cent of the state's population of 3 million. Though their community is tiny by border-state standards, their numbers increased 37 percent be-tween 2000 and 2005, according to the Iowa Division of Latino Af-fairs. The rapid growth of Iowa's Hispanic population, particularly the estimated 55,000 to 85,000 here illegally, has fueled a fierce debate in the state that will hold the first-in-the-nation presidential caucuses on Jan. 3.

Amid the polarizing politics of immigration, the issue is cutting both ways. Regalado said that for the first time since he arrived 15 years ago, he will vote in the Democratic caucuses, possibly for Hillary Rodham Clinton. His reason: anti-immigrant rhetoric from the Republicans. "They don't care about good people," he said of the immigration critics. "Most people come here to work."

In the GOP race, presidential contenders have been taking increas-ingly tough stands against illegal immigrants, favoring, among other things, deportations of convicted felons and hefty fines for employers. Last week, former Massachusetts Gov. Mitt Romney, who holds a narrow lead in the GOP Iowa polls, attacked his two main rivals—former New York Mayor Rudy Giuliani and former Arkansas Gov. Mike Huckabee—for supporting sanctuary status for illegal immigrants and tuition breaks for their children. Colorado Rep. Tom Tancredo, a Republican running on an anti-immigration message, recently began broadcasting a commercial suggesting that open-border policies have allowed terrorists to enter the country.

His spot closes with a man in a hooded sweat shirt in a crowded mall. As the screen goes dark, an explosion is heard. "People here are concerned about stopping the flow of illegal immigrants," said Barb Livingston, chairman of the Republican Party of Marshall County, which includes Marshalltown.

The influx of immigrants has had an impact on schools, health care and taxes, she said. At the same time, Livingston conceded the issue was complicated and that voter anger was not necessarily directed at the Hispanic immigrants living in their communities. "They have compassion for people that are here and don't wish them ill," she said.

Democrats are trying to woo Latino voters. Between 15,000 and 18,000 Hispanics are registered to vote in Iowa and are eligible to attend the state's primary caucuses. They could make up a pivotal bloc in the Democratic caucuses, which drew 124,000 voters in 2004.

The partisan divide over immigration was underscored in a recent University of Iowa poll of likely caucus-goers. The survey found that two-thirds of Republicans rated immigration as either the most important or a highly important issue. Only about one-third of Democrats ranked the issue so high. The poll, however, found Republicans far from united about how to deal with the issue.

Bennett Roth, Houston Chronicle, *November 27, 2007.*
Copyright 2007 by Houston Chronicle Publishing Company.
Reproduced with permission of Houston Chronicle Publishing Company
in the format Textbook via Copyright Clearance Center.

From West Liberty I head east toward Moline, Illinois. While I'm taking a break outside the Casey General Store in Wilton, Iowa, some bikers approach me wanting to know about my trip. One of them says, "Wow, that's a real biker over there." They want to know where I'm going, where I'm coming from. Rick, his daughter Molly, and Chuck Jones had been at Sturgis a few weeks back and are curious, supportive, and impressed to hear details about my ride. They assure me I'll meet lots of nice people along the way. Rick tells me he's just dropped his daughter off at the University of Iowa. They are impressed that I am a professor, and we take a picture together. They offer advice about camping and the roads ahead. I find these spontaneous expressions of support and friendliness from strangers inspiring. Later that evening I cross the Mississippi and arrive into East Moline. Tomorrow I head toward Chicago and should be there by midday Friday. I've decided to postpone visiting Carpentersville until after I visit Chicago. Carpentersville is one of the small towns west of Chicago that have recently passed anti-immigrant ordinances.

Rick, Molly, and Chuck next to their motorcycles on the road in Illinois. Louis Mendoza.

A WEEK BACK ON THE ROAD: AUGUST 30, 2007

I arrive in Rochelle, Illinois, late in the evening after a long day of 100 miles and a couple of unexpected detours. As I go through the small town of Barstow, the road I am on is flooded from recent rains, so I am forced to retrace my route and go on I-88. There is minimal traffic and a nice shoulder, so this route will be much faster. About 30 miles down the road, a trooper pulls me over with a blip of his siren and informs me that cyclists may not ride on the interstate in Illinois. After checking my name in the Illinois database, he sends me up the road to the nearest exit.

As evening approaches I am at a crossroads on a small highway looking for my final turn to the north that will bring me to Rochelle when a woman stops and offers me advice on where my turnoff will be. About that time I see a young woman cyclist with panniers pull up to a restaurant and go inside to eat. I am very tempted to go in and strike up a conversation with her about her trip, but with darkness pending and 20 miles ahead of me I decide to press on since I want to get off this particular highway that is well traveled by 18-wheelers. I am fascinated by this woman traveling alone on a long trip and want to get her story, yet I worry she might find it creepy and uncomfortable being approached by a male stranger. I am curious where she is going to stay that night, as darkness is quickly approaching. I feel a kinship with her, as I have seen very few cyclists thus far, and almost none of them have been women.

Soon darkness descends and hunger, thirst, and fatigue catch up with me. In the distance I see a light and hope that this is my turn. I am completely floored when I get to this light and see a small taco trailer at the intersection with the name Taquería Monterrey emblazoned on its side. Though it is next door to a topless bar, both seem oddly located in what appears to be the middle of nowhere. I stop for a quick taco and to see what I can learn from the proprietor. The young mexicano running it says he came from Chicago to start this business with the hope of eventually opening a full-fledged restaurant. I tell him I am from Texas, and he informs me that he'd lived in Houston off Telephone Road. He explains that the former motel at this intersection had been converted to a migrant camp, and almost all of its residents are from El Valle of South Texas. He gets busy with customers. Another man had heard a bit of our conversation and tells me he is a supplier for many small Latin@ businesses in the region. He lives in Naperville, near Chicago. I tell him I am headed toward Carpentersville, and he says he does business there although it is a place that is bad for Latin@s.

They both advise me to take care because I will be going down a road with no lights, and it is already dark. They are right; it is pitch black, but Sister Moon is rising on the eastern horizon through a cloudy haze. A few miles up the road I begin to see a mushroom cloud of lights from Rochelle refracting off the clouds, and I know I'll reach the town within the hour. I stop at a convenience store as soon as I arrive there for a cold drink. The two clerks see my bike and ask where I've come from. In a gesture of kindness that is to be repeated many times over, they refuse to take my money, saying it is the least they can offer. After getting instructions on where to find motels, I thank them and move on.

CHICAGO LATIN@S BUILDING COMMUNITIES OF RESISTANCE: SEPTEMBER 4, 2007

I arrive in northwest Chicago about midday Friday. Howard and Andi Sass are gracious enough to let me stay at their house even though they are leaving town for the long Labor Day weekend. I take three buses down to Pilsen to visit with Raul Raymundo, the long-standing, charismatic executive director of the Resurrection Project. Its mission is "to build relationships and challenge people to act on their faith and values to create healthy communities through organizing, education, and community development." I am deeply impressed with the success the Resurrection Project has had in reaching its goals and in building a nonprofit that is self-sustaining and not dependent on grant funding. As with my other conversations, I learn Raul's familial history and how his parents' values and experiences shaped him to be a community leader in the very neighborhood he grew up in after coming to the U.S. at age seven.

I learn that a friend and former University of Texas–San Antonio colleague, Rodolfo Rosales, is in town attending the American Political Science Association conference. He is staying with another friend, Juan Mora, so later in the afternoon I go downtown to catch up with them at an outdoor cafe for a few drinks. It is a bit surreal to be in such a big metropolis after spending so much time in rural areas. On my way to our rendezvous point I encounter a Critical Mass demonstration in downtown Chicago. The Friday before leaving on my trip in late June, I'd seen one in Minneapolis. This one is very large, so I respectfully dodge and dart my way through the bikes to cross the street. On Sunday I see news from Minneapolis about a hostile encounter with the police by Critical Mass participants that occurred about the same time as the Chicago ride was occurring.

From Juan I learn about the philosophy of building communities of resistance that is guiding the resistance to gentrification of the Humboldt Park neighborhood. I get contact information for one of the leaders in the struggle that I plan to follow up on at a later time. Rudy and I make plans to meet the next day to hang out with his grandniece, Laura, who has just moved to Chicago from Seattle to attend the Art Institute to study photography. After a nice, long evening with my friends discussing my trip and local community politics in Chicago, I make my way back to northwest Chicago by train.

The next day we meet at the Jumping Bean cafe on West 18th in Pilsen and go to the National Museum of Mexican Art. On the way I'd hoped to stop in at Latinos Progresando, a nonprofit legal aid agency that assists clients in applying for immigration benefits, conducts community education outreach, and advocates for Latin@ rights. My timing is bad, though, as the office closed a bit earlier than I thought. The museo is all that I expected it to be, and after leaving we walk around the neighborhood looking at murals until we hear music that leads us to a Kermes, a seasonal church

An iconic Puerto Rican flag made out of metal stands near the main stage of the Puerto Rican festival in Humboldt Park, Chicago. Louis Mendoza.

festival, at San Pio's Church, where good food, music, and dancing are in abundance.

Afterward we go downtown and make the mistake of going up the Sears Tower to catch the view from the highest building in the U.S. We do see a beautiful sunset, but perhaps because it's a holiday weekend it takes us about three hours to go through the numerous lines for tickets, elevators, and such. From there we pick up a friend of Laura's and go to Grant Park to catch the jazz festival—for all of five minutes before it ends for the night. After walking Rudy to his hotel and the young women back to their dorm, I make my way "home." The next day I am happy to see that I am only about seven miles from Humboldt Park, so I ride the bike there midafternoon and bask in the Midwest's largest celebration of Puerto Rican culture. There are three stages providing everything from traditional and folk music to poetry to hip-hop. I stay a few hours.

Unlike in small towns, in a big city like Chicago it's not about looking for visible evidence of Latin@ life and culture but rather of deciding what to focus on and whom to speak with about the many efforts to sustain and enhance Latin@ life. What is made clear to me about the stakes in Humboldt Park's resistance to gentrification is the very notion of cultural cohesion as it relates to space. Without a neighborhood where the historical, social, and cultural integrity is maintained in an everyday fashion, these folks stand to lose the very soul of their community—a whole way of life.

CARPENTERSVILLE, ILLINOIS

I get to Carpentersville around midday and find that this little township is a very small and very quiet place for all the media attention it has received following the decision in early August to follow in the footsteps of Hazleton, Pennsylvania, by adopting one of the strictest local anti-immigrant ordinances in the country. Even though about 40 percent of the population is Latin@ and a lot of opposition exists to the ordinance to make English the official language, punish employers who hire undocumented workers, and landlords who rent to those who cannot verify their legal status, some of the town's newly elected trustees have decided that this is an issue worth fighting for and made it a wedge issue in their campaigns.

"Our Town," an excellent article by Alex Kotlowitz about the divisiveness caused by Carpentersville's recent anti-immigrant ordinance appeared in the *New York Times Magazine* last month, on August 5. Kotlowitz makes the point that the more than 40 laws passed by local and state governments are "aimed at making life miserable for illegal immigrants in the hope that they'll have no choice but to return to their countries of origin. Deportation by attrition, some call it."

I find some amusement as I ride through the east side of town, where most working-class folks live, that the signature water tower of the town overshadows a Taco Bell. Down the street, St. Monica's Catholic Church advertises masses in English and Spanish, and Meadowlands Elementary School directly across the street from the church advertises back-to-school information in English and Spanish. Since the town is spread out, it looks very much like a suburb; other than a few restaurants and small businesses, I'm not sure how to find a town center where people congregate. I finally decide to go into a small Latina-owned hair salon and speak with the proprietor while I get a trim. In her mid-30s, Adriana tells me that already a number of Latin@s have left town. She finds life there okay but is concerned about a pervasive anti-Latin@ sentiment that she believes affects all Latin@s in town despite their legal status. She assures me that she has no immediate plans to leave; still, she feels that if her business suffers from the hostile climate she'll be forced to consider moving.

After my haircut I spend a long day shadowing Highway 41/94 for 90 miles as I make my way to Milwaukee. It's too late and I'm too tired when I arrive to make productive plans for the next day. Friends are expecting to see me in East Lansing in a few days, so I decide to take the ferry from Milwaukee to Muskegon, Michigan, the next morning. About midday I make the crossing in a high-speed ferry and arrive with plenty of time to get to Grand Rapids. The next day I ride 72 miles and on Wednesday evening roll into Lansing, where I am hosted by my friends Sheila Contreras and Salah Hassan and their two beautiful daughters, Noor and Paz, for a few days. They take me to eat, and afterward we go to a small reception for a Latino politician. There I meet several people including Juan Marinez, an advocate for Latin@ farmers with Michigan State University's extension office. We set up a time to meet the next day, and he agrees to introduce me to his parents, who are originally from Texas and settled out of the migrant trail in East Lansing in the early part of the twentieth century.

I am surprised to learn from Juan about the profound growth of farm ownership in Michigan by people of Mexican descent. He explains that this is driven by Tejanos who have settled out and new immigrants who learn that they can pool their money and buy small farms. Both of these groups, he says, have a long tradition of working the land and feel a strong sense of tradition and pride in being self-employed. He informs me that their growing presence as farm owners has made the agricultural associations rethink their assumptions about who owns and works the land. I am surprised to learn from him that from a global perspective, Latin@s are the world's largest producers of blueberries. The next day he introduces me to his parents, who migrated to Michigan in the first quarter of the twentieth century and have witnessed a lot of change in East Lansing. Mr. Marinez explains how life has not always been easy there but that he always stood up for what was right and fair despite personal risks in doing so.

"THE WORLD GONE CHANGE"

The almost 90-mile ride to Detroit is fairly uneventful—scattered showers and very humid—and a single road alongside the interstate leads me directly to downtown. The inner city reminds me of the industrial neighborhoods clustered together where I grew up in Houston, rough and gritty but very vibrant. I see some great graffiti on the way in. The one I like the most is simple and poignant: "The world gone change." Indeed it has, and this new reality is what people struggle with. It's a dreary morning as I prepare to cross into Windsor, Ontario, Canada, later in the afternoon. I visit the Arab American Museum in Dearborn, less than 10 miles

Chuck on his motorized bicycle at Hart Plaza in downtown Detroit. Louis Mendoza.

from downtown Detroit, where I view an amazing exhibit titled Coming to America. I go back to downtown Detroit to check out my options for crossing into Canada and to see if any of my leads for contacts in the area will pan out. I learn that I will have to take a cab across because bicycles aren't allowed in the tunnel or on the bridge. Bummer.

Before crossing I decide to explore downtown a bit more and ride by the boardwalk to view the lake. There I meet a man on a bike who comments that I am really "geared up." His name is Chuck, and he's riding a bike with a small two-cycle engine over the front wheel. Chuck is interested in my trip and tells me that he co-owns a wine and liquor store with his partner. He says he considers his partner's grandchildren like they are his own and wishes they could meet me because I seem like a nice guy and he likes introducing them to interesting people. Chuck says he's thought of riding around the country on his motorized bike, which gets 100 miles on one-third of a gallon, the size of his tank. I, in turn, am fascinated by his bike, and we discuss the limits (less distance and power) of electric bikes I've seen. Chuck wants to hear stories from my trip, and since he'd lived in the South we speak about our shared Jim Crow experiences, agreeing that they're always in the back of our minds but we can't let them limit us. When I mention I am from Houston, he brings up the brutal killing of James Byrd in Jasper, Texas, in 1998.

Sign pointing the way to Mexican Town in Detroit. Louis Mendoza.

Chuck is heartened to hear about the good experiences I've had, and we talk about the disposition one has to have to interact with strangers and make them feel at ease. He says his dream is to get a mobile home and go "dig for gold in California, diamonds in Arkansas, and fish for marlins in Florida." We ride around the boardwalk, and he insists that I try out his bike. I am sold on it! He asks if I will ride more regularly once the trip is done and I say, "Absolutely." He shares with me how important he thinks it is for people to explore alternate modes of transportation, not just for the environment but for their own health. He says after he leaves work, riding on the bike makes him feel free and alive. He's trying to get the grandkids into bicycling and tries to give them positive affirmations by telling them how good they are because they hear so much about how bad black kids are. I give him one of my cards about the trip and tell him to ask the kids to show him how to access my blog so he can read more stories from my trip and see his picture posted. After about a half-hour together we part ways but not before I let him know how inspiring and important it is to me to meet people like him.

From the boardwalk I go to Mexican Town. When I first heard about it I had to wonder if it wasn't just a tourist trap. It isn't. As I ride down Vernor Street I feel like I could be on Canal Street in Houston, Zarzamora in

San Antonio, pre-gentrified Sixth Street in Austin, or Lake Street in Minneapolis. I buy lunch from a taco truck and sit in Clark Park. I realize that I've left my helmet somewhere. I have no idea where and decide it's too time-consuming to try and figure it out, so I head toward the International Bridge without it. Near the Greyhound bus station I see a line of cabs, and one of the drivers agrees to take me over for a reasonable fee. While I'm loading my stuff, the four or five drivers nearby ask me a bunch of questions about my trip, especially how much it is costing me. When I tell them I'm going to write a book, one guy says, "Well, you tell them us cab drivers that hang around the bus station here in Detroit are hard up."

FROM DETROIT, MICHIGAN, TO LEAMINGTON, ONTARIO, CANADA: SEPTEMBER 4, 2007

Getting through customs in Canada is easy, and the driver lets me off at a McDonald's immediately across the bridge. I ask him about getting to Highway 3, and he approaches a couple in a car who then pull out a map to show me. They are emphatic about welcoming me to Canada and tell me they live near Toronto. By this time it is past three o'clock. After a short stop at a welcome center to get a map and suggestions for a good stopping point a few hours up the road, I leave and ride the 50 kilometers to Leamington.

When I arrive I ride around town looking for a store to get a new bike helmet. I don't have any luck at a superstore, but outside when I am unlocking my bike I strike up a conversation with a Mexican national. He doesn't speak much English, but we meet halfway and I'm able to ask him a number of questions in my imperfect Spanish. Herman Díaz moved here about six months earlier from Tlaxcala. He came here through a recruitment program that brings men to work in the tomato fields and in home construction. He says he'd worked near Jackson, Tennessee, before that, but the constant worry about immigration enforcement made him decide to go back home. He, too, is fascinated about my trip and wants to know my route. I give him a card, which he seems glad to have. He says mexicanos are treated very well here and there is little racism. He also mentions that there are few mexicanas here, as the recruitment programs don't bring women to work. He sports a black eye he got the previous week in a *fútbol* game. He points me in the direction of a store where I can get a bike helmet, and we say our goodbyes.

On the way there I see several Mexican restaurants, and throughout

Herman Díaz in Leamington, Ontario, Canada, pointing to the black eye he received playing fútbol. *Louis Mendoza.*

the rest of the evening I run into mexicanos in the stores or on the streets (many of them on bikes)—all speaking Spanish. Herman told me few of them know English. While I knew there were Mexican and Central American immigrants in Canada, it hadn't occurred to me that they were fulfilling the same roles in the workforce and buttressing small-town economies as they do in the U.S. Later I learn that Leamington has a population of close to 29,000. It's known as the Tomato Capital of Canada. It turns out that the region is also known for the migration of monarch butterflies, which congregate in the fall at Point Pelee before making their way south to their winter home in Michoacán, Mexico. On the road I've seen geese and butterflies making their annual trek to the south.

ACROSS ONTARIO AND INTO NEW YORK:
SEPTEMBER 11, 2007

I leave Leamington on Sunday morning and ride close to
100 miles up the Lake Erie coast to reach the beautiful town of St. Thomas.
On Monday I head toward Dunnville. Outside of the town of Aylmer I come
across a trio of businesses that include the Hacienda produce store and
roadhouse cafe that advertises Mexican and Canadian food. At the time
I don't notice the sleeping Mexican image. I found this picture later on
the web. Much of what I pass are farms along the beach. It's a very pretty,
sparsely populated landscape, and I cycle through a steady light rain. I enter Dunnville slightly after dark. I pick up some food and go back to my
room to relax. A short while later two police knock on the door and ask for
ID, saying they are verifying the identities of all who come into town that
evening because of an incident at a local bar.

On September 11 I cross the border from Fort Erie to Buffalo expecting
security to be extra-tight. It isn't and I sail through fairly quickly. I guess
cyclists don't pose a security threat. When I exit the only road out of the
border checkpoint I know I am back in the U.S. as I head east on Niagara

*I found this image advertising the Hacienda Roadhouse Cafe in Aylmer, Ontario,
on its website in September 2007 while on my trip. I have not been able to relocate
the website when searching more recently, though it appears the restaurant is still in
business.*

Heading northeast on Highway 3 in Ontario, Canada. Louis Mendoza.

A sign pointing the way to the bridge where I will re-enter the U.S. in Buffalo, New York. Louis Mendoza.

Street. Also known as Avenida San Juan, Niagara is lined with Puerto Rican and U.S. flags as the community has just celebrated Puerto Rican Heritage Week. While it may not be fair to compare much about Canada and the U.S. based on the narrow swath of the country I saw in my time north of the border, the poverty and blight I see in Buffalo streets contrasts sharply with the small Canadian towns I rode through. I am reminded immediately of Detroit. It turns out there's good reason for this, as Buffalo and Detroit have the highest poverty rates in the U.S.

I have difficulty finding a motel in town and head toward Highway 20, the road I'll be taking east across the state. Before I know it I am in Cheektowaga, a small municipality about eight miles east of Buffalo that seems to have deep, vibrant Polish roots. I settle in early as it is about to storm and I need to prepare for a graduate student's preliminary exam on Wednesday that I am participating on via phone. Since I have some time before the exam, I get up the next morning and ride about 40 miles to Batavia. I was surprised at the pervasiveness of U.S.-owned businesses in Canada (hotel and motel chains, restaurants, and so forth), and I wonder if this is a post-NAFTA phenomenon. In New York the only sign of Canada I see is the presence of Tim Horton's restaurants.

The weather is noticeably cooler as fall is approaching. Fall colors are beginning to emerge in roadside foliage. I am anxious to get across the state to the coast, where I believe it's still a bit warmer, particularly as I head south. It will take me three to four days to cross the state and enter Massachusetts. I've traveled more than 1,200 miles since leaving Minneapolis, and I've become reacclimated to the road. It's getting dark noticeably sooner now, so I am starting to be disciplined about getting an early start; it's easier to fight off the morning chill than it is the evening one. When I began this trip I made sure to keep on hand a variety of energy gels in tubes to help me when my energy felt low, especially early mornings and late afternoons. I can't say for sure whether they helped me, but at this point I find they make me nauseous, and that is no help at all. I have replaced using these with small bottles of 5-Hour Energy shots, a boost that I find works for me quite well without causing me any nausea or energy letdown.

ACROSS UPSTATE NEW YORK: THROUGH AUBURN, SPRINGFIELD, AND ALBANY, SEPTEMBER 14, 2007

Making my way across upstate New York on Route 20/5 since Wednesday has made for a series of long days of 100+ miles. My primary goal is simply to survive, as I don't have any firm plans or contacts along this stretch. Before leaving Batavia, New York, a few days ago I e-mailed my friend Alan Gómez, a professor of Latin@ studies at Ithaca College, to see if he wanted to meet me for dinner in Auburn, my destination for Thursday. It isn't long before I encounter the steep, rolling hills that comprise the landscape of upstate New York. Though they were difficult, the lessons and strength I gained in the western part of the country are paying off as I am able to maintain my pace, though the rhythm is very different. Stretches of flat land are welcome and enable me to make up lost time.

The farmlands are beautiful, as are the Finger Lakes, several of which I pass as I approach Seneca Falls. Some of the towns I go through—Avon, Stratford, Geneva, and others—were established in the colonial period and are quaint and beautiful, full of tourists and elderly residents. I see very few people of color in any of them, but then again, my brief stops are limited to getting food and drink. I pass through Seneca Falls late in the afternoon and can't resist stopping in at the Women's Rights National Historical Park. The park is on the site of the first national women's convention, held in Seneca Falls in July 1848 and led by Elizabeth Cady Stanton and Lucretia Mott. Many aspects of the museum's exhibits are fascinating and inspiring, but if one judged the women's movement in the U.S. by this museum's exhibits and the titles in the feminist collection of books for sale, one would leave with the impression that only Anglo and African American women have advocated for equality and social change. No big surprise, I suppose, but I am still amazed at the willful ignorance (color-blindness?)

of people about the major and ongoing roles that Native, Asian American, and Latin@ peoples have played in resisting oppression, advancing democracy and civil and human rights, and driving social change in this country. Sigh. It's no wonder youths everywhere think of us as perpetual foreigners or only recent immigrants.

Just past Seneca Falls I begin seeing signs sponsored by the dubiously named organization Upstate Citizens for Equality. That night I look them up on the web and discover who they are and what they stand for:

> We are a growing, not-for-profit corporation of concerned citizens that stand against discrimination, and supports the continuation of free enterprise and equality in our communities.
> Our platform is:
> 200 year old bill of sale treaties between New York State and the Cayuga Indians not formally ratified by Congress were fair, equitable, and just. The land claim lawsuits based on a technicality has resulted in Upstate Citizens for Equality, Inc. taking a stand.
> We believe:
> - NO Reservation should be established.
> - NO tax free residential nor business lands should be allowed.
> - NO tax free businesses should be allowed.
> - NO negotiations should be secret, and ALL people should be equal under ONE set of laws.

Talk about unreconciled history and contradictions! I'm sure these same people also believe this is a nation of laws when it suits their political and economic interests. How convenient it is to choose to ignore this nation's refusal to ratify and/or willingness to break treaties with native peoples! After seeing these signs I can only be amused and curious when I see signs for the Montezuma National Wildlife Refuge and for the hamlet of Montezuma. The only explanation I've been able to find for the source of the hamlet's name is the one given on the town sign.

Alan meets me in Auburn shortly after I arrive and takes me by the Auburn Correctional Facility, a maximum-security state prison that bears a plaque boasting of being the site of the first execution by electrocution in the nation. Though the Latin@ population in these towns is minimal, I suspect that Latin@s are overrepresented in the criminal justice system, as is true all over the country. We walk around the outside of the prison a bit while Alan tells me of recent visits there to see a Black Liberation Army

Sign explaining the origin of the town's name in Montezuma, New York. Louis Mendoza.

Me with Connie Buschman, proprietor of Connie's Tex-Mex Restaurant in Auburn, New York. Alan Gómez.

political prisoner. Afterward we go across the street to Connie's Tex-Mex Restaurant to eat and talk. The owner is originally from Nuevo Laredo and has operated her business here for 13 years. Her Anglo husband, whom she met in Texas, is originally from Auburn, hence their decision to move back here. Connie tells me that business is good. A big proportion of her customers are prison workers and the visiting family members and friends of inmates. When I leave she gives me a magnet of the Virgen de Guadalupe for protection. I place it in my bike bag with the vial of holy water and the St. Christopher necklace my brother and mother gave me for the same purpose before I left on my trip.

LARKFEST: ALBANY, SEPTEMBER 15, 2007

On Friday I make it to Springfield and then arrive in Albany early Saturday afternoon. The days have been overcast and are getting cooler. I stop to get lunch near downtown, and a server tells me about a festival going on nearby. Larkfest, as it's known, has been going on for 28 years. As I walk through the crowd, one of the first booths I pass is run by Henry and Carlos, two *colombianos* who co-own an organic-food restaurant called Peas and Beans. Henry is an avid bike rider, and he tells me about his interest in making a cross-country trek. I record a brief interview with them using my digital camera.

ME: How long have you lived here?

CARLOS: Ten years. We came to go to school. My wife is getting a PhD in Spanish linguistics, so I came to take care of the baby.

ME: What's life like here?

CARLOS: From a Latino perspective we are everything—Puerto Rican and Dominicans and other Latinos. In the suburbs it's all white, but here it's mixed. On Lark Street everyone knows that this is where the action is, so you get a mixed crowd.

ME: Who is your clientele?

CARLOS: We get progressive people who want to change the world.

ME: How do you like life here in the U.S.? Do you miss home?

CARLOS: Yes, but we go and visit. We came from Armenia, a city in the mountains.

ME: And you, Henry?

HENRY: Bogotá. I have a sister down in New Jersey.

ME: Do you teach your kids Spanish?

HENRY: His son is in Colombia but mine is here. We teach them to be bilingual. We only speak Spanish at home, and he takes Spanish in school.

ME: Do all the different Latinos get along with each other?

HENRY: I think it's Colombians with Colombians. Everyone sticks together, but they also stick to themselves. There's a little interaction but not a lot. Puerto Ricans and Dominicans are the strongest here.

ME: What about immigration issues? Is it a problem here? In terms of discrimination?

HENRY: No, we don't see or feel anti-Latino discrimination. Some people but not as a whole, especially if people don't travel much.

Down the street I am approached by a guy who is preparing to go on a cross-country trip. He's just purchased a bike from a man in his 80s who did his first cross-country trek at 68! As we're talking, another guy joins the

Co-owner of Peas and Beans Restaurant, Carlos, at the Larkfest Festival in Albany. Louis Mendoza.

conversation who rode from Seattle to Virginia last summer. We exchange stories, thoughts on the trip, and our suggestions for the newbie. After going through the festival I ride across town and settle in on the far eastern side of Albany so I can head toward Amherst with minimal delay on Sunday morning.

ROAD WEARY

You're traveling from Albany to Amherst, about 80 miles. You're about 20 miles from North Hampton, and from there it's another six or seven miles to Amherst. You've been on the road about six and a half hours today. You're actually feeling pretty good. The hills between Albany and here are rough. You just finished coming down a mountain about 10 miles, so you think you'll take a break. You're not really tired. These are the first hills you've been over since the Black Hills of South Dakota, and you have to get off the bike and walk some. These are steep and last for miles. You've learned by now that rather than wear yourself out you should just get off and walk if that's what you need to do, and that's ok. You're not really tired physically. You're not sure what lies ahead. You think you have one more set of hills to go over.

What is getting to you these days is impatience. Even though you look at a map and realize you've done really well, not quite halfway, you're feeling emotionally drained, and you wonder if you're going to have the stamina to finish this journey. You're bored, even though there are so many things to see. Every day you see something really beautiful—like right now behind you is a babbling brook. Maybe it's the ongoing necessity to move every day and finish this in the time frame you hope to that's wearing on you. You are feeling out of sorts by being on the road so long, not being in your own place, not home. You find that you need to encourage yourself every day to keep going. You say to yourself, "Just make it home," not your real home but the place where you will lay your head tonight, a place to rest.

The weather is really weird, though you've grown accustomed to it. It's been getting very cool. It's warm in the sun and cool in the shade. You wear a coat because it's so cold if you don't. But then the light-weight jacket you're wearing retains heat, and you sweat and get colder. It just makes you uncomfortable and chilly. That's been happening the last couple of weeks. You're hoping you'll feel better once you reach Boston, the milestone of making it coast to coast, and maybe you'll feel a strong sense of accomplishment and get re-energized. You'll see family and friends there, too. You know a number of people on the East Coast. Perhaps it'll be better because you'll see people you know, and it'll be more densely populated and that will keep you on your toes. You are about a week or two from being what you consider the halfway point. The days are full of highs and lows, but you keep moving forward. Such is life, no?

AMHERST, BOSTON, PROVIDENCE:
SEPTEMBER 16–22, 2007

I arrive in Hadley, Massachusetts, on Sunday, September 16. I've arranged to meet my friend Luis Marentes, a professor of Spanish at the University of Massachusetts, after his Monday-afternoon class. I sleep in a bit and then go shopping for some long-sleeve shirts and leggings to help ward off the increasingly cool weather. I make it to the university, and we drive to Luis' home in Lexington, just west of Boston, where we have dinner with his family. We pick up some tequila to sip, and Luis, Negar, and I stay up talking; it's been eight or nine years since we've seen each other.

The next day I visit some Boston neighborhoods—South End, Back Bay, and East Boston. Luis told me gentrification is encroaching in the traditionally Puerto Rican area of South End, and this is fairly evident in the remodeling and construction around Columbus Avenue. East Boston is a visibly strong contrast to South End and Back Bay. As soon as I exit the train I am greeted by the hustle and bustle of a densely populated working-class Latin@ neighborhood—all evident in the people and the tienditas, restaurants, panaderías, and other stores and agencies. I walk around a bit and find a beautiful mural on immigration covering an entire wall adjacent to a health center around the corner from the subway station.

Toward evening I head over to Somerville to visit my niece Salina, her husband, Ryan, and their two young children. They share some of their impressions of life for Latin@s in Boston. After dinner Salina drives me around Somerville and takes me to Foss Park, which I plan to ride by on my way out of town Thursday and speak with day laborers who gather there each morning in hopes of picking up some work. On Wednesday I return to Amherst with Luis and speak to both of his classes in the Spanish and Portuguese department about my trip. The students are very responsive. A consistent message I hear from them is that I should visit the town of Holyoke. I heard the same earlier in the morning when Luis put me in touch

An East Boston mural celebrating the town's rich immigrant heritage. Louis Mendoza.

with Isolda Ortega-Bustamante, a longtime friend of ours from Austin who now lives in the area leading the ENLACE program at Holyoke Community College.[1]

During one of the class discussions, students tell me about persistent police harassment in Holyoke against Latin@s. Some of them live and or work there and have experienced and witnessed racial profiling and condescension from the police. We discuss the collective psychological impact this has on the community, and I tell them of my own experience with harassment growing up in inner-city Houston in the 1970s and the perception of the police this cultivates as them being enemies of the community. I am able to tell them about positive examples of police and community relations that I have experienced on my trip and that the comprehensive language and cultural training some police officers take pays off. One student discusses her experience in a small town in Texas where people were very anti-immigrant, but when the townsfolk worked with the new immigrants, a stronger sense of respect developed. She wonders how to understand that. My response is that over and over a simple but profound truism has crystallized for me: nothing obliterates prejudice more swiftly than actually getting to know others firsthand.

Between classes I interview a few of the graduate students in the department who have immigrated from Latin America. Gloria Caballero from Cuba shares her story of living in the U.S. after growing up in the Young Communist League back home. She struggles to raise her children with the same values she knew then and tries to limit the corrosive impact of consumer culture on them. A reporter from the university's public radio station interviews me and attends one of the classes for a show that airs the next day. In the evening I joke around with the kids and Luis and watch the Red Sox lose another game. The next night, however, they will win the division title.

In the morning I leave town without visiting Foss Park because I have to find a notary public to get an affidavit signed so my car can be released from the impound lot in Minneapolis after being towed from a no-parking zone. Afterward I take a train south out of the city and ride about 70 miles to Providence. I stop just north of downtown to get my bearings, and I'm approached by a cab driver who offers to give me directions. We end up talking for quite a while, and I ask Spencer if I can tape our conversation. He's fascinated with the details of my trip and says "Oh, yeah?" a lot as he code-switches between English and Spanish frequently. He notes that one time he took a short bike trip in Ecuador, but his wife so feared for his safety she made him stop. He says emphatically several times, "It's gotta be nice" and "It's gotta be fun, no?" He tells me about having emigrated to

Spence Núñez, an Ecuadorian immigrant in Providence via New York City, next to his cab. Louis Mendoza.

New York City from Guayaquil, Ecuador, in 1977. His father was American and his mother Dominican, so he had relatives in New York and that made coming here easier; life was very hard in New York, though. He worked for many years there as an auto-body repairman. Over the years, the fiberglass he inhaled gave him a form of cancer, and he had to get a kidney transplant, which he tells me about in great detail. They moved from New York City to Providence in the mid-'80s because he and his wife did not want to raise their son in the "vida loca" of life in NYC, where they felt exposure to negative influences abounded.

Spencer offers to get me a soda or sandwich, and when I decline he tells me to call him if I have time the next day and he'll treat me to lunch at Boston Market. After leaving him I go by Brown University to meet Ralph Rodríguez after his class. I walk around campus and think about my year teaching there in 1995–1996. I have a great visit with Ralph that evening, and the next day I meet another friend on campus, Kisa Takesue. She suggests I ride down Broad Street, where I can find a lively Latin@ neighborhood. I decide not to call Spencer because it is past noon and I want to get as far into Connecticut as I can this evening. It takes me a while to find the small state route I want to take to Connecticut. I make it close to Mystic. The next day I only make it to West New Haven before dark. The New England landscape and the small coastal towns are beautiful, but the roads are consistently hilly and winding. Sunday afternoon I ride into Stamford and take a train into Brooklyn. It is easier than riding into the city, but carrying a bike and bags into the subway and on the trains in New York City is not as easy as one might think, and it's a bit surreal to be doing this in such crowded conditions.

LATIN@S EN NUEVA YORK

I take the C train into Brooklyn and make my way to Quito Ziegler's house. Quito is a photographer I met in Minneapolis in her role as co-founder of the Minnesota Immigrant Freedom Network. She's now attending graduate school at New York University and shares an apartment with her roommate, Enrique, who is from Spain and a grad student in geography. The next day I catch up with my friend and independent filmmaker Cristina Ibarra. It turns out she's moving her things into storage in preparation for attending a monthlong writing retreat in upstate New York. So Rafael Meléndez, another Tejano living in New York, and I help her move on Monday. Cristina is scouting around for another place to live when she returns from the retreat, so we go to Queens, where I meet her potential neighbor Guillermo Vasa, who is from Bogotá, Colombia. He's been living in New York City off and on since 1975. He now owns a successful foreign-car repair shop in Queens.

Guillermo tells me his story of coming to the U.S. alone and leaving his family behind for several years until he got settled here. Driven by economic reasons, he came as an undocumented worker through Laredo. It took him three times to cross using a coyote. Each experience was harrowing. Eventually he brought his wife and then his children. His children were born in Colombia, but they have lived in New York City most of their lives and fully identify with life in the U.S. He tells me he misses his homeland but understands that is mostly nostalgia. His children and wife all have citizenship status, but his prior record of coming to the U.S. and being deported has caused a lengthy delay in the final approval of his application. He now has several relatives here and a strong community of *colombianos* and other Latin@s. We speak of his experiences with racism (stereotypes about Colombians and drug dealing), Colombia's economic and political situation, and U.S.–Latin American relations. He is proud that his two children and three grandchildren all speak Spanish, something he and his wife have insisted upon. They speak Spanish at home and English at school and in public life. Guillermo is in the process of writing a book about his journey to the U.S.

While in New York I finish reading *Enrique's Journey* by Sonia Nazario. I gain a better understanding of the horrific trials youths go through to come to the U.S. on their own—often in an effort to reunite with mothers who came here but could not save enough money to pay for their passage. On Tuesday I have a very full day of meetings. My first appointment is in Spanish Harlem with Dina Montes, a Tejana who graduated from St. Mary's University in San Antonio and went to Syracuse to get her master's in journalism. She now works with UNICEF as a writer and editor in the publications unit. Following that, I meet with Louis Pagan, the creator of *Latino Pundit: A Blog Born out of Underrepresentation*. He contacted me a few weeks before my arrival in New York City and suggested that we meet. I catch up with him at a coffee shop in Times Square, and we interview each other. Louis is Puerto Rican and white. He grew up in NYC without a strong sense of his Latin@ identity, but after completing high school his world grew larger and he began exploring his heritage. While we're talking a woman excuses herself and interrupts us to tell us she thinks what we're talking about is very interesting and important.

I then go to downtown Brooklyn for my appointment with José Ramón

Sánchez, a professor of political science and director of the Urban Studies Program at Long Island University. Earlier in the year José published *Boricua Power: A Political History of Puerto Ricans in the United States.* We have a wonderful interview wherein he shares with me his story of growing up Dominican and Puerto Rican in New York and coming of age during the civil rights movement. His *testimonio* is both idiosyncratic and representative of so many who have little to lose and take risks to demand social change.

After interviewing José I mention to him that someone suggested I go to a park in Washington Heights where one can see the interesting phenomenon of women of color serving as nannies for young white children. José tells me I can see the same thing down the street in a park by the promenade. He walks me down there, and sure enough this child-care arrangement is completely obvious. José leaves to go back to his office, and I hang around waiting for an opportunity to approach some of the nannies. I take some pictures, and I talk with one Guyanan woman briefly. I walk around, gather some courage, and then speak to two Latinas. I ask them if they speak English, to which they reply, *Un poquito.* I explain my research to them and see if I can ask questions about their work as nannies. One looks really shy and hesitant. The other gives me a look that says, "Well, what do you want to know?"

I tell them I want their honest opinions of what it's like to work for people with lots of money, taking care of their children. They're a little hesitant to talk, and I assure them I won't use their real names. We agree to call them Alicia and María. Alicia does most of the talking, while María nods in agreement and listens and scans the area nervously. Alicia says she loves kids and they both have their own children. Alicia's children live here with her. She's from Mexico. María's children are with family in El Salvador. Alicia tells me it makes her a little sad to leave her kids every day, but she and other nannies have made arrangements with another immigrant woman to keep their children while they work. Five of them pay her $40 a week each. She says the combined $200 is a little less than each of them makes in a week working for the *americanos.* Alicia says she likes playing with the kids to whom she's a nanny and that she speaks to them in Spanish. The parents like how the nannies help the children learn Spanish. Most of the parents speak a little bit of Spanish. They treat them very nicely and with lots of respect. Sometimes she has to work late, and this causes problems with child care at her own house, but by and large this doesn't happen very often at all.

I am a bit hesitant to approach others because I don't want to intimidate them by asking questions about their charges. As I leave the promenade I take a shortcut through Albee Square and come across a protest against gentrification. Not only was this one residential building being threatened with seizure for eminent domain to build a parking lot, but so were three houses in the area that were part of the nineteenth-century antislavery underground railroad. The organizational muscle is provided by FUREE, Families United for Racial and Economic Equality, a Brooklyn-based, multiracial organization made up almost exclusively of women of color. I happen to be there while Maritza Pérez, a young Latina, is being interviewed. Maritza reads an open letter she wrote to the mayor:

> Dear Readers:
> Imagine you live in a building where everyone is in the same condition as you having to pay bills like every two weeks and each month. They are also having to take care of their family. But in the meantime someone tells you you have to leave the building because they are going to destroy the building right away and now you have to go. Everyone in the apartments receives a letter saying the building is being destroyed and [everyone] has to leave right away. Imagine how this would make you feel.

Maritza goes on to talk about the dangers of living in the city and how living in a home like they do provides safety because everyone knows them. She tells the crowd that some people are leaving already because they think there is no stopping the destruction of the building. She says she hopes they stay to see what happens. In response to a question, she tells us that her family has been looking into other places to live but also wants to see what happens with the building. They are having more problems every day. They are having to save money in case they have to move. Following the interview I ask to take her picture and tell her that she speaks very well.

TRENTON: SEPTEMBER 30, 2007

After several busy days in New York, I take a train to Newark early Wednesday morning to resume my bike ride. I don't escape the city without having a flat on the way to the subway, so I go to a bike store and pick up some tubes, another rear-view mirror, and an air pump to replace the one I have misplaced somewhere. I fix the flat and hope it's not a sign of things to come. Quito has explained to me that my ride through Newark will take me

Maritza Pérez speaking to the media against gentrification that has led to eviction notices to tear down her apartment building in Albee Square, Brooklyn, New York. Louis Mendoza.

into a heavily industrialized area before giving way to the green New Jersey countryside. I'd hoped to make it to Camden, but a long day, 60 miles, and many townships later I arrive in Trenton shortly before dark and decide to stop here for the evening. I find downtown to be a very bustling place. There are a lot of young people walking around, and they seem to be a very racially and ethnically mixed crowd. People are hanging out, sitting on benches, talking, and having a good time. Trenton is a very clean place. I'm a bit hungry so I search for food. On the east side of downtown I see a place called Latina Americana Pizza catty-corner to the police station. Curious, I go inside and buy a slice and a soda and start talking to the owner, César.

He tells me he is from Guatemala and has been living here for 25 years and before coming here lived in Mexico City for three years. I calculate quietly that this places him leaving Guatemala in '79 or '80—pretty much at the height of the civil war. I ask him why he's opened a pizzeria and not a Guatemalan-food restaurant. He says for many, many years he worked for a pizzeria and learned the trade. So when it came time to open his own place, this seemed the natural choice because he knew the recipes and the business. The menu is straight-up Italian food—pizza, calzones, pasta, and spaghetti. I don't see any Latin@ variation, other than that it is owned and operated by Latin@ Americans. He tells me that though he could cook Guatemalan food, he isn't a specialist in it like he is with Italian food. I find all this fascinating.

I ask César if there are many Latin@s here, and he says, "Yes, lots." He tells me many seasonal agricultural workers are now gone (this may explain signs on several Latin@-theme stores saying they're closed until after the new year), but others remain, such as factory workers, restaurant workers, and owners of small businesses and bodegas. I ask him how people are treated here, and he says, "Very well." Yes, some individuals treat people badly, but he feels by and large Latin@s are treated well and with respect. I tell him about my bike ride, and we chat for a while. He asks where I am from, what part of Mexico my family was from, whether I have family

César behind the counter of his Latino Americano Pizza Parlor on State Street in Trenton, New Jersey. Louis Mendoza.

waiting for me in Minnesota. As I leave he says, "Toma cuidado, Luis," and waves his hand as I walk out the door.

THROUGH NEW JERSEY TO THE WASHINGTON, D.C., AREA: OCTOBER 1, 2007

The next day I leave early and make my way to Camden. When I take a break to examine my map, I realize that I am going to have a very difficult time finding roads to Wilmington, Delaware, without going through Pennsylvania, so I enter Philadelphia from Camden and skirt the downtown area, making it to the far side of Wilmington late in the evening. In Wilmington I'm struck by the proliferation of Dominican businesses. A huge billboard for delawarehispanic.com asks: "Have You Been Sited?" I eat lunch the next day at a place called Burrito Bandido and call my friend Milo in Washington, D.C. We agree that I should make my way toward Baltimore the next day, and he will come get me at some point in the afternoon and take me to his mom's house in Ashton, Maryland. The plan is that I will help him move to his new place in Silver Springs the following morning. (My friends seem to have a knack for deciding to move right when I arrive!) He picks me up mid-afternoon on Friday in a small town, and we make our way through a heavily congested I-95. That evening I meet his mom and siblings. His mom, a military MD, is originally from San Antonio. Her father had been an active member of the GI Forum, a World War II–era Mexican American civil rights group.

Saturday is all about moving but a nice, leisurely day nonetheless. On Sunday, after some great homemade *papas con huevos* tacos, we go to Adams Morgan to check out the Latin@ population there and to make a quick trip to the bike shop because I need to replace the battery in my bike computer. Luck is with us, as it turns out that the annual Latin@ festival is being held that day. We are treated to a cornucopia of food, music (on several stages), and art at one of the most truly pan-American festivals of this sort I've ever seen. The festival has been going on every year since the early 1970s and has become increasingly diverse over the decades as the countries of origin that shape the demographic makeup of Latin@s in the D.C. area have changed to include many more Central Americans and Caribbeans.

Monday is a busy day. I take a train to meet Elaine Chalmers and her mom in Alexandria. Elaine, a former student of mine in San Antonio,

Organizers proudly proclaim the festival's long history of acknowledging Latin@s' presence in the D.C. area. Louis Mendoza.

works with the USDA. She was the first graduate of a collaborative program we worked on with Texas A&M, the Hispanic Leadership Program in Agriculture and Natural Resources, designed to build a pool of potential employees for the U.S. Department of Agriculture to expand the diversity of people and research within the agency. Her mom is visiting during this time, and they show me some of the Latin@ization occurring in the area. Our lunch is fairly quick, as I have an appointment with a University of Minnesota alumnus, Ed Landa (PhD in soil science in 1975), who read about my trip in the alumni magazine. Ed made the generous offer of housing and feeding me as well as showing me around Langley Park, Maryland, where he lives. This is only my second offer of housing from a stranger, and I am touched. However, he only lives one metro stop away from Milo's new apartment, so we agreed to meet on Monday afternoon for a tour of Langley Park. Ed meets me at the metro stop and is able to identify me from the picture in the magazine. He is a very affable man, and we get along quite comfortably. He works as a geologist for the U.S. Department of the Interior in Reston, Virginia, but lives in Langley Park because he and his wife love the

Taco trucks lining a street in Langley Park, Maryland. Louis Mendoza.

diversity there. He informs me that Reston is one of the areas where people are trying to gather support for the town's own version of local anti-immigrant ordinances.

We drive to Langley Park and then spend a couple of hours walking around the neighborhood. He treats me to a pastry from a local panadería and tells me a lot about the neighborhood dynamics and the work of organizations like Action Langley Park and Casa de Maryland. Some tensions among ethnic groups have arisen as neighborhood organizations and churches have directed more of their services to new immigrants to the detriment of other underserved groups. He shows me around some of the apartment complexes that have a dense population of Latin@s and the empty parking lots of closed businesses where a spontaneous flea market has begun forming on weekends, and we marvel at the proliferation of taco trucks in the vicinity. Many of these are parked on the side of the street and, Ed says, serve residents in the apartments. We see one or two in motion, but there is a hustle and bustle as many vendors are preparing for the evening rush. These vendors have also been a source of tension because they are unregulated and unlicensed, and some of the local restaurant owners, including Latin@s, say this places them at an unfair advantage. We see 25 or more trucks in a four-block area.

SIMMERING ISSUES IN THE MELTING POT

Simmering tensions of crimes against Hispanics and Latinos in a triangle of southeastern Montgomery County [Maryland] and adjacent Prince George's neighborhoods were the catalyst for a community meeting earlier this month that brought about a renewed commitment for greater police cooperation and communication. . . . The police commanders from both counties stressed that they don't aggressively enforce federal immigration laws and encouraged crime victims not to remain in the shadows. Casa [de Maryland] has estimated as many as 60 percent of all crimes go unreported. Any reluctance by immigrants to talk to or be interviewed by government authorities carries deeper consequences, since data is needed to provide core government services and funding. The meeting also provided a fresh reminder that Congress has turned a blind eye to needed reforms in workers visa programs and an expedited pathway to citizenship, and that tolerance for illegal immigrants has been rubbed raw. In some communities, anti-immigration undercurrents are getting swifter and more dangerous. The police are investigating twisted telephone messages to Casa of Maryland, including a veiled bomb threat, and the organization has asked the Maryland attorney general for assistance.

The Gazette, *op-ed, June 25, 2008. Reprinted with permission.*
Copyright © 2011 The Gazette.

We drive to Casa de Maryland, but like the other agency we've tried to visit, it is closed for the day. I am impressed with the listing of educational and social services they offer. Likewise, the abundance of local Latin@ print media is quite impressive and bespeaks an active, informed, and alert community. As Ed gives me a ride to Silver Springs, I can't help but ask him what has motivated him, a product of New York City streets and Russian Jewish background, to be supportive of recent immigrants when so many others feel threatened. I find his answer refreshingly honest—both simple and profound.

> ME: *I have one final question I want to ask you. I am curious about what motivates your open-mindedness about immigration, about newcomers to this country. Does this derive from values you learned*

*from your parents or your sense of our immigrant heritage as a
nation?*

ED: I think part of it for me is knowing that if it wasn't for immigration, I
wouldn't be here. That is certainly a big part of it, but I have to say I have
frustrations about immigration issues so I wouldn't say I am dogmatic, that
every issue I come down on the pro-immigration side, but I would say my
general feeling is that there is a selfishness about the argument "I am here
and it is time to close the doors." Plus there is an economic reality—without immigrants, we are doomed economically. I think it is mostly the fair-
ness issue, really. When I hear these right-wing nut jobs on the radio, it just
makes my blood boil.

ME: *I appreciate that. It is good to hear.*

ED: I like diversity, not in the kind of canned government sense. When I
moved here I found it fascinating that I could go to a Cambodian market,
go to a Latino market, go to an Indian market. I just loved it. For me, it was
like going on a foreign trip every weekend. I used to call it my ethnic tour.
I would go down to that corner there and I would go shopping and I really
liked that aspect of it, and the one thing I have to say is I wish Langley Park
could maintain more diversity. It is becoming one culture, and I wish it
could maintain a multicultural identity.

In the evening, Milo makes a fabulous meal of *carne guisada* to go with
some fresh, homemade tortillas I picked up from a local Mexican restaurant. It's a great way to end my visit. The next morning I wait for rush hour
to subside, and with my bike and gear I catch a train to Alexandria and begin riding south.

INTO THE SOUTH! OCTOBER 2, 2007

My plan is to go through Virginia on Highway 1, also called Jef-
ferson Davis Highway. The name of the highway and the numerous rebel
flags on city signs and on bumpers are constant reminders of being in the
traditional South, but I also see numerous Mexican businesses. By Thursday I hope to be in North Carolina, where I plan to meet with members of
a farmworkers union. Next Monday I'm scheduled to give a short talk at
Piedmont High School in Unionville, North Carolina. Sherry Edwards, a
teacher I met in San Antonio at a 1999 National Endowment for the Hu-

manities seminar on Integrating Latino Literature into the Secondary Classroom, teaches there and thought my trip would be an interesting topic for her students to hear more about. I make it only as far as Fredericksburg, Virginia. There, as I am looking for lodging, I ask two guys who have just finished a jog for directions, and after a brief conversation I learn one of them is a University of Minnesota graduate. He doesn't say much, but his friend is interested in my trip. I end up having to go a little farther down the road to Spotsylvania to get affordable lodging.

The next day I get only as far as Richmond when I begin to get a series of rear-tire flats. I am exasperated, as I have only had minimal tire trouble since leaving Minnesota. Virginia is beautiful. Highway 1 passes through a series of long, winding hills. At times I am able to manage these quite well, particularly when they are spaced in such a way that I can keep my momentum if I pick up lots of speed going downhill and use that to get me most of the way up the next one. I am feeling very inefficient at times because my chain is rubbing and my gears slip from time to time in a way that recalls the difficulties I had in Wyoming. I change my tube three times and decide I should find a shop to see what is going on. I am concerned about being delayed, as I am expected in Monroe, North Carolina, on Monday, and my timing is being jeopardized.

It's too late to find a repair shop open, so I make my way toward hotels near the airport in case I need to rent a car. I get another flat, and I end up having to walk the last four miles. The next morning I call a couple of bike shops in the area, and none can look at the bike right away. I decide to take a car to Raleigh, North Carolina, the next big city up the road, where I will have more choices. I arrive in the afternoon and go to the All Star Cycle shop. The guys there are great about prioritizing repairs on my bike, given the trip I'm on. Even before I get into the details of my trip, they begin rattling off the many things that need repair. They can only work on it at the end of the day as they have a commitment the next day, so we agree that they will replace the derailleur and the rear tire and repair my rear-wheel spokes. They tell me I also need to replace the chain and the rear drive train as well as the brakes.

When I pick up the bike the next day, I am amazed at the vast improvement! It feels like a new bike. I hadn't realized how much I had gotten used to the slow build-up of problems. Riding is so much easier, smoother, faster, and stronger. I spend the next three days covering the 150 or so miles to Charlotte—camping a couple of nights in the North Carolina foothills. The roads are as hilly as in Virginia, but the riding is definitely a lot easier.

Props to the quality service I've received at bike shops along the way.

An Ingles (pronounced eng'ulls) Food Market in North Carolina with a sign making sure customers know the store is American-owned. Louis Mendoza.

The folks at shops are usually avid cyclists and are eager to hear about long trips and to share their own experiences. Both in Raleigh and in Cherry Hill, New Jersey, where I had the latest work done, the owners were there and shared their own cross-country trip stories with me. Both told me they made the ride with their spouses a long time ago. At Elkton's in Cherry Hill, the guy told me they biked a lot at night to beat the heat, and farmers accommodated them if they knocked on their doors and promised to leave the place cleaner than when they arrived. The heat and humidity are out in force, but I find that easier to embrace than the cold. I am particularly struck by the blue skies of North Carolina.

On Sunday, Sherry Edwards takes me to visit her friends Magda and Rocky in the Hickory area of western North Carolina. As we drive toward Hickory, Sherry points out a chain of food stores to me in western North Carolina, and we muse on the name Ingles (pronounced *een-gulls*, not like the Spanish word) and the special effort the store owners made to note on signs that the store was American-owned.

Magda is Colombian American born in Colombia. She and her brothers and mother moved here to reunite with her father after he had been here in North Carolina a few years working on farms and as a horse trainer, an expertise he brought with him and cultivated into a highly successful family enterprise over the years. She is a high school Spanish teacher and continues to help with the family business—training riders and breeding and selling paso fino horses, a rare breed that has earned international acclaim. Magda and Rocky's children are being raised bilingually, something the parents want and the grandparents insist upon. Rocky is Native American and Scotch-Irish from northern Michigan. As we sit in their kitchen, Magda shares her family's history of moving to the U.S. and their early struggles adapting to a new country, language, culture, and society. Magda notes that when she was young there was only a small handful of Latin@s in the Hickory-Conover-Newton area of North Carolina and in the state at large.

This demographic has changed dramatically, though she also notes that most white North Carolinians don't bother to learn the distinctiveness of each Latin@ group, and all of them tend to be perceived the same way—for better or worse. Rocky says that given his own background and the region of the country where he grew up, marrying a Latina was not an issue for his family. Magda relays an instance within the past few years in which Rocky took a day off work to participate in a sit-in held on behalf of Latin@s when local tensions about new immigrants began to emerge.

Magda Iriarte with her husband, Rocky, and two of their children at their home in Hickory, North Carolina. Louis Mendoza.

Me with students and teacher Sherry Edwards (center, in polkadot top) at Piedmont High School in Unionville, North Carolina. Louis Mendoza.

At one point, as their daughter Hannah is about to leave, I ask her about race relations in school. She attends a suburban school with youths from the larger towns as well as from the rural areas. In her very strong opinion, tensions do exist because some of the rural youths bring in attitudes about race taught to them by their parents, and this manifests itself in "old-fashioned" ideas about race, race-mixing, and being biracial. She places herself in that third category and clearly claims both her parents' cultural heritages. Her strong and vocal personality makes her a good advocate for the New South, as she appears ready and able to challenge her peers.

That night I sleep in Monroe and prepare my presentation for the students the next afternoon. On Monday morning I ride the ten miles from Monroe to Piedmont High School in Unionville. Staff members at the school are expecting me, as a front-page story about my visit appeared in the Monroe *Enquirer Journal* the day before. Since I arrive early, Sherry asks if I can visit the tail end of her midday class because the students are a bit envious of the other class, the one I will address. I give these students an abbreviated talk and take their questions. Both here and in the larger presentation in the library, with two classes for a total of about 65 students and some administrators, staff, and teachers, the questions are quite good. They are interested, invested, and apparently engaged with the issues. They are especially pleased that they are the first high school I've visited on my trip.

One student asks if my ride is like Che Guevara's. I compliment her on knowing this history and tell her that a friend of mine has recently learned of a cross-country ride across his homeland that Che took on bicycle. I appreciate their sincerity, their curiosity, and their hospitality. Another article on my visit runs in the local paper the next day, and Sherry tells me she has received a number of positive comments on the visit from students, teachers, and parents. She encourages me to engage high school students more since they are in a position to reach their parents and communities on the issues and to help foster a stronger sense of our commonalities and histories. That afternoon Sherry gives me a ride across the North Carolina border so I can head out early the next day.

BUILDING A NEW WORLD IN THE MIDST OF THE SURREAL: OCTOBER 16, 2007

The next day I cycle to Columbia, South Carolina. The ride is quick as expected because, as one of the cycle shop employees has told me, the road going toward the ocean is a steady decline. As I ride through the city I see some graffiti stenciled with spray paint on a wall, and I smile: "you are so beautiful," it proclaims, and I think of how many people must find daily affirmation in seeing it as they pass by. By now I have passed the halfway mark of my trip, and though I have miles and miles to go, even now I feel like I am on the way home. I suspect I will feel this even more strongly when I begin heading west. I've no doubt that seeing family and friends in Tejas will renew me even more, as having seen so many dear friends along the East Coast has.

I rent a car in Columbia and begin making my way back to central North Carolina to visit with the folks at the Farm Labor Organizing Committee in Dudley before driving to Philadelphia. I'll be taking a break from riding for several days, as I am scheduled to present at the American Studies Association conference in Philadelphia over the weekend. While I'm in Pennsylvania, I plan on going to Hazleton to see the birthplace of these small-town ordinances that have been cropping up the past few years. Sherry had told me to be on the lookout for South of the Border, a tacky place near the South Carolina–North Carolina border, as I drive north on I-95. There's no way I can miss it because for at least a hundred miles out

Taken at night, my own pictures of the infamous and iconic South of the Border's sign were not so clear. This one was acquired online. © 2010 Rokusfocuspix, Dreamstime.com

there are numerous billboards advertising this gaudy tourist attraction. Though it seems to be so many things, I can't quite figure out what it is until I see it with my own eyes.

I arrive at the neon monstrosity fairly late—around 11 p.m. It's not a town, at least not in the typical sense, but a stop about one mile south of North Carolina that includes restaurants, campgrounds, a gas station, a tobacco store, an amusement park, shops, an ice cream parlor, and so on, all based on some godawful South of the Border theme that makes Taco Bell look sophisticated in comparison. Here you can find Pedro's Campground next to larger-than-life images of sleeping Mexicans. This is among a variety of other caricatures and images meant to evoke someone's idea of Mexicanness intended for amusement and easy consumption. It's otherworldly, all right. No wonder the alien moniker has such enduring force in regions where one-dimensional, ahistorical caricatures reign supreme. This so-called oasis is a living testament to how people's ideas can live outside of time. Most of the places are closed or closing when I get there. I decide to go into the gift shop to take a look, and I swear the two young clerks do a double-take when I walk in. Seeing a real Mexican in their midst must have confused them!

FARMWORKER JUSTICE IN NORTH CAROLINA

My co-worker Lisa Sass Zaragoza helped me make contact with Farmworker Labor Organizing Committee (FLOC) executive director Baldemar Velásquez to give the folks at FLOC a heads-up about my desire to stop in and visit with them. FLOC is a legendary farmworkers union, with headquarters in Toledo, Ohio. It opened a permanent office in the small town of Dudley, North Carolina (just outside of Goldsboro), after winning a huge case against the Mt. Olive Pickle Company following a five-year campaign. In 2004 FLOC signed a collective-bargaining agreement with Mt. Olive and the growers. More than 6,000 of the state's 10,000 guest workers joined FLOC. As Leticia Zavala, the young union organizer (and mother of an infant son), tells me, one of the reasons this was such a historic victory was that more than 1,000 growers agreed to form the North Carolina Growers Association. In doing do, they also agreed to act as the employers' collective-bargaining agent. More importantly, this agreement marked the first time an American labor union represented guest workers. FLOC quickly established a program to bring guest workers into the United States under U.S. government H-2A temporary guest worker visas. According to Leticia, FLOC is the nation's largest utilizer of the H-2A visa.

Leticia immigrated to the U.S. in the mid-1980s with her family. They became part of the migrant stream, working throughout the Midwest. Eventually they came to North Carolina, and the family stayed year-round on the East Coast. After high school she attended Florida Southern College and majored in business administration. She got a job as a union organizer after graduating. When I ask her if she uses her degree, she laughs and says it's been helpful in organizing economic boycotts. The FLOC offices are run by a small staff, but it is clear that this is much more than a

Angelita, the honorary madrina of FLOC in Dudley, North Carolina, beneath a painting that pays tribute to her important role at the union offices. Louis Mendoza.

union—the workers, union staff, and community members see themselves building a social movement of workers and advocating for fair and humane working conditions but also social justice in the largest sense of the term. FLOC is one of the few unions that successfully operates transnationally. It organizes guest workers in Mexico by recruiting them as well as informing them of their rights as workers and meeting with extended family members in Mexico so they can feel secure that their loved ones are part of a larger community here in the U.S. when they come to work.

FLOC's latest campaign is focused on the tobacco industry, seeking fair wages and addressing some deplorable working conditions. Many workers suffer from nicotine exposure in the fields and receive no health protection or compensation when this occurs. Leticia and I speak briefly about tensions between immigrant workers and African Americans. She says most of this tension revolves around manufacturing jobs; there is little competition for fieldwork since it is not work local people want to do. More than 90 percent of agricultural workers in North Carolina are Latin@.

FLOC's offices are housed in a beautiful multifunctional building and property that serve as playground, community gathering space for *quinceañeras*, picnics, church services, and so on. The land was donated by a highly respected elder of the community, a woman diminutive in stature but huge at heart, Angelita, who is originally from San Antonio. As Angelita explains to me, she has done any and all kinds of jobs possible. She left San Antonio and became a migrant worker because she was worried about her children being susceptible to big-city influences of crime and drugs. Several years back she opened up a store, Las Palmitas, to serve the needs of the small but growing migrant community in this part of North Carolina. The business is successful, but some of her other ventures, including a construction company that pursued state contracts, have not fared as well. As I leave FLOC, I find myself recharged by the humility and power the staff exhibit and by Angelita's generosity.

ALL LEGALS SERVED IN HAZLETON, PENNSYLVANIA

I arrive in Philadelphia very late Wednesday and check into a motel in Bellmawr, New Jersey, to take advantage of having a car as a way of saving money on a downtown Philadelphia hotel. I spend most of Thursday preparing for my presentation the next day. On Friday morning I go to the conference, find a place to print my paper, and attend our session called Connected, Grounded, Surrounded by Academic Freedom? Still Changing the Languages and Cultures of the Academy, sponsored by the Minority Scholars Committee. I see several colleagues and friends at the conference, some of whom I haven't seen in quite a long time. The truth is, however, that it feels very odd to be around this many people after spending so much time alone. I'm a little discombobulated—both wanting to connect to people and feeling overwhelmed by the crowd. I decide to split the conference early and get back to the solitude of being on the road. Hazleton is about

A bar on West Broad Street in Hazleton, Pennsylvania, with a sign declaring "All Legals Served." Louis Mendoza.

three hours away, so I figure avoiding traffic the next morning is a good thing. I go north to Bethlehem, where I stay for the night—thinking not of the religious connotations of the town's name but of Bethlehem Steel, a business near the neighborhood of my youth.

There's much to say about Hazleton. As I follow the news about the continued battles being played out in small-town USA where local leaders have tried to "do what national leaders won't do" by creating and enforcing laws against undocumented workers. Hazleton is the birthplace of the modern anti-immigrant movement that has some towns undermining their own self-interests. This is evidenced in a recent *New York Times* article on how many of these towns, Hazleton included, have experienced dramatic unwanted economic consequences as people have gotten the message that they are not welcome here and have sold houses and businesses and gone elsewhere. The battles continue although most of these ordinances have been struck down and declared unconstitutional. In this particular article, the mayor of Hazleton proclaims that the ordinance achieved its purpose. In towns with leaders who aren't so willing to proclaim victory in the face of defeat, which is to say they have been able to admit that maybe immigrants were a beneficial economic force, they are making changes to their stances on immigrant presence in the hopes of drawing workers, consumers, businesspeople, and homeowners back to these towns.

I still see lots of indications of Latin@ life, but there is also evidence of the recent departure of Latin@ entrepreneurs. A number of closed businesses that were formerly owned by Latin@s sprinkle Broad Street. I eat lunch at a Latin@-owned deli and see a group of people hanging around a barber shop. I am particularly perturbed when I see several rebel flags lining Broad and wonder how this icon has become so popular outside of the South.

A sign outside exclaims: "We serve all legals." I go in the otherwise empty bar for a few minutes and ask the lone bartender what this refers to. He gives a sly smile and says, "We just want to make sure people are of legal age to drink. But it's also a joke because of the attention we've received with all the debates about illegal immigrants here." I want to believe him, I really do.

Return otra vez

4,000 miles of pedaling have
gotten me a long way to nowhere in
Hazleton, Pennsylvania.

No spokesperson need announce the town's
revolving door policy toward
much-needed workers and entrepreneurs of a
dead economy, but a cruise through narrow
downtown streets tires one out
as rebel flags blow in the wind
and dust gathers on closed-
down Latin@ businesses

Small-time, small-minded
politicians make national headlines
as they race to push people
out even as they fail to admit
they are in a state of dependence.

Pero, la gente sabe que ellos no los quieren.
So they steer clear and move elsewhere,
until the cycle renews itself
and they are asked to return
otra vez.

MOVING ON

I leave Hazleton on Saturday afternoon and spend two long days driving more than 1,200 miles to get to South Florida. I marvel at the distance I can cover driving marathon days in a car in contrast to on a bicycle; I think about how my average cycling days are equivalent to a little more than an hour by car. On my way I go to St. Augustine and then on to Fort Lauderdale. I've come down here and will return by car to resume riding on Wednesday evening from Savannah, Georgia. From there I can ride south to Jacksonville and then begin traveling west across the country.

My time in Florida is a real bust. While in St. Augustine I walk around the tourist center in the evening to see how the "oldest city in America" presents its Spanish colonial past, which was not necessarily any more benign than the American colonial past of Jamestown or elsewhere. I am very disappointed in all the attention paid to mythical elements like Ponce De León's quest for the fountain of youth. With the exception of the visitor center, everything is behind walls and requires an admission fee. It's a quaint town, but the city center is one big tourist trap. I spend two nights in Fort Lauderdale, and with constant rain, deadlines to submit letters of recommendation for students and colleagues, and some other obligations including catching up on blog entries, I never make it to Miami or have many conversations with people. Though I'm staying across the street from the beach, I only walk down there one evening. My time here is not productive for my project. I'm disappointed and feel like it's best to get back on my bike in Georgia and continue the trip.

FREE-WHEELING FLORIDA? OCTOBER 20–26, 2007

I return my rental car on Wednesday evening in Savannah and leave the next morning down Highway 17 to Kingsland, about 110 miles south. About halfway there I stop at a roadside attraction, a tiny church proclaimed to be the Smallest Church in America. I find this miniature church peaceful, and I can't help but think about a news story I read a month ago that discussed the changing nature of race relations in the South in the face of immigration and how this is presenting challenges to many churches where the all-too-convenient black/white paradigm is no longer as useful or easily applied for determining who does and does not belong. I remember the preacher dealing with integration saying something like, "I tell people, 'America is changing. Get over it'" to those who decry change.[2]

I rest and take a few photographs, and in the comments section of the visitor register I call on my Catholic upbringing about how every stranger in our midst may be a test by God and write: "May we always remember the least fortunate among us and welcome the stranger in our midst."

On Friday I cycle 97 miles from Kingsland to Lake City, Florida. I encounter several short but intense storms that require me to pull off the road because my vision, and I'm sure my visibility on the road, are impaired. There is no chance of staying dry, so I pull out my tarp, cover my bags and bike, and smoke a cigarette as I sit out the rain under some trees. The rain is part of a front connected to a hurricane in the Gulf. Saturday's ride is a bit shorter, to Perry. Though I am more than 50 miles away from Tallahassee, the chain motels in town have jacked up their prices due to the Florida State University football game. This annoys me, as it's obvious that people don't regularly flock to Perry for lodging. I stay at a smaller motel across the street from another independent one declared "American Owned."

Since seeing the Ingles store in North Carolina advertise this so blatantly, I've noticed it more and more, particularly with motels. I can't help but feel that underlying it is a race-based appeal to the sentiments of travelers (*Hey, stay here and be a patriot—not in one of those places managed or owned by them other [non-white] folks.*) Given a choice, this has the opposite effect on me. The next day as I head toward Apalachicola, in the Panhandle, I take some photos. If you've never seen the Gulf Coast, you should know that the water is not beautiful blue but murky brown because it gets stirred up from being contained in the Gulf.

Today is a nice day, and the overcast skies keep it cool. I go through a series of small towns, not very populous. I'm feeling super-strong, having fun, and enjoying the scenery. It's nice to be riding west and on flat terrain. The East Coast is beautiful, but almost all of it has big, rolling hills. Somewhere near Carrabelle, Florida, a motorcyclist slows down as he cruises past me and shouts, "I really respect what you're doing, man!" I flash him the peace sign and then a power fist. He raises his fist in solidarity and speeds past. To my chagrin, in Apalachicola I've no choice but to stay in a place called the Rancho Inn that has the same American-owned message scrolling on an electronic sign. While there's no immediate competition in the vicinity, I think as with Ingles, its owners don't want its name to prejudice would-be customers; yet I guess they still want to appeal to those who like the Spanish quaintness of the name. I'm staying here because all the other places are about twice as expensive, given the coastal location.

I should arrive in Panama City tomorrow. I plan to stay there an extra day or two before heading to Pensacola. Lisa, my friend and colleague from

Minneapolis, will be joining me on Friday for a few days. We'll ride to New Orleans and spend a couple of days there before she heads back on Día de los Muertos. I'm looking forward to being in New Orleans. I haven't been there since Katrina. I've since heard about an influx of Latin@ workers. It should be extremely insightful. A former UM student of mine, Emily, recently contacted me. It turns out she took a year off school to ride down to New Orleans by bike with two friends. They worked with Habitat for Humanity for a while, and she became so enthralled with the work that she took a supervisor job with Habitat and postponed school for a year to stay there. She's promised to hook me up with some contacts in exchange for a commitment from me to work with Habitat for a day. I admire her and her friends' courage riding there from the Midwest. She has shared some of her experiences, including police abruptly waking them up in the middle of the night while they slept in a tent. Once the officers discovered they were all women, one told them they couldn't stay there, but he did let them stay in the jail.

After a couple of days of rest in Panama City, I arrive in Pensacola on Thursday afternoon and find a place to stay relatively near the airport so I can meet Lisa when she arrives on Friday. I go to dinner at the Cuban restaurant housed within the Days Inn off Highway 90 and have a conversation with a man sitting at the next table. It turns out he's from Australia. He has lived all over the States since 1961, when he moved here out of college to work for Ford Motor Company. He doesn't much like living in Florida (he calls this part the Redneck Riviera), but he owns some properties here. He is happy to be at this relatively new restaurant and tells me the food is great. He's right. He gets pretty excited when I tell him about my trip, and he says he is continually disappointed at the narrow-mindedness of people who don't know much about the world. He says he's done business in Latin America for decades and feels safer there than here.

MAKING OUR WAY TOWARD N'AWLINS:
OCTOBER 27, 2007

About midday Friday I meet Lisa at the airport, and we decide to forge ahead to Mobile even though we are getting a late start. The ride is a bit hilly, but otherwise all goes smoothly. She's trained for the trip, carries a lot less weight than I do, and keeps a good pace. We ride about 72 miles to the far side of Mobile, arriving about 9:30 that evening. There isn't a lot of traffic when we enter Mobile through the two-lane Bankhead Tunnel un-

Me underneath the Welcome to Mississippi sign. Lisa Sass Zaragoza.

Lisa under the sign upon our entrance into Alabama. Louis Mendoza.

der the Mobile River as we are advised to do by our maps and by clerks at a local store about five miles out of the city. It goes without incident until my chain gets jammed in the lowest gear and I am unable to pedal. This is a problem I've had before, and I know immediately that fixing it will require loosening the back wheel to free the chain—something I cannot do in this risky situation. It couldn't have happened at a worse time. I advise Lisa to go ahead. My only choice is to run and push the bike out of there as fast as I can and hope traffic will simply get around me with care. Right about then, a male voice booms loudly over an intercom system and says repeatedly, "No biking in the tunnel. Do not stop. Get out of the tunnel." They must have a surveillance camera in place. I haul it as fast as I can, but it isn't easy or fun. As I exit the tunnel where Lisa waits for me, the voice on the intercom says: "Don't come back!"

What a way to enter the city!

On Saturday we ride into Biloxi with little fanfare. The weather is nice and cool. As we are getting settled for the evening, I realize I've broken a link on my chain, probably from the jam going through the tunnel the previous night. Fortunately, I have the parts and the tools to fix it. In Biloxi and for the rest of our ride through Mississippi, we begin seeing stark, lingering evidence of Hurricane Katrina along the shoreline drive—Highway 98—where businesses, homes, and roads were swept away and only hollowed-out frames or flat foundations were left behind. Some bridges are closed, but others are being reopened this fall. It is apparent that many of these were wiped out, though it is also clear that some folks rebuilt right away while others had only small trailers on otherwise empty lots with some debris of their former homes still on the land.

As we head into New Orleans on Sunday, I continue having flats and realize that my wheel needs to be replaced again. We're only about 15 miles out of town, so Lisa rides ahead to find us a room and I push the bike until I find a bus that has a bike rack that can get me to downtown. We get a hotel near the French Quarter, and once we get settled in we tour the scene for a bit. We'll be here until Thursday morning. I should be in Houston by Sunday at the latest. On Monday I find a bike shop first thing and get my rear tire replaced again. It's been nice, if a bit unusual, to have company to share thoughts and feelings along the way. I'm accustomed to internalizing my experiences, so this is a welcome break from that practice.

A MERGING OF THE OLD AND THE NEW:
OCTOBER 29–31, 2007

Unfortunately, my contact with Habitat for Humanity doesn't pan out. I probably waited too long to call the supervisor to get us scheduled for a volunteer assignment for one day's worth of work. I also hoped to meet with a Chicano from California who is working with Habitat as well, and we made plans, but we're unable to coordinate a time that works for him. It happens. I do have occasion to have some good conversations with various workers. Lisa and I strike up a conversation with Juan, a Honduran immigrant who has lived in New Orleans for 25 years. He tells me he is retired and receives a pension, but he continues to work two jobs, one full-time and one part-time, as a parking valet. He says that though he had a decent job in Honduras, he didn't foresee a good future for his four children, so he came to the U.S. on a guest visa and decided to stay. His kids are all grown, and he no longer visits his home country because his life is here. He has a resident visa now, and he has not filed for citizenship.

On Wednesday morning I get up early and ride alone out to Robert E. Lee Circle, where we heard day laborers gather each morning. By the time I arrive at 7:30 it's pretty empty, though I do see one small group of men hanging around and one lone Latino standing off to the side by a gas station. I approach him and strike up a conversation. His name is Francisco Gutiérrez. He is a bit wary to talk to me and asks that I not take his picture.

I learn from him that he just arrived from Mexico (near Mexico City) the week before. He never left his hometown before coming to the U.S. and has only done so because there was no work for him to feed his family there. He has come to New Orleans because he knows other men from his hometown who arrived here recently, and they offered to let him stay with them while he finds work. He speaks no English, and he seems both earnest and anxious about being here. Thus far no one has messed with him, and he hopes to start getting work regularly.

I leave Francisco and ride over to Claiborne and MLK near the Super Dome, where I've heard a health agency is planning to build a clinic. Here's where the real action is, as this intersection is crowded with day laborers— mostly African Americans and Latinos. I feel a little bad for Francisco, as he seems to be in the wrong place. It's an intersection comprised of several burned-out and otherwise vacated buildings with men mostly on one side of the street gathering under trees, on the stoop of a charred house, talking and eating food from the two vendors in the area: two women work out of their car selling tamales and cool drinks; the other is a more typical taco truck, though this vendor, too, only sells tamales ($2 each) and cold drinks.

As the men gather around I hear some of the African Americans ordering their food in Spanish, and I compliment one of them on his really good accent. He tells me, "Yeah, my homeboys here have been teaching me to speak it right." Around 10 a.m. the traffic around the taco truck starts easing up, and I have a chance to speak with the young owner, Ezekiel. He tells me he's been in New Orleans about a year and came here from the Mexican state of Tabasco because he has family members who have been in this area for about 10 years. He says he was *un contador* (an accountant) in Mexico, but that work was unsteady, so he and his wife decided to make the move. Like the two women vendors, he started off in a car selling food to day laborers at different sites around the city (near Lowe's, Home Depot, and such), but by March he'd earned enough money to buy a truck, and he found that they could stay in this one spot and do well on a daily basis.

Ezekiel says they make the food really early each morning and sell out shortly after 10 a.m. every day. They seem to do well if the wads of cash he has stuffed in his pocket are any indication. I ask him if he has any regrets about the move, and he says, "No, not at all." He tells me life in Mexico is anywhere from 10 to 70 on a scale of 100 and here life is 100 for him because he and his wife can work hard and get ahead—buying the truck, saving money, having a reliable source of income. I ask him if he is ever harassed by anyone, and he says no, but his truck is *un lugar de historia* (a place of history), that is, he hears everyone's stories here. Some of the guys

Ezekiel Hernández in New Orleans holding his broom while talking to me. Louis Mendoza.

have told him stories of being robbed, often when they were by themselves at night. I ask if there are tensions with *los africanos*, and he says no, that most of the problems were with *los morenos*. I am a bit confused by this. Perhaps my question to him was muddled by the way I phrased it, though in my experience African Americans are often referred to as *negros*. So I'm not sure if he means *morenos* in reference to darker-skinned Latin@s or if he is referring to the local African American population. I later learn from several people that he was definitely referring to African Americans.

I ask if he has trouble with the police or racism in the city, and he says the police leave them alone. He points to the signs from the day-laborer association in the area that list rules for workers. He says association employees are really good about coming around and letting the workers know their rights—and their obligations for everyone getting along. The association provides trash cans and bags and asks that the workers not litter, clean up after themselves, and respect each other. It works. As I speak with Ezekiel he is sweeping the area around his truck. He tells me his younger cousin was picked on in school for speaking Spanish, and the family didn't feel like the school had a very good policy for Spanish speakers. I tell him about my project, and he asks for a card and my phone number so he can call me sometime.

That afternoon Lisa and I take a bus out to the lower Ninth Ward, where we walk up and down three blocks. On one, we count 27 empty, abandoned, or otherwise shut-down dwellings, many of them duplexes. Two years after Katrina, the devastation to people and communities is still palpable. Federal Emergency Management Agency trailers are everywhere, sometimes in clusters, sometimes next to single-family dwellings where it is difficult to tell which is the primary dwelling, though in some cases it appears that people are living in the trailers as they fix up their flood-ravaged homes. The streets are full of debris, often neatly piled, but one has to wonder where the trucks are to haul this unhealthful and unsightly trash away! We are both surprised at the economic and racial mix of the neighborhood. Brick homes stand next to narrow, wooden, shotgun homes, but the ability of the owners to repair seems to hit across economic sectors. One has to see the devastation to believe it and to comprehend the permanent impact the disaster has had on this historical city. We leave disheartened but with a better understanding.

The French Quarter appears to be making a stronger and quicker comeback, and here more than anywhere else we see evidence of the in-

Latino workers painting a building in the French Quarter. Louis Mendoza.

A sign dedicated to those who lost their lives in Hurricane Katrina, in a median near the entrance to the Ninth Ward. Louis Mendoza.

flux of Latin@ laborers working in the construction and service industries. In some of the neighborhoods outside of the French Quarter we see thriving Latin@ cafes and restaurants. The emergence of a Latin@ population in this city reminds one that it is a rich cultural palimpsest with a French, Spanish, Italian, American, Cajun, and now Latin@ presence. Who knows what the future holds?

I leave New Orleans under a clear blue sky the next morning after seeing Lisa off at the airport. My plan is to cycle close to I-10 into Baton Rouge, where I will then go down Highway 190 to Opelousas and eventually come to Lake Charles. I'm familiar enough with I-10 going through the swamplands that I'm concerned I might not have access to rest stops and restaurants if I stay on the interstate. I get to Baton Rouge by four o'clock, much more quickly that I expected, so I decide to keep moving. Not too far out of the city I am racing down the road about to cross the Mississippi when a man in a white pickup on the side of the road tries to hail me down. I initially think he's just waving, and I wave back as I pass him. He drives past me and pulls to the side of the road where the shoulder is beginning to disappear. This time he sticks his hand out and says, "Wait!" I pull over and he tells me in a thick Cajun accent, "I really wouldn't ride across that bridge coming up. It's very dangerous. My wife and I had a friend killed recently going across a bridge just like this one on her bike 'cause there's no shoulder." The traffic is thick and fast, so I look at him and ask, "How else can I get over the river?" He says, "Well, you can't really without going to one of the other bridges just like this. Put your bike in back of my pick up and I'll give you a ride across the bridge." By this time, I've had too many acts of kindness extended to me to be shy, and I say "Thanks" and quickly heave my bike and gear in the back of his truck.

As we go across the river, I realize just how dangerous it would have been crossing this long bridge with traffic going 60 miles an hour and me riding on the edge of the road with no shoulder. We talk only briefly, and he tells me he's going to work second shift in a factory not too far down the road. We talk about places to stay, and he says they will be few and far between before getting to Opelousas. He lets me off with good-luck wishes, and I begin cycling hard, as I figure I only have a few hours of daylight left. I am, once again, humbled by this stranger's kindness and feel like he may well have saved my life. What happens next makes for one of my more challenging and enlightening days on the road.

After 20 or so miles I begin having a series of tire flats because the road is not very clean—lots of trash and glass on the shoulder. I have two new tubes with me and a bottle of Fix-a-Flat for cycling tubes, but the flats happen so quickly and often that within an hour or so I am unable to do anything else with my rear tire. I am in what feels like the middle of nowhere, and I have to push my bike. I stop at a little cafe with a few slot machines and learn that I have zero chances of getting a taxi ride but that the town of Erwinville is only about three or four miles up the road. I push on. An hour or so later I get there and find that there aren't any hotels or taxis and that I'll have to continue on to Livonia to find lodging for the night. Livonia is about 10 more miles up the road. By this time I've cycled about 90 miles and walked three or four more. I grab some food at a gas station and resume walking-pushing. Darkness descends and I realize it'll probably take another three or four hours to walk ten miles at this slow pace.

I'm slowed down even more when the rear tire begins to come off the wheel because it's carrying the burden of my loaded panniers. I'm finding it really hard not to feel sorry for myself and begin to wish that I could call someone for help. I'm bored as can be but begin to start thinking about what, if anything, I have to be grateful for at this moment. I realize that the road has become a lot cleaner and that the shoulder is wide, so this makes walking-pushing more bearable. I realize that the sky is clear and the temperature is nice and cool, when rain or Louisianan humidity could have made this walk much more terrible. Despite resenting having to walk at the end of a long day, I marvel at how strong I feel and realize that I have gotten in really good shape—and that I am physically prepared to do this. I make a deliberate decision not to feel bad and to move forward. Still, I ponder sleeping in the woods not too far off the road, but I don't find the deep darkness and unknowns of the marshy land appealing at all. So I stick with the road and begin counting how many steps it takes me to walk each mile and multiply that by the miles left and focus on taking one step at a time. There is little traffic on the dark road, but when I see lights approaching from behind, I stick my hand out, hoping someone might stop and offer a ride. It doesn't happen. It's close to midnight when I get to the motel on the far side of Livonia.

My relief at arriving there is dispelled when the women at the desk tell me that there are no rooms available. I know my face must have dropped, as they apologize, and I tell them I'm going to find somewhere nearby to sleep on the ground and will try to check in first thing in the morning after someone checks out. As I am walking away, one of the clerks shouts after me and tells me they have one reservation that hasn't shown up yet, and they will give me that room. I've never been so happy to have a roof, a room, a shower, and a vending machine!

I don't sleep in too late since I need to check out and get the bike fixed and don't know what's available in this town. I soon learn there is little and that not even a bus travels through here. The rental car dealers in the surrounding towns don't have any cars available, either, so it finally dawns on me to call for a cab in Baton Rouge. They agree to come get me and take me back there and drop me off at the airport so I can rent a car and go get my bike fixed. While I wait for the cab, I walk around the town and within 30 minutes I am approached by a local policeman in his car who asks: "Who are you? What are you doing here? How long do you plan to stay?" By now, this is an all-too-familiar routine, so after we talk, I go back to the hotel and wait for my cab. Though I have had my preconceptions about small-town police blown wide open a number of times on the trip, this experience reminds me once again that in the eyes of many I remain suspicious-looking.

> *La Chota*
>
> *Getting stopped by the police*
> *(a.k.a. la chota)*
> *in East Houston was as certain*
> *as humidity on a hot summer afternoon.*
>
> *We learned to see the underneath*
> *a raging red tempest of*
> *resentment against the*
> *red, white, and blue lights*
> *in our rearview mirror.*
>
> *No way to win.*
> *Complain? Risk elevating*
> *the situation to a physical confrontation—*
> *your word against theirs—*
> *a vacation behind bars for sure.*
> *Run? At least a beating,*
> *perhaps an underwater excursion*
>
> *in a local bayou with*
> *handcuffed wrists.*
> *A sure recipe for death.*
>
> *Taking it*
> *meant learning your place*
> *when a cop says:*
> *what, YOU a student?*

When all I have is a university ID and
I had to be lying.
You're expected to know
that frisking is their special way of saying hello
and that being meskin
is probable cause
enough to pull you over . . .
for being brown in H-town.

In Baton Rouge I get my tires and tubes replaced, and I am left wondering how I'm going to get past the same territory without encountering the same problems with the narrow bridge across the Mississippi and the debris on the road that caused all my flats. As I look at a map, I can't see an alternative route, so I make the decision to take the car to Lake Charles. From there, I ride into Texas the next day with a sense that I am entering a new phase of my journey as I re-enter the Southwest and the borderland states.

GUEST BLOG ENTRY FROM LISA SASS ZARAGOZA,
NOVEMBER 8, 2007

Upon her return to Minnesota, I invite Lisa to submit a guest entry to my blog to share her "outsider-insider" experience on the trip. Here is what she wrote.

I had the good fortune to be able to bike from Pensacola to New Orleans with Louis last week as part of his "Journey Across Our America" ride. What follows are some thoughts that I'm digesting about the trip. Overall the biggest theme that emerged for me revolves around balance and perhaps imbalance needed to complete such a trip. Here are a few examples:
- Balancing trust/faith with risk taking;
- Balancing moving with staying put and engaging;
- Balancing being connected with others and being alone.
    A few things that might not be as balanced or as proportional for many of us in the privileged life of stability:
- The extraordinary amount of patience and flexibility it takes when you do not know where you are going to sleep that night, eat your next meal, if you are going to be able to fix the broken bike part or

what the heck to do if you can't and just need to stick with it and see it through because qué más se puede hacer? What else are you going to do? You have to figure it out and you have to stick it out.

- The extraordinary strength—physically, mentally and emotionally—it takes to commit, recommit and execute such a trip. Punto. Again and again.

- The vulnerability it takes to commit to such a trip—and then to have it out on the Internet for the world to know about it! (Thus my trepidation to write this piece, but part of why I wanted to ride was to help lighten the load, offer some support during a difficult stretch and follow through with a commitment to a friendship, so if he's going to put his stuff out there, then for me to follow through on trying to understand/share a bit of the experience, I'll do my best!)

What else? I think the title of Louis' project, Journey Across Our America, is really a very fitting and telling title—Journey to me conveys something much deeper and far reaching than a Trip. I thought about that Our America part more than once as I was pedaling across the Gulf area. I was embarrassingly surprised to see and understand a bit better about how Katrina had impacted such a large part of the Gulf area—not just New Orleans. I was drawn to and impacted by the consequences of the storm and the need to re-build so much of area and how that impacts not just the local area, but all of us. For me in Minnesota now, it seems harder, less tangible, but the whole thing about an injury to one is an injury to all struck home with me as it was obvious that so many fellow compatriots suffered and are trying to re-build. What is my responsibility to them and how do I exercise that from Minnesota? How does one claim and assert one's rights as a resident and citizen—national citizenship or cultural citizenship, within an area or region not your own? How does one decide to claim or not claim being part of a larger identity—family, community, region, country? What the heck keeps this country together and what keeps us apart/separated? Are we by and large more together or more apart as folks living under the same roof?

Finally, I was excited about being in shape—it was FUN to ride, great to feel strong and capable, to have a bike in good working order and my body in good working order. That sense of confidence and joy combined with intense family history of bike injuries, death and near-death experiences on two wheelers got me pondering about the risk, trust and faith mentioned earlier. Who has a right to do this? Do some people get injured for some reason under the sun and others not? Ultimately, I believe in free will in our lives, and I am grateful for the privilege and choices that I have had and have to live the life that I do. I thank the universe for the opportunity, my sister for helping to gear me up and Louis for letting me join him for a piece of the road on his Journey Across Our America.

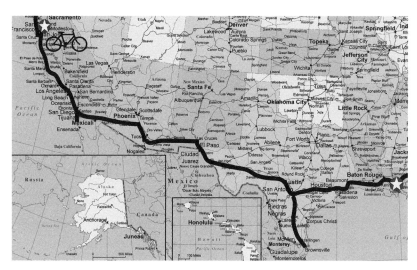

The last leg of the trip, through Texas and back to northern California. Louis Mendoza.

PART FOUR

REDEFINING THE BORDERLANDS
Uncharted Waters in Familiar Territory

I SOON REALIZED THAT NO JOURNEY CARRIES ONE FAR UNLESS, AS IT
EXTENDS INTO THE WORLD AROUND US, IT GOES AN EQUAL DISTANCE
INTO THE WORLD WITHIN.

Lillian Smith

REMEMBER THAT YOU WOULD NOT HAVE DONE THIS HAD YOU NOT
HEARD YOUR HEART CRYING OUT FOR THE FREEDOM OF IT, HAD YOUR
ANCESTORS NOT FILLED YOU WITH THE DESIRE AND ABILITY TO LIVE
AN ETERNITY IN ONE JOURNEY, HAD YOU NOT KNOWN THAT YOU
ARE ALREADY WORTH MORE THAN THIS TASK, AND HAD YOU NOT
SUSPECTED SOMEWHERE INSIDE YOU THAT THE ROAD WOULD NOT
BREAK YOU.

Edén Torres, inspired by Carlos Santana

INTO TEXAS: NOVEMBER 3, 2007

On Saturday morning I call my parents in Houston and let them
know that I should make it somewhere between Anahuac and Houston
after a long day's ride and that being so close, I may want to be picked up.
They live on the far east side of the city and insist on picking me up as soon
as I cross the state line. They worry about me riding through some of the
small East Texas towns like Vidor where a hostile racial climate is pervasive and the KKK is still very active. While they don't express their fears directly, I understand their plea and think of how it feels to stop late at night
in these towns where some people give you grueling stares. Having just cycled through the South, I'm less concerned about riding in daylight, but I

My father giving my sister Gilda a push as they take turns riding my bike during my visit in Houston. Louis Mendoza.

know my mom in particular has a lot of anxiety about my safety on this trip (every time we speak she tells me she's praying for my safety), so I agree. I ride along small roads shadowing I-10 until I get near the Sabine River, where the only place I can cross is I-10. Perhaps because this is my home state, I feel a special thrill when I cross the state line and exit at the welcome area. My reunion with my parents is exhilarating, and we stop for lunch at a cafeteria on the way back to Houston.

The next day all six of my sisters and several of my nieces and nephews come to my parents' house for a big meal. My sisters, my father, and one of my nephews take turns riding the bike up and down the block where my parents live. My sister Gilda gets a push-off from my dad—just like when we were kids first learning how to ride!

For the next few days I relax and prepare to give a presentation at the Selena Quintanilla Center in Denver Harbor on Wednesday. My sisters have invited a lot of family and friends to the event, and we have quite a crowd and lots of food. While the building is relatively new, this is the park in the neighborhood of my youth. Being here is one of the highlights of my trip thus far. This is the barrio where I grew up, and therefore it always holds a special place for me. Presenting in the neighborhood park where I played my first baseball games, learned to swim, went to the library, hung out with friends, and romanced my first childhood girlfriend is very special. I share pictures, video, stories, and insights I've gleaned thus far.

In addition to meeting so many new people throughout my journey, another benefit has been the way it has reconnected me to family, friends, and neighborhood folks I haven't seen in many, many years. I strive to make the talk come from the heart and still be informative about my trip as well as the larger context in which it's occurring and the issues that permeate our lives and the national news. A good discussion and set of questions ensue. During my week there, I also speak at George I. Sánchez and César Chávez high schools. My sister Mary Ann works at the former, and my friend Freddy Porras teaches history and economics at the latter. The students and teachers at both are very interested and receptive. An ABC network affiliate reporter visits one of my presentations and incorporates an interview with one of the students at Sánchez into a story that airs that evening. I am humbled by the attention.

Between presentations I drive to visit familiar places and reflect on how the neighborhood, the city, and my life have changed in the past 30 years. I visit some day-labor sites and set up a meeting with folks at Casa Juan Diego, though that appointment is cancelled by the directors at the last minute due to a scheduling conflict. Houston is a 20th-century Latin@ city—meaning that unlike San Antonio, its roots are not connected to Spanish colonization but to an influx of immigrants coming to escape the Mexican Revolution and work in the shipyard, construction, and agriculture industries. Until the 1980s Houston's Latin@ population was mostly comprised of Mexicans, Puerto Ricans, and Cubans, but since then, in the aftermath of the U.S.-backed civil wars in Central America, there has been a huge influx of economic and political refugees from El Salvador, Guatemala, and Nicaragua. My time in Houston passes quickly.

- -

TAKING BORDER BATTLES TO THE STREETS

It's become a Saturday morning ritual on a street corner in Spring [Texas]. Two dozen U.S. Border Watch volunteers, some wearing combat boots and military-style garb, face off with Hispanic day laborers and a half-dozen of their supporters. "Stop the hate! Stop the fear! Immigrants are welcome here!" boomed a woman's voice recently over a portable loudspeaker. "Thou Shall not Steal America," reads a sign waved by a member of Border Watch, a group based in Spring.

A similar scene has unfolded over the past months at the busy intersection of Steubner-Airline and Wimbelton Estates Drive in northwest Harris County. The day laborers, many of them undocumented, gather each morning in the Speedo gas station parking lot. And nearly every Saturday morning since September, dozens of Border Watch members have attempted to drive them away. They chant slogans, wave signs and film employers who pick up immigrants for work.

Far from the halls of Congress and the front lines of the Southwest border, the divisive immigration debate is being played out in local neighborhoods, including the Houston area. A number of groups have upped the ante by moving from debate to confrontation, attempting to take immigration duties into their own hands.

Since the Minuteman group staged a border surveillance operation in Arizona in 2005, more than 250 new anti-immigrant groups have formed, said Mark Potok, director of Southern Poverty Law Center's intelligence project, which monitors such organizations. . . . In April, the center listed 144 "Nativist Extremist" organizations that go beyond debate and target individuals, Potok said. There are 13 immigration-related activist groups in Texas, and Border Watch was among three in the Houston area.

"The most significant danger posed by these groups is the poisoning of the democratic debate" about immigration levels, Potok said. Instead, the groups have turned "the discussion into a diatribe about how Mexicans are destroying our culture, bringing diseases to our country and killing dozens of Americans every day," he said.

'IT'S ABOUT BEING ILLEGAL'

The president of Border Watch, Curtis S. Collier, said his members don't have a racist agenda. Their goal is simple: Expel the millions of illegal immigrants in the United States. "To be racist, you have to target someone because of their race," Collier said. "We don't care who you are. If you're here illegally we want you to go home. It's not about being brown-skinned, it's about being illegal."

Doris Meissner, who headed the Immigration and Naturalization Service during the Clinton era, said groups such as Border Watch have proliferated due to frustration over the government's inability to control illegal immigration. And while Meissner characterized the groups as "spot outbreaks," she considers them a threat. "They are dangerous because they do border on vigilante activity," said Meissner, a senior fellow at the Migration Policy Institute, a think tank based in Washington, D.C.

But groups lobbying for limited immigration see the growing activism differently. Dan Stein, president of the Federation of Americans for Immigration Reform, said the explosive growth of immigration as a domestic issue—fueled in part by the Internet—and the formation of activist groups was triggered by the Bush administration's failure to crack down on illegal immigration. "It is a truly magnificent populist action, in a way we haven't seen in decades," he said.

THEY KEEP CLOSE WATCH

Border Watch was co-founded by Collier, a 47-year-old Spring resident who spent eight years as a U.S. Army policeman before opening a small pest control company. He claims 1,628 members nationwide, with chapters in El Paso, San Antonio and Arkansas. Twice a year, Border Watch tracks illegal immigrants crossing the Texas-Mexico border

Collier, who speaks about border security at events across Texas, repeats claims that 25 Americans citizens are killed each day by undocumented immigrants. Islamic terrorists are slipping across the Southwest border, he says, camouflaged as illegal immigrants. "There have been reports of Spanish-speaking schools popping up in the Middle East and teaching people in that part of the world to speak Spanish so they can blend in easily," Collier said.

Potok, with the poverty center, said those claims are common to this new breed of anti-illegal immigration activists. "These are the paranoid fantasies of people with difficulty handling reality," he said.

Border Watch monitors some of what Collier said are 57 day labor sites in the Houston area. . . . So when church leaders in the Spring area proposed a center for day workers who use Stuebner-Airline as a gathering place, Collier and his group pounced. "All hell broke out," recalled pastor Franklin Moore, part of a local interfaith group working to establish a center. "All we wanted to do was get a place for day laborers to be safe, to get out of the sun and rain, to get a drink and go to the bathroom," Moore said.

SAN ANTONIO: NOVEMBER 12, 2007

After we have a hearty breakfast on Friday morning, my parents drive me to Sealy, Texas. They are somewhat wary of seeing me get back on the road, so they insist on driving me a ways down the interstate instead of just to the outskirts of Houston. I think if I would have let them they would have driven me halfway to San Antonio! I make my way to Flatonia down Highway 90 through a steady wind from the west. I arrive in San Antonio on Saturday evening. Riding parallel to I-10 is both familiar and new, as I see a different side to a route I've traveled dozens and dozens of times over the years. On Highway 90 I see roads leading to unfamiliar places and the centers of small towns I've never seen before, as I mostly knew them as rest stops and gas stations between Houston and San Antonio and nothing more.

My brother, Bobby, and I go on a brief excursion to Lake Medina on Sunday morning for a relaxing couple of hours of feeding the fish. No luck catching any. Later that afternoon back at the house he grills a "chickan"— a new concoction that involves standing a whole chicken atop a can of beer as you cook it—that tastes quite good. Besides talking to folks here, I plan to visit Austin and a couple of towns in the Valley with the hope of learning more about the work of people resisting the erection of the border wall.

I suppose I've been riding with good luck for a while so that, like my tires, good fortune was bound to wear thin at some point. After meeting with Elaine Ayala from the *Express-News* and taking advantage of having my brother's car to drive around town, I return his car before meeting friends for dinner. As I ride my bike back to Bobby's house before going to dinner I have a collision with a pickup while going through an intersection. We are both going east on Bandera Road, and the pickup driver turns right and I go straight as he cuts in front of me without ever seeing me. I hit the back of his truck and use my hands to push myself away from the vehicle so I won't go under his wheels. I manage to slide along the truck's bed until it passes, and then I fall forward hard, bruising my hands, wrist, and elbow on my left side and scraping my left knee and elbow. I bounce up with post-accident adrenaline and yell at the driver. He stops and comes back, completely unaware of what has just happened. Once I see that his concern is genuine I calm down, inspect my bike and body to make sure there is no serious damage, say goodbye to him, and go on my way. Though he should have been aware of my presence, I should have made sure to make eye contact with him before entering the intersection. Fortunately for me, neither one of us was going fast, and in the big scheme of things I got off easy.

I am able to ride home and put ice on the elbow and wrist immediately to help with the swelling.

Funny thing is, I was just telling Elaine and Helen, the *Express-News* photographer, that I need to make sure I stay sharp and focused so as not to have something like this happen as I begin the final leg of the trip. Little good it did to knock on wood! I'll be sore for a few days but much more street-aware.

SOUTH TEXAS AND THE LOWER RIO GRANDE VALLEY: NOVEMBER 18, 2007

I attend The Soul of San Antonio, an open discussion on issues relevant to the San Antonio community that is exploring how faith and politics can be translated into effective social change. I am invited to this event by former Texas United Farm Worker Union executive director Rebecca Flores. One of the group discussions is on immigration. Though a small group, we have a passionate discussion about how the quality of public discourse on the issue can be improved and humanized so as not to focus solely on its legal, economic, and political dimensions. I participate in the morning and afternoon discussion sessions, in which many concerned citi-

Wayne Romo, Sister Elizabeth Riebschlagel, and Vanessa Torres (left to right), round-table participants at The Soul of San Antonio. Louis Mendoza.

zens participate. Among them is Sister Elizabeth Riebschlagel, a nun from the University of Incarnate Word, who says that some nuns from the order in Mexico are not being allowed to visit the U.S. Vanessa Torres, a graduate student in political science from St. Mary's University, Wayne Romo, the director of ministries from St. Mary's University, and Heidi Flannery also participate. One powerful idea that emerges is to hold an immigration summit that would bring together local politicians, faith leaders, and other community members including undocumented residents to discuss how San Antonio can be a more welcoming city for new immigrants and to provide factual information that addresses misconceptions about the problems often associated with a rise in the immigrant population. It is felt that such a summit might allow for people to better understand the common humanity we share and the role everyone plays in building an inclusive social and cultural climate. An excerpt from our discussion follows.

SISTER ELIZABETH: If we get an inspired leader who understands this is what needs to happen, that's when change is going to happen. Individual things need to happen, but I don't think they're going to happen until there's a change in the psyche among people and how we think about leadership and we accept the fact that immigration is what it is. We need to deal with immigration as a reality and to deal with it in a humane way.

WAYNE: I agree with you. I think that there's a generation of our young adults today who are much more willing to articulate what's important in terms of basic human dignity, much more so than their parents. When it comes to the table of politics for law and reform for immigration, the questions for me are: What's known by those who are at the table and what's not known? Who's not at the table to represent the reality? If we use the gang-summit initiative as an example, political leaders, church leaders got together and said, "We need to sit down with the leaders within the gangs to talk about what it's doing to our family lives. We need to listen to where they're coming from, where their needs are." The question that remains for me in immigration, this is a fabric of American life that's breaking the health-care system, because of the funding that's required to care for illegal aliens. Well, how do we know what those family realities are if they're not at the table of conversations when we're making decisions politically about laws and regulation and we don't know if we're really addressing the need?

HEIDI: The other thing is that we need to have people at the table from the business community. We need to talk about what immigrant labor, whether legal or illegal, is contributing to their business, what it's contributing to the economy. We need somebody to inform the American public that these folks pay taxes. And they pay Social Security fees into [the] Social Security system, yet if they choose to go back to their countries, they can't take it with them, so it benefits us. So there's a lot of deliberate deception of the public in terms of the reality of immigration. We need to finally get an accurate picture of what we're talking about.

> ME: *One of the common things you hear from conservatives on this issue is that we're a nation of laws. Too many will not listen to any discussion other than saying, "That's my starting point, end of discussion." The problem is that they've allowed law to supplant morality. If we look at law as a framework for morality, then we're in deep trouble. How do we have a discussion around the morality of immigration that focuses on what we have in common as human beings?*

HEIDI: I think we need to talk on a level of ethics, which has a lot in common with morality.

> ME: *But we don't talk about that. They want to say that ethics is determined by "Did you or did you not break the law? Are you illegal?" In this way they can shape the discourse to dehumanize people by labeling them as "illegal aliens" so they are not even at the table. They put that tag on people and they become persona non grata.*

HEIDI: I think it's at the level of common values that we can come together to address this. And that's why to a certain extent we have to talk about faith in politics, because it's a reality. Faith motivates some people into the political arena and what they do when they get there, and nothing has demonstrated that more effectively than Pat Robertson and the guy from the American Family Association. And they really have a nice hold on the country and on politics in the last years, but I think that that's falling apart. The very fact that they cannot come together in terms of who to endorse, the very fact that Pat Robertson endorses one guy and somebody else endorses another, says that that's not coming together anymore. I really feel sorry for the people that went into this with a deal of sincerity and simple faith, and they have seen what George Bush has done to the country. I see the people coming together on the basis of common values. If I can identify with that person, then we can work together.

SISTER ELIZABETH: Do you think part of the reason polarization happens is because people feel so insecure in this day and age, in society? They feel like there's so little of their life that they have control over, that they're look-ing at issues in black and white rather than . . .

HEIDI: I think it's more the fact that people in this country, down deep, believe that this country belongs to them. I expect it to be messy at the lo-cal level, but I think what's important is that we learn to dialogue respect-fully. I think it's important that I be allowed to respond to someone I dis-agree with and say, "I'm not comfortable with that perspective. Here's my perspective."

SISTER ELIZABETH: And be positive, because I think positive values are what's going to save the country, not the negative knee-jerks.

WAYNE: I think we should be asking ourselves, What would we like to see happen, not so much what needs to be done?

> ME: Do you mean nationally, or are you talking about at a micro
> level?

VANESSA: I think we should consider getting people together, getting the politicians and getting the faith-based organizations and talking to them about it and coming up with a solution but also bringing in those people that have immigrated and see how can we as a society help them make that connection.

WAYNE: If our politicians can't decide on reform, then somebody needs to help them. What are we as citizens of San Antonio doing to help them?

HEIDI: To me the primary thing that needs to be happening at any type of summit of leaders is that we need to have a presentation of some kind that would give us valid information, that would not allow us to come and go into the same discussion we're having at the national level with half-correct information, incorrect information, prejudicial information. It would be an educational summit where we really learn the necessity of what the situa-tion is . . . like unpaid taxes and things of that nature.

WAYNE: With that I would add what I heard us all talking about is that in-stead of looking at the negatives of what immigration may be resurrecting for us, why aren't we articulating the positives—What economic contribu-tions are the immigrants contributing to our own city's economy, what suc-cesses have come from illegal immigrants who are now legal? One of the questions that has always been of greater concern to me is that I can talk about immigration issues but not as an immigrant, even if my ancestry is one. I can't talk about it as a lived experience. My interest really is, when we sit at the table and talk about immigration, all the circles that I've been in, there's never been a person that's an immigrant, illegal, at the table. And it's people getting together to talk about how do we serve, but we don't have the people being served.

> ME: *Talking is how we build compassion. We build understanding by placing ourselves in the shoes of others. We can't experience everything there is to experience in the world, but we can speak from that perspective when we have true compassion.*

WAYNE: The issue for me is that institutional churches have separated us from open dialogue because institutional churches have gotten to the point of saying, "This is black and white; don't waver either way," and it's not healthy living.

HEIDI: Well, some institutional churches are also changing. What about including in this particular immigration summit a challenge that churches come to a common statement of belief on the issue? If we can come up with a statement of common values to give some direction to a certain extent, this can shape a humane vision.

I find the discussion helpful and reassuring, though I wish that opponents to immigration reform had been in attendance so we could have explored the issue more deeply with opinions from the entire political spectrum. The next day I put my bike in the shop to get yet another replacement wheel, which has to be ordered. With a couple of days off, I decide to rent a car and go down to the Rio Grande Valley. Without an advance appointment I go to visit Rogelio Núñez of Proyecto Libertad in his office in Harlingen. Proyecto Libertad is a nonprofit community organization that promotes and defends human rights among the immigrant community. I'm initially screened by staff who call him in his office. Once he discovers that we have mutual friends in Raúl Salinas (Austin) and Susana De León (Minneapolis), he welcomes me with open arms and takes time out of his busy schedule to tell me about the work of Proyecto Libertad with immigrants and as advocates for women facing domestic violence. He also shares his perspective with me on the climate for progressive action on behalf of the Mexican American community. A former professor of sociology, Rogelio is a lifelong Valley resident who laments the lack of culturally relevant education for youths of the region and the resulting dearth of leadership that could challenge the dominant power structure that sustains inequitable social, political, and economic relationships.

Me with Elizabeth García (left) and Leide Martínez (right) at Casa Digna in Colonia Cameron Park. Kamala Platt.

Rogelio recommends that I speak with Elizabeth García at Casa Digna in Colonia Cameron Park, just outside of Brownsville. Elizabeth is an active participant in the No Border Wall coalition being organized in the Valley. Originally from Matamoros, she's lived in Brownsville for approximately 20 years. She runs Casa Digna in conjunction with San Felipe de Jesús Church in Brownsville. She works part-time as coalition organizer for organizations seeking *colonia* empowerment. One of the more successful projects the coalition has taken on is to register voters in the colonia to force elected officials to address their concerns. Cameron Park is situated in one of the poorest zip codes of the country, but its residents have recently had some success in getting streets paved and other services into the area. On the night we go by, the group is screening a segment of Michael Moore's film *Sicko* that addresses health issues in the Valley.

I go see Elizabeth García with a friend of mine, Kamala, who is teaching at the University of Texas–Pan American and brings along a student of hers to introduce to me, Leide Martínez. Leide is a first-year student at UT–Pan Am in Edinburg, Texas, where she is studying to be an accountant. Originally from San Luis Potosí, Leide has lived in the Valley for six years. As we drive to Casa Digna, she tells me how her move to Texas was very much against her wishes when her mother married a Tejano. Now, however, she can't imagine returning to San Luis even though her *abuela* and *tías* are there. Here is part of a conversation we have in the car.

ME: *How did your family come to be in the U.S.?*

LEIDE: We were supposed to be in Reynosa just for a little while. Then my mother told me that she didn't want to stay over there, that she was going to get married to someone here.

ME: *Did that surprise you?*

LEIDE: Yes. I got really, really mad at her. And I wanted to go back with my father, but she didn't let me.

ME: *So do you talk to your father? Have you been able to go back home and visit?*

LEIDE: Yes, we went back home, but he was already sick. We stayed like three years over here, then go back with him, then he died.

ME: *Besides your sister, does everybody else live here?*

LEIDE: Yes, everybody. My brothers and sisters are over here, except for one. He's with my *abuelita*. He doesn't want to come here.

ME: *Do you live at home now with them?*

LEIDE: Yes, with my mom.

ME: *When you came here, were you in some kind of English classes?*

LEIDE: I went to ESL classes. They are bilingual. And I stayed in bilingual classes for three years.

ME: So what do you want to study?

LEIDE: I was going for criminal justice, but I already changed. I want to do accounting.

ME: *What's your status? Are you a resident?*

LEIDE: No, my stepfather has just put in for my papers. He adopted me. I'm in the process right now.

ME: *Do you pay in-state tuition? Or do you pay out-of-state?*

LEIDE: They count me like a resident.

ME: *After being here seven years, do you feel like this is home?*

LEIDE: I really feel that this is home. I really wouldn't like to go back home. (Me: Why?) 'Cause nobody's over there.

ME: *Have you met many other recent immigrants?*

LEIDE: Yes, in the ESL classes.

ME: *What do your brothers do?*

LEIDE: Landscaping. My mom, too.

LOUIS: Does she work for somebody else?

LEIDE: My mom and my stepfather work together. My brother works for a company, and my other brother, too, works for the company.

ME: *So what do they think about you being in college?*

LEIDE: *Que le heche ganas.* [Give it all you got!] [Laughter]

ME: *Do you keep in touch with anybody back in San Luis, any relatives?*

LEIDE: Only with my abuelita.

ME: *Do you think of yourself as americano or mexicano?*

LEIDE: No, *¡mexicano, cien por ciento todavía!* [No, Mexican 100 percent still!]

ME: *So do you follow the news on immigration? What does it make you think?*

LEIDE: It makes me think a lot of things. At the same time it makes me sad and mad.

ME: *Do you think most people that come over here really want to come, or do they feel like they have to come? What do you think the Mexican government thinks about that?*

LEIDE: They always talk and talk about it. But they never do something to stop that or produce something that is going to produce good for the people. They just make promises and never do nothing.

ME: *What do you think they have to do? I mean it's a big question, so don't think you have all the answers. What would make people stay there?*

LEIDE: Provide them good work to support their families, because I think that nobody wants to leave their families. If I would be able to have the money to live over there, I would leave. And I think most people would.

ME: *What do you think about the building of the border wall?*

LEIDE: It's very embarrassing.

ME: *What do you think or feel when you see all the Border Patrol?*

LEIDE: I don't really have anything against them. They're doing their work. But I don't like when they don't train people right. I just read an article about an agent from the Border Patrol, and I think he take one lady and raped her; it was like two months ago.

ME: *Were there many indocumentados in your high school?*

LEIDE: Yes.

ME: *What do they think? I mean you're in a little bit of a different position since you have your stepfather, right?*

LEIDE: I have *esperanza* [hope] but most of them don't. When I was a senior, the school knew who has [a] Social Security number and who doesn't. They call us and put us all together and take us to the universities, and they helped us with registration and all that. And most of the times the ones in the high school who [are] immigrants like me, they are the people that want to have the higher GPA. I was in the top 10 percent. There were like 25 to 35 of us in the top 10 percent who didn't have papers. A lot of them have scholarships to universities that are out [of] state. But for their situation, they don't go; they decide to stay here. The second-best student in my class, he was in the same situation.

ME: *Do you think your friends that don't have papers live with fear of being caught, or do they feel like if it happens it happens?*

LEIDE: Yeah, if it happens, it happens. The good thing is if it does happen, it's right across the border. But for people that are out of state, that's hard.

ME: *Do you feel like your mexicanidad [Mexicanness] is the same thing here that it is in Mexico? What makes it different?*

LEIDE: The traditions are not the same. Halloween is not the same. Thanksgiving we don't celebrate it. The music is very different. And the food is thoroughly different.

ME: *What about your language? Do you feel like you've changed?*

LEIDE: No, I don't like to speak English because it's hard for me. I try and try.

ME: *You do pretty good. How about when you have to write in English, your essays?*

LEIDE: It's different because I can write English better than I can talk.

ME: *Do you hope to have kids someday? (Leide: Yes.) Do you think they'll be able to grow up feeling mexicano, or you think they'll be more American than you?*

LEIDE: I would make them feel more mexicano.

ME: *Do you know the word* pocho?[1]

LEIDE: Yes.

ME: *Do you think that's happening to you?*

LEIDE: I really don't know. [Laughter]

ME: *So now you've been here some while, do you think that you agree with your mother's decision to come?*

LEIDE: Yes. At some points yes and other points no.

ME: *But if you had to come you're glad you stayed close by, right on the border.*

LEIDE: I don't go to Mexico, but I know there are people that have passed through worse things. Like *guatemaltecos.*

Before leaving the Valley, I go see my aunt who is a nun at the Virgen de San Juan del Valle Shrine, also known as Our Lady of San Juan, near McAllen, Texas. I meet with Aunt Patricia and her friend Letty. I am surprised at what they have to say, and I record part of our conversation after they tell me that lately some of the nuns have been having trouble returning to the U.S. and are frequently detained at the border.

SISTER LETTY: We used to go to Zapatecas, [Mexico,] and we would help out the *zapatecos*. The [Mexican] government is not for that. Not because you wanted an uprising, but you instruct them, and the government does not appreciate it *porque el gobierno del PRI quiere seguir dominando* [because the PRI (ruling party) government wants to maintain dominance]. And they're very unfair to the people, especially with their land, and people, that's what they will kill each other for is for their titles, because they know that much, that they need to have titles for their land.

> ME: *But you were also saying that nuns coming into the United States were having trouble getting their visas approved as well, right?*

SISTER PATRICIA: I think it's just lately.

SISTER LETTY: After the news in English here I like to go to and hear the other Spanish news at 10:30 *porque te dan un poquito de national o* [because they give you a little national or] international news.

> ME: *You get a different perspective from international news?*

SISTER LETTY: You do. That's how I got to learn about all the flooding that was going on in Chiapas even before it was announced here.

> ME: *Did you grow up in this area, Sister?*

SISTER LETTY: No, I grew up in San Antonio. I was born in Luling, which is a small town between Houston and San Antonio, and my parents moved to San Antonio when I was two years old, but I was raised in San Antonio, and then in the early '60s I came to San Benito. I was here for three years in San Benito; then I went back to San Antonio for health reasons, and then I came back in the early '70s because by that time, in 1971, for the first time we were going to go do missionary work in Oaxaca. We had to go to Salina Cruz, you know, around the Isthmus of Tehuantepec. Then we were going to go to the missions, to the mountains, so that's when they sent me here, 'cause the sister superior needed somebody to work at the nursing home.

SISTER PATRICIA: Our sister started the St. John's Catholic School, and that's like how many years ago, 40? And the nursing home, and it's still going on strong and growing, but not the school.

SISTER LETTY: The thing is the people wanted the children to have Catholic schools.

> ME: *So you spent time in Oaxaca?*

SISTER LETTY: We used to go in Greyhounds from San Antonio to Laredo. We even came through Matamoros or Reynosa, or we'd come from, *para que no los conocieran* [so they wouldn't know us], we would go through a different border not to get known too much *porque* sometimes when they would know you too much and you knew that they were religious, especially on the Mexican side, they would give you a hard time [to] get in. *Te daban* [they would give you] three months or 30 days.

ME: *Because you were going to help the poor?*

SISTER LETTY: Yes. And we found out that the ones that gave you the roughest times was in Matamoros. So we would go through Laredo or through Reynosa, so for me it was convenient to go through Laredo because I lived in San Antonio. But then they started to go where the bus didn't cross you over. You had to pay like $30 just to cross it over on the bus, and if they felt like giving you 30 days, they would give you 30 days. And I needed those days.

Are you biking completely on your own, *porque* there's so much gang members, so much evil going on, *que haga peligro* [it's dangerous].

> ME: *I had to accept that that was always a possibility, but it's a possibility walking out of your own house. I'm not going to be starting arguments with people, even if I disagree with them. What I am doing this trip is listening to people. I don't think you can live your life afraid of the worst things. I've needed help. My bike has broken down, I've been stuck in the middle of nowhere, and something good always happens. I've been given rides, so people have trusted me, and that's been a good thing. Every time that happens, then we talk and I get to learn about them and I tell them who I am. It's a lesson, an opportunity to learn from them.*

SISTER LETTY: That's good because so much is happening, so very much, not like the old days. There's more danger now. I'm happy that you're doing fine. We'll keep on praying for you. We're spreading more devotion to your guardian angels, so pray to your guardian angels that they protect you and we'll do the same thing so you can complete your ride and finish your goal. There's some learning and some message that you're bringing, more than just you're biking about.

Our parents leave, and leave children behind because children are legal. Or even to see this wall and you go and start other walls *porque* we see it as wrong, *aqui nosotros* [here we] in America are building the same wall they tore down. It doesn't make sense how this is happening. At the same

My tía Sister Patricia (left) and her friend Sister Letty (right) outside their residence in San Juan, Texas. Louis Mendoza.

time, instead of getting a better message, it gives a wrong message and creates more antagonism between the two sides of the border *porque* the children grow up with negativity.

I leave after a short visit but not before they find the resident priest and ask him to give me a blessing.

- -

OUR WALL

Borders everywhere attract violence, violence prompts fences, and eventually fences can mutate into walls. Then everyone pays attention because a wall turns a legal distinction into a visual slap in the face. We seem to love walls, but are embarrassed by them because they say something unpleasant about the neighbors—and us. They flow from two sources: fear and the desire for control. Just as our houses have doors and locks, so do borders call forth garrisons, customs officials, and, now and then, big walls. They give us divided feelings because we do not like to admit we need them.

Now as the United States debates fortifying its border with Mexico, walls have a new vogue. At various spots along the dusty, 1,952-mile (3,141 kilometers) boundary, fences, walls, and vehicle barriers have been constructed since the 1990s to slow the surge in illegal immigration. In San Diego, nine miles (14 kilometers) of a double-layered fence have been erected. In Arizona, the state most overrun with illegal crossings, 65 miles (105 kilometers) of barriers have been constructed already. Depending on the direction of the ongoing immigration debate, there may soon be hundreds more miles of walls.

. . . The boundary between Mexico and the United States has always been zealously insisted upon by both countries. But initially Mexicans moved north at will. The U.S. patrols of the border that began in 1904 were mainly to keep out illegal Asian immigrants. Almost 900,000 Mexicans legally entered the United States to flee the violence of the revolution. Low population in both nations and the need for labor in the American Southwest made this migration a non-event for decades. The flow of illegal immigrants exploded after the passage of the North American Free Trade Agreement in the early 1990s, a pact that was supposed to end illegal immigration but wound up dislocating millions of Mexican peasant farmers and many small-industrial workers.

. . . Perhaps the closest thing to the wall going up on the U.S.-Mexico border is the separation wall being built by Israel in the West Bank. Like the new American wall, it is designed to control the movement of people, but it faces the problem of all walls—rockets can go over it, tunnels can go under it. It offends people, it comforts people, it fails to deliver security. And it keeps expanding.

Charles Bowden, National Geographic, *May 2007*

THE FINAL PHASE: NOVEMBER 19, 2007

Early in the morning a few days later, Bobby drops me off at the southern edge of Boerne, Texas, about 20 miles outside of San Antonio on I-10. I've decided to ride the interstate rather than smaller Texas highways across the vast expanse of West Texas because it feels safer to trek across the Texas landscape on the interstate than it does on roads where the rest stops and towns are incredibly far apart. Having spent two weeks in Texas, leaving San Antonio is both exciting and daunting. It's exciting because I now sense that I'm definitely going to finish what I've started. Being on the road this long has taken its toll on me. I am tired and long to be in my own bed in my own house and in familiar surroundings. Seeing so many friends and family members the past couple of weeks has been really good. Meeting new people and hearing their stories continue to energize and inspire me. I'm not tired of that. I feel that though my mind, eyes, heart, and soul have been opened by all that I have witnessed and experienced, I also have to acknowledge that there's so much I still don't know, so many people I didn't get to speak with, so many times when the urge and decision to move has resulted in missing out on something important. I have to come to terms with the limits of this journey.

Though I can practically see the end goal (I've bought a ticket home from Oakland for December 19, a month from now), I have to bear in mind that the ride from here to there is no cakewalk. If nothing else, my little accident in San Antonio serves to remind me that I have to keep my guard up. Crossing the beautiful but barren Hill Country across Central Texas heading west demands that I plan each day carefully because places to rest and refuel are few and far between. My plan is to reach El Paso by Saturday. If today is any indication, I'll manage the hills just fine. As I get closer to El Paso, I'll cross some mountains. It's been a while since I've driven this road, so I cannot recall if the road goes through or around the mountains, though I do remember that the entry into the city is very steep.

Riding this road brings back childhood memories of "backwards" rural towns where Mexicans were not welcome and were confronted with a Jim Crow small-town culture as harsh as existed anywhere in the South. But I also know that reality has changed. Mexicans now live in substantially larger numbers in these small towns, and social, cultural, economic, and political inroads have been made. Though I suspect this hasn't necessarily translated into real power or a progressive social order based on equity and respect, one can reasonably say that the quality and character of life is different, less tense, and more bicultural if not multiethnic. I record myself while riding one day.

> This is the Texas Hill Country. Right now I'm about 100 miles west of San Antonio. It's been a good day. Had some problems with my tires yesterday on my way toward Junction, Texas. I had to call a friend of mine to bring me a new front tire even though I just had the rear wheel replaced. That was a real bummer. There are few stops out here. They are about 80 to 100 miles apart. Looking at the map I can tell that it's going to be tough going through West Texas. Some mountainous areas. The Hill Country hasn't been that bad. Steady inclines and declines,

My shadow against the hillside as I ride through West Texas. Louis Mendoza.

lots of big trucks and brush. It's supposed to be low 40s on Thanksgiving morning. I'm not looking forward to that.

EL PASO: NOVEMBER 22, 2007

Over the next couple of days I ride through Sonora to Ozona to Fort Stockton. Monday, Tuesday, and Wednesday are long days of 85, 100, and 108 miles. As I am riding into Ozona something quite beautiful happens. Earlier in the day, two sheep ran along the fence with me until they could go no more. Several hours later now, after the sun has set, I'm riding in the dark. For the past five or six weeks I've been making it a point to get an earlier start to have as much daylight as possible, but I'm not always able to reach my goal before the sun sets. As often happens at the end of a long day, I am riding a steady but not fast speed. My mind is numb, and I am counting the minutes until I can get somewhere to rest and eat a good dinner. As I'm riding along this evening, I begin hearing a rustling sound in the brush alongside the road. At first I think it's just the wind, but it sounds like something moving. It's pitch dark. The only light is the glow from my light attached to my steering wheel and the occasional headlights from a car passing in either direction. Some evenings I wear a head lamp, but I haven't done that this evening as the traffic is minimal and the shoulder of roads reasonably clean. Road kill is all too constant, but my lamp is sufficient for me to see anything large in advance.

The sounds in the brush persist and I began to worry. I stop a couple of times to listen more carefully, and when I do, there is only silence. I check my wheels to make sure some brush hasn't gotten stuck. None there. I move forward and hear it again. This time I stop and point my steering wheel into the brush, and the light shines on a big, beautiful deer staring right at me. I find myself overwhelmed with emotion as I realize that she has been keeping pace with me—accompanying me for some unknown purpose. I say, "Hi, there." She stares placidly back at me but doesn't make a move to run away. We hold a stare for a few more moments, then she ducks her head and walks into the brush away from the road. I've no other way to understand this than to feel a communion with nature, a connection to something much larger than myself, as if I was being watched over and kept company on this long, lonely road. Feeling comfort, strength, and peace emanating from within, I press on.

As I work my way westward, I keep my eye on the weather because I saw that a cold front is due on Thursday that will take temperatures down into the 40s. No problem, I think. At least not until I see that projections have changed to temperatures in the high 20s and low 30s with snow or freezing rain in Fort Stockton and Van Horn. Uh oh. I'm not interested in riding in that at all, given so little shelter, food, or resting places out here. This is something I'm keenly aware of and concerned about. I decide I have to make a plan since my goal is to be in El Paso for the weekend and in Tucson by the end of next week. Now that I have an end date set, I feel some pressure to keep my schedule. I plan ahead and get a Motel 6 room for two nights in Fort Stockton and a bus ticket for Thursday. No snow or rain today, but the cold wind is steady. In fact, my ride to Fort Stockton is slowed down considerably because I can only go about six to seven miles per hour for six hours as the road winds into the very cool but not yet cold north wind.

I regroup and rest in Fort Stockton. If you ever read the book or saw the movie or television series *Friday Night Lights*, you'll know what I mean when I say that high school football is where it's at in these small West Texas towns. As I sit in a small store and eat, I read the *Fort Stockton Pioneer* and marvel at how in a story about a local high school football game in the Permian Basin, between Fort Stockton and Odessa, 12 out of 13 athletes named as stars of the game have Spanish surnames. The rest of the newspaper is also full of news of the Mexican American community: reports from the docket of a Spanish-surnamed judge, arrests, and a profile of Leonor Villegas, a famous mexicana living in Laredo at the turn of the 20th century and active in supporting the Mexican Revolution from this side of the border—she is featured as a famous Texas pioneer woman. As I surmised earlier, this is not the West Texas of old. Twice on my ride here, folks have pulled over on the highway and offered me a bottle of water and inquired about my ride.

STRUGGLES IN THE BORDERLANDS: THANKSGIVING DAY, 2007

It's Thanksgiving and I spend my day riding a bus to El Paso, renting a car, and going back to get my bike. As I ride on the bus I can't help but wonder if I should have tried riding. When we stop in Van Horn and I feel the strong winds, I can't imagine how I would've made 120 miles today. My time in El Paso is short but intense at multiple levels. It is made particularly productive and easy by the presence of friends and family. I spend

A sign protesting the plans to use eminent domain to take over and develop some of Segundo Barrio in El Paso. Louis Mendoza.

Friday evening and part of Saturday as the guest of University of Texas–El Paso Chicana historian Yolanda Chávez Leyva and her artist-photographer friend Lucia. Over a wonderful home-cooked breakfast on Saturday morning I interview Yolanda about her work with Paso del Sur, an emergent organization founded to resist the urban renewal plans crafted by the city's political and business elites for the downtown area and the historic Segundo Barrio adjacent to it. The plan was developed and subsequently adopted by the city council without input from residents and has proven to be quite controversial because it involves the displacement of numerous people and a substantial redesign of the neighborhood that would destroy the barrio's structural and historical integrity.

Thanks to my father I also have the wonderful opportunity to meet some third cousins of mine for the first time while in El Paso. Lupe and Jesse Vega and their mother, Paula, my paternal grandmother's sister, spend part of Saturday with me sharing familial history and their views on how El Paso has changed since they moved here in 1946 from Houston.

In "New Guidelines Issued for Immigration Raids," an article by Anna Badkhen appearing in the *San Antonio Express-News* on November 18, 2007, I read the following: "A study released last month by the Urban Institute, a Washington think tank, showed that many children whose parents are arrested in immigration raids face mental health problems, including post-traumatic stress disorder, separation anxiety and depression."

Veronica Carbajal, a former student of mine who is now a lawyer with the Texas RioGrande Legal Aid (TRLA) office and chair of the local ACLU chapter, also hosts me in El Paso and takes time from her busy schedule to give me a tour and set up meetings with people. Born in El Paso, Veronica grew up in Ciudad Juárez just across the border and attended schools in El Paso. She has returned to her hometown to provide leadership and advocacy in several areas, including environmental justice and housing. I have an inspiring and informative discussion with Carlos Marentes at a farmworker center and safe haven in Segundo Barrio near one of the bridges and next door to a Border Patrol office. In addition to his many other astute insights about Americans' ambivalence and contradictions when it comes to immigrants and immigration, Carlos makes a chilling, sad, and eloquent analogy:

To me the immigration policies of this country resemble a case of domestic violence. The man beats the woman, does whatever he wants to do with the woman, and it's not because he wants the woman to leave. It's because he wants the woman to stay under his control. So, this is where we have immigration policies that attempt to have an immigrant population under control. But we don't want them to leave—we want them to do the dirty jobs.

I've had a very full Monday speaking with many people. It ends with a fantastic discussion with the amazingly committed staff at the Paso del Norte Civil Rights Project who take time to share their work—legal cases they pursue on behalf of individuals—and tell me about their advocacy for policy reforms and why they do this seemingly endless work.

GROUPS FIND HATE, RACISM LURKING IN IMMIGRATION DEBATE

A local TV crew was shooting a live morning report about Lisa Dupre's Sacramento preschool, where toddlers can learn yoga, etiquette and Spanish as a second language. The phone rang—the first response, Dupre thought, to an on-air invitation for parents to get more information. She let her answering machine pick up. "I thought this was America, not Mexico. This is English only," she heard a voice growl when she later listened. "That's why we've got a problem with illegal aliens—because people like you are trying to change California into Mexico."

CNN's Lou Dobbs comes under fire for what the group calls "false propaganda" about undocumented immigrants and disease that he refused to recant. TV pundit Pat Buchanan is criticized for spreading xenophobia in his book "State of Siege," in which he describes Latino immigration as a mortal cultural threat: "The crisis of the West is of a collapsing culture and vanishing peoples."

. . . Mark Potok, a lead researcher at the Southern Poverty Law Center, said, "One of the most obnoxious elements out there are mainstream media talk-show hosts perfectly willing to popularize ideas that have no basis in reality."

Rep. Steve King, R-Iowa, is cited by the Anti-Defamation League for calling undocumented immigration a "slow motion terrorist attack." He also wrote on his Web site that "murderous illegal immigrants kill 12 U.S. citizens every day," a claim Potok called "extreme hogwash."

The Anti-Defamation League cites comments by D.A. King of Georgia, who founded an anti-undocumented-immigrant group called the Dustin Unman Society. He has appeared on CNN and testified at an Education and Workforce congressional committee hearing in 2006. In April, a newspaper report said, King told a gathering of Georgia Republican Party members that undocumented immigrants are "not here to mow your lawn—they're here to blow up your buildings, and kill your children, and you and me."

Susan Ferriss, El Paso Times, *November 23, 2007*

ACROSS NEW MEXICO AND INTO ARIZONA: NOVEMBER 29, 2007

I leave El Paso on a beautiful Tuesday morning. I ride out Mesa Road until it turns into Highway 2 and then link to Highway 478 heading north toward Las Cruces. From there I go west on I-10 toward Deming, New Mexico. It's a great day for riding, with the air cool and the sun out but its heat muted by passing clouds. I'm amused when I have to ride

About 10 miles west of Las Cruces, I went through a Border Patrol checkpoint on I-10. It was surreal to do so on a bike. The officers just waved me through. Louis Mendoza.

through a border checkpoint and the Border Patrol officers just wave me through. Throughout the entire trip, road kill has been constant—a wide variety of snakes and birds, rabbits, armadillos, indiscernible small animals, and deer. What stands out in New Mexico is the number of beautiful white owls I see on the side of the road. They are big, their chests full and plump. Though I know that for many people owls are ominous signs portending death, I try not to dwell on this, as they have already met unfortunate deaths as they were trying to feast on other victims of highway traffic.

All day long I am happy that my tires are holding out—until about five miles from Deming when my back tire gets low on air. I decide to just add air and ride fast so I can wait to change it until I find lodging for the night. At the Motel 6 off the first exit in Deming, I eat, work on some student graduate school recommendations, then sit on the curb of a gas station so I can hitchhike on the La Quinta Internet. When I finally get around to fixing the flat I notice that my rear wheel is no longer true. It's wobbly and rubbing against the rear fender. I spend some time trying to adjust it to no avail. A quick look on the Internet reveals that there are no bike shops for miles and miles around. I take off and discard the rear fender and decide I have no choice but to try and ride it into Tucson—still two days away.

I have an ambitious day planned for Wednesday. My goal is to go 135 miles to Willcox, Arizona. About 15 miles out of Deming I realize that I've left my CamelBak in the motel. No way am I going back. I don't think it's prudent to add 30 miles (two hours or more) to my trip on an already long day. I make a note to drink and refill my water bottles at every stop. I actually feel lighter and cooler without this on my back. The wobbly wheel feels okay, but my speed is decreased by this and the steady upward climb as I once again pass over the Continental Divide. *Ni modo*, I think, whatever. I'll just go slow and steady and get there by eight or so.

And then it happens. I have my first flat of the day about five miles from the Arizona state line. No problem, I have three more tubes. Well, even though I added a new tire liner for flat protection the night before, I start having a series of flats that makes me adjust my goals for the day. By the time I get to San Simon, I've used all my tubes and am riding and adding air every 10–15 minutes. I end up walking the bike the last five miles to a truck stop on the far side of San Simon. Small town. Very small. No lodging. At least there's a 24-hour truck stop. After several hours of resting, eating, and fiddling with the bike some more, I realize I am stuck for the night. I go behind a vacated gas station and set up my tent in the desert

One of many signs about a controversial case in Arizona involving the arrests of humanitarians who provide food and water to border crossers. Louis Mendoza.

Sandy Soto and Miranda Joseph giving me a bike tour of Barrio El Hoyo in Tucson. Louis Mendoza.

brush. It is cool but ultimately okay. I am more worried about getting hassled by some of the multitude of Border Patrol agents in the area than I am about animal life in the surrounding desert—though the next day I learn that there are lots of wild javelina in the area. What you don't know can't scare you.

I am up by seven the next morning, eat breakfast and shower at the truck stop, and try to look at my problem from a fresh perspective. The people at the tire shop next door tell me there is nothing they can do for me, so I set up a sign on my bike asking for a ride and call my friend Sandy in Tucson to let her know I might need a ride. One of the clerks tells me that if I don't get a ride by two, when she gets off work, she'll take me 35 miles up the road to Willcox. So that's what happens. I give her gas money and thank her profusely for taking the time. It is rainy and very cool all day, so I sit in a truck stop and read while I wait for Sandy and Miranda, her partner, to come get me after their classes that evening. Once again, I end up not making it all the way into the city on my own leg power—this time due to mechanical problems.

In Tucson I discover that the rear wheel has to be replaced again. Turns out that the one I got in San Antonio was only a single-wall frame, and it is warped beyond repair. I pick up a new rear tire for good measure and more tubes. I am tired and frustrated beyond belief with these ongoing problems. The only consolation I get is to learn that it's not something I'm doing that's causing the problem. I meet a young woman working at the Ordinary Bicycle Shop in Tucson who tells me about a solo trip she took this summer from Columbus, Ohio, to Tucson. We trade stories.

TUCSON: DECEMBER 2, 2007

Arizona Daily Star columnist Ernesto Portillo gives me an amazing tour of the city and history of Tucson on Monday morning. On my tour with Ernesto, we stop at the Pascua Center and speak with Rebecca Tapia. I learn from her that the community was established around 1921. The city ceded land to the community, and people started building homes there. The center is city-sponsored as well, as is the recreation center. The center of the Yaqui community is just south of Tucson in New Pascua. Some of the land here is being sold to outsiders so they can obtain deeds. Part of this is because people aren't keeping up their payments, and it becomes a way for outsiders to gain control because they turn around and rent the houses to people as absentee landlords. Some mexicanos are doing this, too. We talk about the local community.

ME: *How long have you been working here?*

REBECCA: Twenty-eight years, but I grew up here. My great-grandparents walked here from Mexico.

ERNESTO: What year was it named Pascua and received the land?

REBECCA: [In] 1921 the Franklins owned the land and were doing a survey.

ERNESTO: When the Yaquis were being persecuted in the late 1800s and early 1900s they came up here and got arms and supplies. Even the American military came after the Yaquis here with the Mexican military.

REBECCA: But an international incident arose here due to encampments, and they decided to provide the land to the Yaquis as a way of settling the crisis.

ME: *What do you all do here?*

REBECCA: Primarily this is part of the establishment of the Yaqui community, and the owner took the plaza. It was decided to make it a cultural plaza where special events are held. In the '50s it became city property, but in the late '60s [and] early '70s it became recognized by the city of Tucson as Native land. Meetings are held here, religious services, health fairs, and education services. Recently an elder passed away, and we're going to hold his wake here. I don't know if they are going to have a traditional *pascuaro* for him or not.

ERNESTO: Does he have a Pascuala family?

REBECCA: No, but he's an elder of our community.

ERNESTO: Fortunately, the Yaquis still recognize their elders as elders.

ME: *How does the community retain its sense of cultural integrity?*

REBECCA: Through traditions and maintaining our community lands.

ME: *What is the relationship between the Yaqui community and the immigration debates?*

REBECCA: It's somewhat cut off, but it's a big subject due to the cultural ties. We rely heavily on people on the other side [in Mexico]. It's a great inconvenience for us—the paperwork.

ME: *There is a lot of exchange across the border?*

REBECCA: I would say yes. On the reservation there is a cultural exchange and language office that helps younger folks learn Yaqui. The ceremonies and ritual are even more strong on the other side. So in order to preserve our way of life to the best of our ability, having strong ties to traditional lands across the borders is crucial.

ME: *What language do most kids know here?*

REBECCA: That's complicated. Most of them know English first, now. When I grew up we had to speak English in school. We try to promote at least bilingualism if not trilingualism. If it wasn't for family and tradition we'd be swallowed up. I always tell people that when the old church was torn down by our own Enselmo Valencia, he didn't do it alone, but he participated in it. He thought that if he tore the church down people would follow him south to a town in the desert. What happened was that people stood around and watched and cried. And of course the people didn't go with him, and they rebuilt the church. He thought he could save the community from bad influences here in the city—away from the urban zone. He thought the he could prevent change by moving us away.

ERNESTO: The community politicized some of the leadership.

REBECCA: But even before the casinos we were struggling with issues of poverty, health care, identity, and survival. Identity is what has saved me from being swallowed by American culture. I always knew who I was.

Rebecca Tapia speaking with Ernesto Portillo and me in her office in the Pascua nation. Louis Mendoza.

When we were growing up here in the community we would be taunted by some of the Hispanics. This happens today.

> ME: *That's really sad since you share a language, a religion, and many aspects of the culture.*

REBECCA: Yeah, we are considered the lowest of the low by some.

> ME: *Is there a new generation of leaders coming up?*

REBECCA: Yes and no. We have people who are smart and strong, but they aren't stepping up as leaders per se.

ERNESTO: It's a bad political situation for the [Yaqui] nation right now.

REBECCA: We need people to get involved.

Late this day I have a powerful interview with an elder, Adela Marmion, about her 93 years of life in the U.S.-Mexican borderlands. I meet Sandy, and we end the day with a stop at the Estrella Bakery, where I have some of the best *pan dulce* I've ever tasted.

HAPPINESS IS THE WARM SUN, WHEELS THAT ROLL TRUE, AND A SMOOTH ROAD: DECEMBER 4, 2007

I leave Tucson today well rested and ready to keep on moving west across the Sonoran Desert. I make my way 122 miles up the road on I-10 and I-8 to Gila Bend. The next morning I head out toward Yuma, about 115 miles from Gila Bend. Three small things bear mentioning.

At a rest stop on Interstate 8 my bike is leaning against a picnic table, and a couple of older men come by and start talking to me about my bike ride. It turns out they are avid cyclists. Eventually their wives come over and join the conversation. They are all very nice and interested in what I am doing. They are from Washington state. In response to hearing about my research, one of the women says, "Oh yeah, it's a good place to be doing that kind of study because they're building that crazy fence down here that no one wants and it won't work. It's a bad, bad idea." They wish me luck. Before they leave, each of the men gives me $10 to buy a meal and a beer or to donate to whatever cause I want. I try to refuse, but they insist. They say they work for Boeing and are here on some kind of job but have taken the day to ride the highways and see the landscape. I find out later there's a Boeing plant in Yuma that does work for the military base there. I take the money to honor their gesture of kindness and solidarity.

It was cool to see the sign for Aztec, Arizona, although there wasn't much there but some gas-station ruins. Louis Mendoza.

After crossing a steep mountain pass on the way into Yuma I want to stretch my legs in a different way, so I go for a walk down Redondo Road, a dark, industrial street that runs parallel to a fence on the south side. A big ravine lies between the fence and some railroad tracks. There is very little foot or vehicle traffic on this road. I see two young men run hard across the street, jump the fence, and disappear into the ravine. My first thought is that they are running from something, so I keep my eyes open to see what's up. All I see is a man in a car who seems to be shuffling things in his trunk. Later I realize they weren't running from something but to something. They were probably running to the trains because a couple of minutes later the train horn sounds. I realize they are probably hopping it and the man in the car has dropped them off for that purpose. How they knew that train was about to go, I have no idea, but it's probably on a regular schedule. I surmise that they are heading toward L.A., and I wonder and worry about their fate atop the train.

Shortly after this, a man in a Ford pickup stops and asks if I want a ride. I say no, but we get to talking and I learn he is a local probation officer who works with folks in rehab—he tells me he is a former meth addict himself. He is from Chicago. He starts talking to me about the large Mexican population in town. Yuma's a big lettuce town. He informs me that right now there are lots of temporary workers in town for the harvest, lots of "illegals" among them. This explains why I see so much lettuce scattered across the highways today. He says lots of Mexican cowboys work in the cattle industry in the area. I passed a bunch of slaughterhouses yesterday. Overall he is very nice. He tells me to be careful and goes on his way.

On Thursday I cross into California and change time zones for the final time on this trip. I don't know how long I can ride on this highway because California law doesn't allow cyclists to ride on the interstates. I decide to do the best I can and see what happens. About 20 miles into the state I am forced to get off the interstate by state troopers, so I ride on Plank Road, which appears to be the highway that preceded I-8. It is extremely bumpy and full of potholes, but I've no choice but to ride it about 12 miles into El Centro. It is hard on my body and harder on the bike. I go about 15 miles past El Centro this evening and set up my tent off the mountain road. It is a cold and rainy night, and I am unable to enjoy the darkness. My plan is to head south and follow a smaller road just north of the border because the interstate directly into the San Diego area is getting very steep very fast. I had picked up some food during the day, and I go to bed fairly soon. The rain is hard and the darkness intense. I get up early, and the mountain is shrouded by fog and rain. I ride to the next exit, where I am able to get breakfast. I'm advised that staying on the highway will be dangerous, as would going on the smaller road that is narrow and heavily traveled by tractor trailers. I am already soaked and cold, so I decide that the most sensible option is to work my way back to El Centro and rent a car I can drive into San Diego.

MEXICAN IMMIGRANT WHO SAVED BOY HONORED FOR HEROISM

NOGALES — An illegal immigrant who rescued a 9-year-old boy from the southern Arizona desert will be recognized for his actions at a ceremony Tuesday morning in Nogales. The ceremony is set to begin at 10 a.m. for Manuel Jesus Cordova Soberanes. Beatriz Lopez Gargallo, Mexican consul general for Nogales, Santa Cruz County Sheriff Tony Estrada, and other officials are planning to present Cordova with certificates of recognition.

Authorities say if it hadn't been for Cordova, 9-year-old Christopher Buchleitner might be dead. Cordova was two days into his journey to Arizona from Mexico when he spotted Christopher, alone and injured in the desert. Christopher's mother had just died after she crashed their van. Cordova says he gave the boy his sweater, fed him chocolate and cookies and built a bonfire until hunters found them 14 hours later and called for help.

Associated Press, December 5, 2007. Used with permission of

SAN DIEGO: DECEMBER 7–10, 2007

I arrive in San Diego on Friday afternoon and get settled into a motel, where I take a hot shower, get my bearings, and start making contacts. After a few phone calls I am invited to dinner at the home of recent Texas transplants Crissy Rivas, a UC–San Diego grad student in sociology, and Dave, a filmmaker, where we are to be joined by Calaca Press cofounders Brent Beltrán and Consuelo (Chelo) Manríquez, also a vice principal at a local middle school. Before dinner I find a bike shop in National City that can replace some broken spokes and realign my rear wheel, which got out of balance on the road to El Centro. Brent calls Cecilia Brennan, a local lawyer who has recently relocated from L.A., to join us at dinner so she can share insights on some of her work in helping to challenge the local anti-immigrant ordinances in Escondido, which has been in the news again this week as it is attempting to pass laws targeting day laborers. The food is great and the company better.

Early the next day I fly to Houston to spend a couple of days with family to celebrate my mother's 80th birthday. When I return to San Diego on Sunday I am picked up by Brent and Chelo, who will be my hosts for the next few days. Monday morning, Chelo gives me a ride to the airport, where I rent a car for the day so Brent and I can have wheels to get to the many appointments he's set up for me. Our first stop is a quick visit to San Diego Mesa College, where newly hired professor Manuel Velez meets with us for a little while before his morning Chicano Literature class. Manuel recently moved from El Paso to take this position, but he's not a newcomer to California, having grown up in Salinas. Manuel eloquently shares his perspective on life in the geographic, cultural, and political borderlands. After leaving Manuel we go to a little restaurant in Barrio Logan called Las Cuatro Milpas that specializes in bowls of beans. Yes, they sell other food, but this is the primary dish with rice or chorizo. It's inexpensive but extraordinarily rich in taste! We then walk around Chicano Park for a while, and I take many pictures while Brent tells me about some of the years-long struggle to establish and maintain the park.

Our next stop is a visit with Mónica Hernández of Casa Familiar in San Ysidro. Mónica is a Berkeley ethnic studies graduate who grew up in Tijuana, went to school in San Ysidro, and has decided not to apply for citizenship even though she has a permanent work visa and could be eligible. She is soft-spoken but powerful in word and deed as she contributes to bettering her community from the ground up through this powerful agency. San Ysidro, established in 1908, is situated at the U.S.-Mexico border between Tijuana and downtown San Diego three miles east of the Pacific Ocean. It is the busiest border crossing in the world. Monica shares her own experience of being detained at the border and sent back to Mexico because of a bureaucratic glitch. We speak briefly with Andrea Scopica, the executive director, who recounts for us the intensification of border security during her lifetime. She tells us of a time when the family would send their dog with a note tied to its neck to her mother's house across the border to deliver messages.

ANDREA: I can remember when Lou Dobbs was a financial guy, and now he's become this immigration demagogue. How did that happen? Well, it's the same with our city council person too, Roger Hedgecock, who used to help us but now he's made a name for himself for being anti-immigrant.

> ME: *So in your opinion are we on a trajectory of things getting worse, or is it part of a cycle?*

ANDREA: Well, if you look at it historically, it's part of a cycle. We went through this in the '20s and the Chinese faced this, too. But if you look at it recently, with just what's happened during our lifetime—the environment that sustains it is getting worse. Because of 9/11, things will never go back down to pre-9/11 levels. This has left a lasting impression. I really believe they're going to change the constitution and other things because of the way politics have changed. We have Bush and he is the most innocuous of the way things have changed. We got rid of Gonzales, but he wasn't the whole problem—he was only a symptom of the problem. There are all the lawyers who came out of Oral Roberts University who hold our future in their hands.

I tell people if you're not a citizen, if for no other reason than securing your own future you should become one because the first thing that's going to happen if you're not a citizen is that you're going to be targeted for deportation. They're going to say, "Anyone not born here is no longer a citizen." This is going to be the easiest one to change. It's already happening in Germany.

> ME: *That's interesting that you say that because you think if anything it would be more difficult to change because it's part of our national legacy—it's foundational to the country. I didn't realize until recently that the reason they made that birthright law was to grandfather in slaves because they weren't born here.*

ANDREA: After that they are going to start shutting down more and more employment opportunities. Already there are certain jobs that require citizenship—such as defense. These areas are going to grow exponentially. This is the way they are going to shut down economic mobility for immigrants. Even if immigrants are here for just a generation, their children tend to be better off than their parents.

> ME: *So you don't think there's a way to interrupt the debates? That it's inevitable?*

ANDREA: Well, yes, dialogue is necessary, but you have to force it. MLK was able to get as far as he got because of SNCC. Compared to them, he sounded logical. They were scared of black power.

M E: *Your point is even more poignant because the Democrats aren't willing to stand up and push the debate to the left—we get pushed further to the right.*

A N D R E A: Yes, it's really sad. When things swing back it's never to where it was before. It's also sad because it's not a BIG issue for those from, say, Indiana. It's big but you don't feel it the same as if you were here. During the Vietnam War, the draft affected anyone who could be drafted anywhere in the country. There are mexicanos everywhere, but they aren't going to be able to stand up and make a difference. It has to be a broad cross-section and coalition of the population.

B R E N T: Among us we're divided, too.

A N D R E A: Yes, but when 187 Prop came up, I was against it, but I was happy because all these people who had been passing after all these years were approached for their opinion. It was a good reminder that in the eyes of the world, when you're this color, you're this color. Credentials don't matter; they're not important in a racist situation.

From Casa Familiar we go to central San Diego to meet with immigrant-rights activist Enrique Morones, the founder of Border Angels and radio talk-show host of Super-K 1040 AM's *Morones por la Tarde.* A simple web search of his name reveals that Morones is no stranger to talking loud and clear about his stance that a more humane and honest means of dealing with immigrants is necessary. He has debated with Lou Dobbs and Bill O'Reilly a number of times and pushes them in a confrontational style that has seemed to earn him their respect. The extreme dislike of him by anti-immigrant groups only strengthens his credibility in the eyes of more reasonable folks.

Border Angels is a nonprofit organization founded in 1996. The organization consists of volunteers who work to stop the unnecessary deaths of individuals traveling through the Imperial Valley desert areas and the mountainous terrain surrounding San Diego County by offering humanitarian aid and assistance, including supplying water stations in the driest places. Enrique is passionate about his work and confident that comprehensive immigration reform will eventually come to pass. He is a reservoir of data and has many anecdotes about sacrifice, loss, and a search for basic human dignity to humanize these otherwise harsh debates surrounding undocumented immigrants. After a short break, Brent and I go to artist Victor Ochoa's house and sit and talk in his garage-studio as the sun goes down. As a lifelong resident of Southern California, he brings some historical perspective to local struggles and the role of art in social movements. He was an integral part of the movement to establish Chicano Park and teaches art in the schools while continuing to produce public murals. He gives me a copy of a textbook on murals he uses in teaching and shows us a new book on Chicano art that features a section on his contributions.

In today's debates, considerations of public goods are too easily cast aside in an effort to draw bright lines around citizenship. A better way of thinking about what immigrants ought to be allowed to access is to sever presumed connections of certain rights and privileges to citizenship, and instead regard them as something beneficial to the common good.

The obsession with protection of these rights and privileges is in some way understandable. Immigration and illegal immigration in particular, challenges our understanding of which rights belong uniquely to citizens and which can be shared by all, even illegal immigrants. But as the protectors tighten their grip, what oozes between their fingers poisons the potential good that arises when access to certain privileges is broadened. . . . But this reasoning fails to see the forest of common good for the trees of protecting citizens' privilege.

Tomás R. Jiménez, op-ed, San Diego Union-Tribune,
December 7, 2007. Permission granted by the author.

The day ends with an evening trip to Tijuana. Brent, Chelo, and I are accompanied by artist and scientist Nuvia Crisol. After a quick stop at Tijuana's Costco for some tequila and et ceteras we go to the infamous Tacos Salceados, which I have heard Brent brag about in what I thought was pure hyperbole. No hype. The real deal. I concede that these are some of the best tacos I've ever had. Simple but fancy and rich in taste to the extreme.

Chelo and Brent cross over frequently and have a SENTRI card that expedites their return drive into the U.S.[2] Passengers are not allowed on the pass, so on the way back Nuvia and I hop out of the car, as does Brent to accompany us, and we three cross the border on foot while Chelo drives across. Even late in the evening the lines are extraordinarily long due to the holiday season, we surmise. Chelo says that in the mornings the radio says lately the line for *peatones* (pedestrians) is 1,500 long. My Border Patrol officer apparently lived in Minneapolis, as she keeps asking me specific questions about streets where I live—though Brent seems to think maybe she

Nuvia Crisol's hand over the border marker at the crossing in Tijuana, Mexico. Louis Mendoza.

is just trying to catch this pocho in a lie. Meanwhile, in the line Chelo is pulled over on a spot check, and we witness *indocumentados* in a van driven by a woman get busted. The Border Patrol officers stand around laughing at them as they pile out barefoot and disheveled. Chelo is righteously pissed when she meets us on the U.S. side. We go back to Nuvia's, where I interview all three of them for an hour. Well-fed, full of information, and tired from a full day of meeting wonderful folks, I begin to pass out.

In the morning I return the car to the airport, get back on the bike, and head north. I record these notes:

> It's Tuesday the 11th of December. I'm approaching Oceanside, California. It's about one o'clock, and I'm enjoying the nice sunny, cool ride along the coast. It's nice to finally see the Pacific Ocean again. It means that I'm getting close to where I started, and then I'll be done. The weather has been a little bit cooler than I expected it to be at this point but not horribly bad. The nights are really cool, much colder than I would have thought. I hope I don't have to sleep outdoors much this week. The temperature in Central California this week has been in the high 30s. One way or the other I will make it into L.A. today. I probably won't ride the entire way. At some point I'll catch a commuter train to Rita and Raul's. I'm feeling good.

I ride up the coast on Old Highway 101. I only make it to Irvine before deciding to catch a commuter train into Los Angeles. I arrive shortly after sunset in Glendale, where Rita Alcala picks me up. I'll be staying with her and her husband, Raúl Villa, and their son, Joseph.

L.A. AND THE LAST LEG: DECEMBER 12, 2007

Today I visit staff and students at Cal State University–Los Angeles in East L.A. Luz Borjon, a counselor with CSULA's Educational Opportunity Program, instructor in Chicano studies, and part-time counselor at another university on Fridays and Saturdays, takes time from her packed schedule to host me on Wednesday. Luz introduces me to Steve Texleira, the director of the Student Support Program and adviser to Students United to Reach Goals in Education (SURGE). Like Luz, he is an L.A. native whose commitment to improving educational opportunities for Chican@s is lifelong and deep. He shares a lot of information with me and speaks enthusiastically of students' evolving political maturity and commitment. Afterward I am invited to attend the Equal Opportunity Program's holiday celebration (lots of great food!) and birthday tribute to longtime EOP director David Sandoval. It is beautiful to see such respect and admiration for an administrator!

After the celebration Luz introduces me to student leaders of SURGE, who allow me to sit in on a meeting for a holiday action they are planning with students from Cal State–Dominguez Hills. It is clear to me they are well organized and committed. The students begin their meeting with a round of introductions. They quickly transition into a brainstorming session to develop a strategy for the protest action they call A Dream Christmas. They discuss slogans for posters and agree to be in uniform agreement on certain things even though their message is complex. They will use Santa Claus and Grinch figures to illustrate meanness and the exploitation of immigrants by government figures as we near the Christmas holiday. They utilize an open process of deliberation and decision making, and they agree to be present at the event for 30 minutes. They will make posters exposing and educating the public about immigration raids, the separation of families, police brutality, the federal DREAM Act, the extension of the California Dream Act, educational access issues, the broken immigration system, and corporate reliance on immigrant labor.

I hope to get a chance to interview some of the students individually, but our schedules don't allow time. Steve shares his pride in the sophistication of the politics of undocumented students. He says students have learned that they cannot and should not give their uncritical support to a politician just because he or she is *raza*. We discuss the need for scholarships for undocumented students—and how financial aid solutions must stand in for legislative action to address this tuition gap. Steve tells me how a Korean restaurant's owners funded some scholarships because they own a Mexican restaurant and have Mexican employees. Luz discusses SURGE's passion and intelligent approach to organizing. Steve ends our meeting by saying, "What we have bequeathed this generation that hasn't done them any good is the romance of revolution. We really want reform, not revolution. In a global economy we need immigrants. . . . Chicanos cannot ride this out alone. We cannot volunteer to be the sacrificial lambs . . . the modern Jews. We need to fight vigorously for reform, for change that promotes a more inclusive society."

DON'T CALL ME CRIMINAL:
IS THE IMMIGRATION DEBATE READY FOR
"COMING OUT OF THE UNDOCUMENTED CLOSET"?

César A., 21, is a junior at San Jose State University and the community liaison of Students Advocating for Higher Education (SAHE), a statewide campus-based association started by undocumented college students. . . .

"After 14 years of being in the shadows, you reach a point where you say, I don't care, I'm fighting for what's right," says César, a hunger striker who says the decision was not hard to make. "My picture and full name were in newspapers, I was on television, and yeah, I wondered if the eyes of la migra were watching, but I figured instead of waiting for others to do for me, I had to do for myself."

The irony that César is using a very American do-it-yourself ethic to fight against an anti-immigrant backlash that does not consider him American is not lost on him: "The difference with us versus our parents is that we grew up here. I have been hearing for 14 years that everybody in America has inalienable rights. It is education that makes us fight."

SAHE's public call for the rights of undocumented students has not only brought supporters, but has been a lightning rod for virulent anti-immigrant anger, that now has faces, names, and organizations to target. When SAHE and a number of other undocumented student groups across California held their hunger strike, popular ultraconservative shock-jock Michael Savage told his listeners, "Let them fast until they starve to death."

The student groups launched a series of protests against Savage, but his attacks only got more vicious.

Raj Jayadev, Metro Silicon Valley, *December 12, 2007*

- -

COMPLETING THE LOOP: DECEMBER 15, 2007

I leave L.A. on a beautiful Thursday morning. My host Raúl drops me off at the Metrolink station in Glendale where I catch a train to Lancaster. I arrive there before noon, and after a quick lunch I ride 53 miles to Frazier Park. I am feeling very cold today. It has been cool, but this cold is more internal, a chill I can't seem to shake. My bones are hurting—my wrists, my elbows, my forearms and knees. I wear two shirts, a vest, and a windbreaker as well as a cap under my helmet and long gloves. Hitting the road actually makes me feel better. As I get near Frazier Park the road begins going uphill as I expected, but it isn't too bad. What surprises me a bit is the snow that I begin seeing on the side of the road and on the hills. When I see signs in Frazier Park for buying and renting ski equipment, I realize that snow is no stranger here. I check into a room about 6 p.m. with a strong urge for hot soup. Once I undress I get miserably cold again and feel feverish, so I crawl into bed expecting to rest a bit and plan to get up for dinner after a while. It is 4 a.m. before I wake up. I drink lots of water, take some aspirins, and go back to bed for a few more hours. I haven't slept this long or hard my entire trip. When I wake at 6:30 a.m. my fever has broken and I feel rested, so I go for breakfast and get ready for what I know will be a hard ride to McKittrick.

I've severely underestimated the difficulty of the route from Frazier Park to this little mountain town. Having looked on the map from my atlas and Google Maps, I knew I would be going through a hilly region, but I thought I would be staying on the edge of the peaks. Though I can still remember vividly the Oregon and Wyoming peaks that caused me so much physical pain in the first part of my journey, I have to say that this day rivals those in difficulty and misery. There is snow and ice on the road much of the way. Signs proclaiming that tire chains are mandatory for cars are prolific and ominous. The temperature is somewhere in the 30s when I leave, but it isn't until I am about 10 miles up the road that I realize the cool air and altitude will have a cumulative impact on me. The road is curvy, steep, and sometimes very narrow, though it is both a blessing and a curse that there is little traffic. It is easy enough to hear cars coming if I can't see them, but the lack of traffic provides me with a sense of urgency for getting through the ride lest I get stuck in the cold overnight. It's not that it is so cold that I'll be in danger, but I am confident I will be utterly miserable and uncomfortable if I have to sleep out here.

I am forced to walk several steep, climbing curves but take very little time to stop and rest because I am afraid that my legs will tighten up and I won't be able to go on. I try to appreciate the beauty of the scenery I see from this high road of the seemingly endless rolling hills. I have to work at beating back thoughts of regret for choosing this route. It was either this way, riding directly up the coastline (memories of the hard winds from the north at the start of my trip dissuade me from making this choice) or going to the east of I-5, which seemed much too far out of the way to get to Oakland. When making a choice, this route seemed to be the most practical. My mantra for the day becomes "Don't think, just ride. Push!" I know it has to end eventually. It is after 2:30 when I exit the Los Padres recreation area and begin to feel a steady decline and flattening of the road. I've only gone 40 miles in seven hours. I make it to McKittrick as the sun is going down, happy that this little town does indeed have a motel and diner, as this is the one town on the map. I hadn't found any lodging on the Internet. There is no cell phone or Internet service to be found, but I am happy to get some warm food and several bottles of water before taking a steaming-hot shower and resting my aching back and legs. I remind myself to talk to people about the route from here to Paso Robles in the morning so I can better grasp what to expect before taking off.

Getting to Paso Robles proves to be a cakewalk compared to the previous day's ride even though it is 40 miles longer. Most of the road is flat. I go through three mountain passes, but these are spread out and long, steady inclines as opposed to the steep, curvy, shoulderless, icy roads of yesterday. I leave Paso Robles early the next morning. The hotel clerk confirms my hunch that the side roads will take me through the hills, so I decide to hop on Highway 101 right outside of town and ride it as far and fast as I can so as to shave off a few miles and benefit from the flat road. Some parts of my directions have me getting on the highway, so I know that riding parts of it on a bike is permissible. Overall, I do very well. I am stopped by a local policeman who tells me he won't force me to get off but a Highway Patrol officer might. This happens a few miles outside of Salinas in the afternoon, so I exit and go to a gas station to see what route I can pick up. While I'm here, a couple in a pickup says they saw the trooper talking to me and ask me if I want a ride. They are going to San Francisco and offer to give me a ride the entire way. I say I'll take a ride to San José. They leave me off somewhere between downtown and the airport, and I make my way toward Milpitas as it gets dark so I can be on the road that will take me to Oakland.

ON THE EVE OF MY LAST RIDE, A TRAVELER, NOT A TOURIST: DECEMBER 16, 2007

Tomorrow I will reach my final destination for this journey. I'm excited, tired, and feeling a little disoriented. *What a long, strange trip it's been.* Getting an unexpected ride today was a nice surprise and wonderfully typical of the many acts of kindness that have been extended to me on this trip. I didn't get a chance to speak with or take a picture of the couple who gave me the ride, since I sat in the back of the truck. Though it was cold, I enjoyed looking at the road unfurling behind me for a change and appreciated that it would cut my riding time by more than half on the last day so I can enjoy the ride even if it does rain as it is expected to. I've still work to do when I get to Oakland—and much more when I get home—but this phase of the project is just about over. It will feel strange to ship the bike home. At some point I have begun dubbing it the Dream Machine—not a very personalized name nor one I have ever articulated to others. It seems a bit funny to me, like I stole it from Hakeem Olajuwon (my Houston roots coming out), but it also makes perfect sense given that it is the dream of acceptance, citizenship, and opportunity that drives so many immigrants.

In Milpitas I pick up some food from a new restaurant in the evening; the Filipina owner is a recent immigrant. Somehow we start talking about my ride.

HER: How many miles is that?

ME: *Well, I'm not sure, but over 8,000.*

HER: Wow. So you lost lots of weight, no?

ME: *Well, yes, some, but at some point I stopped. I still have more around my stomach I wish I could lose, but I've been told that without doing other kinds of exercise this happens.*

HER: Yes, well, I guess you don't work your upper body as hard as you do your legs.

ME. *Yeah, that's true.*

HER: So what's next? You going to ride the Tour de France?

ME: *(Laughing) No, I'm not that kind of rider. I haven't really been going fast, just slow and steady so I can keep riding the next day. And there are lots of days where I stay over so I can take time to talk to people.*

HER: Yes, you're a traveler, not a tourist, right?

ME: *I like to think so.*

HER: So tell me your last name. Maybe I'll hear about you.

ME: *It's Mendoza. Louis Mendoza.*

HER: Oh, yes, in the Philippines we have that name because the Spanish were there. You take care, okay?

MY LAST DAY OF TRAVEL: DECEMBER 17, 2007

The next day I make the short, 40-plus-mile ride to Oakland. I take my time and enjoy the scenery. Cristal García, a friend and former student living in San Mateo, has kept track of my trip and decides she will greet me with balloons at the home of my friends Beth and Antonio, my final destination for this ride. She calls me several times as I get close to ensure she's ready to record my arrival on her computer's camera. Much to my surprise, she manages to round up some neighbors and passersby to whip up noise for my arrival. It's funny and sweet!

I didn't plan it at all, but I've completed my journey on the eve of International Migrants Day. I'm humbled by this synchronicity and find it a great way to end my trip with a few more interviews and an opportunity to attend local events commemorating this day. Here is a description of the purpose of the day I found on the National Network for Immigrant and Refugee Rights website:

What is International Migrants Day?
December 18 is a day when the international community recognizes the rights of migrants around the world. The UN General Assembly approved the International Convention on the Protection of the Rights of

Me with Cristal García at my destination in Oakland, California, on the last day of the trip.
Beth Ching.

All Migrant Workers and Members of Their Families on December 18, 1990, and the day was officially designated International Migrants Day by the United Nations in 2000. In the U.S., International Migrants Day is a day when we can express our support and solidarity with all immigrants. In a period when national crises have stirred public anxieties about immigration and when unfair policies and discrimination against immigrants have intensified we need to call for respect, tolerance, and justice. December 18 provides an opportunity to highlight important issues affecting immigrant communities. It is also a reminder of the right guaranteed to all migrants by the International Migrant Convention, and the need for all nations to approve the convention and adopt its standards.

The next evening I go with Beth, Antonio, and Antonito to an event held at the Asian Resource Center co-sponsored by several organizations serving immigrant communities in the Bay Area. The event features food and music, and several advocates of immigrant rights speak. Among them are Arnoldo García, executive director of the National Network for Immigrant and Refugee Rights, and David Bacon, an acclaimed photographer and author of numerous books focused on the people most directly impacted and the dehumanizing impact of free trade and foreign policies. In this crowd of people whose origins and networks are global I feel at home and more grounded. While in Oakland I go with Antonio to his office one day and interview him and two other key staff members at People Organized to Demand Environmental and Economic Rights (PODER), Teresa Almaguer and Oscar Grande, about their work to preserve and advance community integrity by promoting collective action and advocacy among the San Francisco Mission District's residents.

On December 19 I ship my bike home and board a plane back to Minneapolis. Marianne picks me up in my Jeep. Seeing her at the beginning and end of my trip provides nice closure and re-entry to an everyday life that I feel somewhat estranged from by being on the road for so long. Just sleeping in the same bed each night and seeing the same places and people every day seem strange because I've lived with this nagging feeling that I should keep moving. It's disconcerting that I've nowhere to go or new destination to aim for. Returning home with school out and Minneapolis enshrouded with snow allows me to reacclimate slowly. It's good to be back home, but for a couple of weeks I find myself making minimal contact with people and enjoying my time alone. Because I have been invited to the University of Utah to spend the first week of January with honor students studying immigration and to share my experiences, I opt to stay home for the holidays and prepare.

As I reflect on my experiences and readjust to being home, I find it hard to imagine how I will organize all that I have learned from people along the way. For almost six months I've been on the road, often traveling, but meeting many, many people who have reshaped my understanding of the complexity, longevity, and importance of Latin@ life in the U.S., Latin@s' yearning to be seen as an integral part of the fabric of the U.S., the impact of our incoherent immigration polices, and many, many aspects of our life in the U.S. that I've never before encountered. I've interviewed more than 90 people, met hundreds of others who connected to me as a cyclist, fellow traveler, Latino, scholar, and perhaps most importantly just another human being whose mode of travel made them want to reach out and speak with me. The almost 8,000 miles I have cycled, along with another more than 4,000 by car, train, and ferry, have both worn me down and strengthened me, and I feel blessed with so many gifts—basic survival among them. But I also feel, and rightfully so, an enormous sense of responsibility to use this experience to help promote better understanding and solutions for resolving the immigration and immigrant crisis.

I believe we all must own the issue. We must understand that if we persist in framing our immigration policies unilaterally, we will only defer, if not exacerbate, a global human crisis. While there are indeed economic, political, social, and cultural consequences to the outcome of these debates, we must also understand and hold ourselves accountable to the moral issues at stake.

If there are two lessons I can cull from my experience as standing out, they are:

- First, we live in a world in which we are increasingly interdependent on others—that is, our well-being is not something that can be considered independent of someone else's because our destinies are intertwined.
- Second, the notion that information trumps ignorance seems so basic as to be banal, but whether in conversations, in the media, or in public discourse, all too often people continue to base their judgments of people and of issues on little correct or firsthand knowledge. Yet, as I witnessed over and over on this trip, when people truly get to know others, be it through work, community networks, religious connection, or new familial ties, they can began to have compassion and to develop a sense of common ground for how our experiences across time and space connect us to others, as workers, as members of the same community or church, or through a common immigrant heritage.

As I ponder these points, I am struck by how far I have had to travel to find the words to articulate this small yet seemingly insurmountable distance between people. I know that my role is to help bridge this distance, and I hope that this journey is neither so hard nor long as my own.

EPILOGUE

LIKE ALL GREAT TRAVELERS, I HAVE SEEN MORE THAN I REMEMBER,
AND REMEMBER MORE THAN I HAVE SEEN.

Benjamin Disraeli

ONCE YOU HAVE TRAVELED, THE VOYAGE NEVER ENDS, BUT IS PLAYED
OUT OVER AND OVER AGAIN IN THE QUIETEST CHAMBERS. THE MIND
CAN NEVER BREAK OFF FROM THE JOURNEY.

Pat Conroy

In the four years since I completed my Journey Around Our America, the challenges associated with immigration, xenophobia, and Latin@ educational, economic, and cultural inclusion have only increased. Comprehensive immigration reform continues to be elusive, and anti-immigrant sentiments are pervasive in political and popular discourse at the local and national levels. Even before the economic crash of 2009, there was an alarming increase of hate crimes against Latin@s, especially those who "looked" undocumented. Much of this violence has been enacted by youths who have been inundated with messages that Latin@s are unwelcome, criminal aliens, and thus as outsiders they should not have any legal, civil, or human rights. With this mind-set, they perceive their acts of violence as justifiable acts of patriotism.

The animosity toward immigrants is so deep and the fear of Latin@ social integration so palpable that not only are politicians gridlocked with fear about how to address the issue lest they risk voter backlash, there are also serious movements afoot to alter the U.S. Constitution to eliminate birthright citizenship. Efforts to establish local ordinances governing the regulation and control of immigrant employment, housing, education, and health care have mushroomed to the state level, with Arizona taking the lead. The Support Our Law Enforcement and Safe Neighborhoods Act, otherwise known as Senate Bill 1070, passed in Arizona in 2010, contains the broadest and strictest anti–illegal immigration measures ever seen. The intent of SB1070 is overt—to push immigrants out of the state. The new law makes it a crime for an "alien" to be in Arizona without carrying required documents demonstrating his or her legal status, and it paves the way for state and local officials and agencies to become agents of federal immigration laws. It also contains punitive measures for those who shelter, hire, or transport undocumented immigrants. Though many of the most controversial aspects of the law were blocked from being enacted by a federal judge's preliminary injunction, the law's passage has generated copycat efforts in 20 states across the nation.[1] Moreover, such a public declaration of anti-immigrant and anti-Latin@ sentiment has already produced some of its intended impact, as a significant relocation of Latin@s out of Arizona occurred just months following passage of the bill, with some studies showing 100,000 fewer Hispanics living in the state.[2]

National outrage by Latin@s and many others across the country toward this measure is grounded in the adamant belief that it will exacerbate racial profiling of all Latin@s and violation of civil rights by law enforcement agencies. The bill has drawn international criticism as well for promoting xenophobia. Yet, despite the national and international ire that the bill has drawn, polls show that 55–60 percent of Americans support its passage. There is little doubt that the polarization of public opinion regarding SB1070 also influenced the debate and rejection of a 2010 mid-December vote on the DREAM Act, an immigration-reform measure that provides a path to citizenship via educational attainment or military service for those who came to the U.S. with their parents as undocumented immigrants.

What does all this mean? I would argue that these fierce debates about immigration are not only about immigration, just as they are not really about national security or jobs, but instead they reveal deep, latent fears about people's perceptions of who "we" are and who "we" are becoming. The operative word here, of course, is "we." As I ponder this, I am reminded of a popular Mexican *dicho, Dime con quien andas, y te diré quien eres* (Tell me who you walk with, and I'll tell you who you are). People's sense of self is enormously complex. In the U.S., I would argue, the idea that we are self-made, autonomous individuals is deeply rooted if not synonymous with democracy itself. I can't think of a popular saying that expresses this sense of individualism in the U.S. other than the iconic character Popeye's declaration "No matter what ya calls me—I yam what I yam an' that's ALL I yam!" But our beliefs, values, and views of the world don't arise in a vacuum.

It's been said by many, many immigrant-rights advocates that the struggle for fair and comprehensive immigration reform is the new civil rights struggle of our time. This is predicated on the belief that the earlier civil rights movements, of the '50s, '60s, and '70s, had a deep, pervasive, and positive impact on U.S. society to advance the inclusion of women, ethnic minorities, and gays and lesbians so they can live lives full of hope, respect, and dignity. The assertion that this is a parallel struggle for new immigrants may well be challenging for those who see immigrants as outsiders or newcomers to the national imaginary and not in a position to claim equal rights. I suggest, however, that the inability to see them as having rights or as part of society only makes sense if one exists in denial or ignorance of the role of immigrants in the U.S., as workers and members of communities throughout the nation.

Two things are worth noting here. First, a great many people don't see and understand our *dependence* on immigrant workers. Second, many people don't understand how we as a nation have contributed to the circumstances that make it necessary for people to migrate here in search of basic human needs. U.S.–Latin American relations do not begin and end with the U.S.–Mexican war, the Spanish American War, or even U.S. support of oppressive regimes in Latin America. We have been an integral part of the political and economic landscape in Latin America since the 19th century, even if it hasn't been made explicit to the average citizen here that U.S. wealth has been built on the raw materials and natural resources extracted from Latin America and the labor of Latin Americans. Nor do our history books document or teach about the essential labor of immigrant workers in building the U.S. economic empire, both in times of boom and periods of hardship. Rather, as has been prevalent throughout U.S. history, we often view the immigrant as an interloper, an undesirable foreigner whose difference from some imagined unified "us" we find threatening.

Something very basic needs to be said here. New immigrants and the internal migrants who have changed the cultural geography of the U.S. in recent years are real people with real lives. Though they relocate for survival or in pursuit of dreams of success, safety, or happiness, they often do so at great peril. And in this way, they reflect our immigrant heritage even as they have their unique motivations, experiences, and dreams. In doing so, they extend our vitality as a nation.

In fall of 2010, while the U.S. Senate was debating the DREAM Act, some undocumented high school and college students in the Twin Cities found themselves inspired by a monthlong hunger strike being held by students at the University of Texas–San Antonio. In solidarity with these compatriots, five of them decided to launch their own hunger strike until the Senate addressed the issue. Lisa Sass Zaragoza, our outreach coordinator in Chicano studies, and I met with them to offer assistance and advice to make sure they were safe and to help them develop a communication plan to broaden their base of support. When it was announced that the Senate was going to vote on the bill a few days later, we began to plan a local rally to show solidarity. But within a day the idea emerged that the students should go to D.C. and witness this historic event. Understanding how this could be a life-changing experience for them, we helped gather funds to get them a rental car and food, and we identified a community member and ally who could drive them there.

Several days later they returned, having witnessed the bill's defeat. A small group of us gathered at a local charter school to greet them, share a meal, and hear about their experience. Without our having to prompt them, each reported on how despite the disappointment, this had indeed been a life-altering experience. They expressed joy at being part of a large group of youth who attended the hearing in Senate chambers. They expressed admiration for the bill's advocates who did their best to humanize the lives of young people whose futures were at stake. They expressed disdain and shock for the bill's detractors like Senator John McCain, who callously mocked the measure's sponsor, Senator Dick Durbin, as he held up pictures of youths who would benefit from passage of the legislation. They cried as they spoke about how empowering it was to see themselves as part of a national movement and how much they wanted an education and the possibility of using that education to be lawyers, teachers, or doctors. Their passion, commitment, and maturity brought tears to our eyes as they spoke of how despite defeat they had won something that could not be taken away from them—a stronger sense of dignity and belonging, that they were on the right side of history, and that this struggle to belong to the society in which they were raised and were striving to become full members of was one worth fighting for.

I think I can say that along with others there I felt humbled by their courage, emboldened by their confidence, and extraordinarily proud of them. I'm not so foolish as to think that if only their detractors could have heard the students, their opinions would change. The work that needs to be done to move people who view these young people as outsiders is harder than that. And this is why we need national and local political, religious, community, and educational leaders to understand that they are

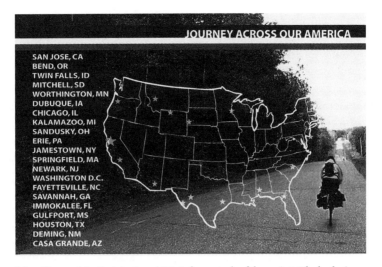

JOURNEY ACROSS OUR AMERICA

SAN JOSE, CA
BEND, OR
TWIN FALLS, ID
MITCHELL, SD
WORTHINGTON, MN
DUBUQUE, IA
CHICAGO, IL
KALAMAZOO, MI
SANDUSKY, OH
ERIE, PA
JAMESTOWN, NY
SPRINGFIELD, MA
NEWARK, NJ
WASHINGTON D.C.
FAYETTEVILLE, NC
SAVANNAH, GA
IMMOKALEE, FL
GULFPORT, MS
HOUSTON, TX
DEMING, NM
CASA GRANDE, AZ

My calling card for the trip. I used it to inform people of the project. The back gives a brief description of my goals and the address for my blog. Photo by Lisa Sass-Zaragoza. Design by Kelly MacDonald, College of Liberal Arts, University of Minnesota.

called upon with urgency to find or forge common ground and to dissipate the fears of the larger U.S. society that Latin@s, be they indigenous, multi-generational inhabitants, or newcomers, are a threat.

I returned from my bike trip somewhat dazed and confused and perhaps a bit too hopeful that what I had witnessed along the way portended an imminent resolution. I look back at my experience as one of great affirmation. I was changed by what I was able to do, what I saw and heard, and how the support I received along the way inspired me when I wanted to quit. Though I lost weight and gained enormous physical, emotional, and psychological strength, I can't say I became a committed cyclist, though it's not insignificant to me that I am keenly aware of my capacity to handle challenges.

In the dozens of presentations I've done about this journey, one of the most common questions I face is "What was your most memorable experience?" To the disappointment of those posing the question, my usual response is to refuse the question. I cannot choose among the great moments of natural beauty I witnessed, the spiritual encounters I faced, the psychological and emotional lows and highs I went through, the amazing sense of strength and accomplishment that surprised me at times, the conversations I had with people from so many walks of life, and the unanticipated acts of kindness I received from strangers when I needed them to be there for me.

I began the journey with a lot of anxiety about the unknown and fear of personal limits I might face. I experienced enormous wells of solitude but found an expanded sense of community. I was prepared to face hostility and met such kindness that I returned feeling unexpected hope, pride, and a stronger sense of belonging. I will always carry some of that with me in honor of all those who made this trip what it was, who, like the great natural beauty, are there to be encountered around the next bend or over the next hill. I believe all this to be true. There is no doubt that I had the experience of a lifetime and learned much about Latin@s in the U.S. and about the country in general beyond my wildest expectations. We, all of us on the entire political spectrum, are faced with resolving this issue. I want to believe that we will find a way to wrestle with our inner demons and call forth our better sense of self to do what is humane and right for this country's well-being, and for humanity, by setting an example for the world to follow. Do we have it within us to do so?

NOTES

INTRODUCTION

1. Throughout this book I use "Chican@(s)" and "Latin@(s)" as gender-neutral ethnic identifiers. "Chican@" refers to people of Mexican descent living in the U.S., while "Latin@" refers more generally to people of Latin American descent now living in the U.S. As a term strategically selected and deployed out of the civil rights movement, for many people "Chican@" has a very nuanced definition that signifies ethnic pride, critical race and gender consciousness, and an embrace of the ideals of social justice. It can be and is used as a politically charged term of identification for people of Mexican descent in place of other terms like "Hispanic" and "Mexican American." The use of the "@" instead of "a/o" has gained prominence among scholars in the past few years as a gender-inclusive signifier to address what is viewed as a privileging of the masculine in Spanish-language nouns that are intended to be gender-neutral or gender-inclusive.

2. I qualify my use of "citizen" here because it is often deployed as a term connoting the so-called natural rights accrued by legally recognized members of a nation-state. The dehumanizing label of "illegal" applied to undocumented immigrants erases the complexity of their lives as active and constructive members of their communities, those whom we might otherwise label "good citizens," by reducing their human worth to their immigration status.

3. A complete copy of the text of Martí's "Our America" in English can be found online at http://www.csus.edu/indiv/o/obriene/art111/readings/JoseMartiOurAmerica .rtf. All references here are drawn from this source.

PART TWO

1. See http://www.farmworkerjustice.org/ for information regarding the labor history of farmworkers in the U.S. The National Center for Farmworker Health maintains an excellent website and fact sheet on occupational health issues faced by farmworkers and their children, at http://www.ncfh.org/docs/fs-Facts%20about%20Farm workers.pdf.

PART THREE

1. ENgaging LAtino Communities for Education (ENLACE) is a multiyear W. K. Kellogg Foundation initiative designed to strengthen the education pipeline and increase opportunities for Latin@ students to enter and complete college.

2. Warren St. John, "Wave of Immigrants Helping Boost Church Integration," *The Day* (Clarkson, Georgia), September 22, 2007.

PART FOUR

1. *Pocho* is a word often used pejoratively to refer to Mexicans who have become assimilated to American culture as a result of loss of Spanish language or sense of detachment from their traditional culture.

2. The Secure Electronic Network for Travelers Rapid Inspection (SENTRI) program of U.S. Customs and Border Protection provides access to dedicated commuter lanes where prescreened applicants and vehicles are allowed to cross the border northbound into the U.S. usually more quickly and efficiently.

EPILOGUE

1. For a list of these states see VotoLatino's "Copy Cat Legislation" page, http://www.votoLatino.org/sb-1070-copy-cat-legislation/.

2. At http://www.rawstory.com/rs/2010/11/hispanics-fled-arizona-law/.